THE DECLINE AND FALL OF
REPUBLICAN AFGHANISTAN

AHMAD SHUJA JAMAL
WILLIAM MALEY

The Decline and Fall of Republican Afghanistan

OXFORD
UNIVERSITY PRESS

OXFORD
UNIVERSITY PRESS

Oxford University Press is a department of the
University of Oxford. It furthers the University's objective
of excellence in research, scholarship, and education
by publishing worldwide.

Oxford New York

Auckland   Cape Town   Dar es Salaam   Hong Kong   Karachi
Kuala Lumpur   Madrid   Melbourne   Mexico City   Nairobi
New Delhi   Shanghai   Taipei   Toronto

With offices in

Argentina   Austria   Brazil   Chile   Czech Republic   France   Greece
Guatemala   Hungary   Italy   Japan   Poland   Portugal   Singapore
South Korea   Switzerland   Thailand   Turkey   Ukraine   Vietnam

Oxford is a registered trade mark of Oxford University Press
in the UK and certain other countries.

Published in the United States of America by
Oxford University Press
198 Madison Avenue, New York, NY 10016

Library of Congress Cataloging-in-Publication Data is available

ISBN: 9780197694725

Printed in the United Kingdom
by Bell and Bain Ltd, Glasgow

Dedicated to those courageous and steadfast members of the Afghan National Defence and Security Forces, and their families, who in the face of tremendous odds gave so much to Afghanistan and received so little in return.

Dedicated to the Afghans and their friends who shared the dream of a republican and democratic Afghanistan and worked towards it in their own ways.

Dedicated to the Afghans for whom hope died on 15 August 2021. And dedicated to the Afghans resisting the Taliban's tyranny and keeping the nation's aspirations for a more just country alive.

CONTENTS

ACKNOWLEDGEMENTS

The authors would like to express their deep appreciation to Michael Dwyer and his colleagues at Hurst Publishers for supporting the writing of this book. For literally decades, no publisher has done more to foster serious analysis of Afghanistan and its travails.

Ahmad Shuja Jamal would like to thank the individuals who spoke to us in the research for this book and offered other assistance. He would also like to thank his co-author, William Maley, for the valuable opportunity to work together. And, of course, he offers special thanks to Homa for her constant love and companionship that sustained him in difficult times.

William Maley owes a special debt to his co-author Ahmad Shuja Jamal, not just for the intellectual engagement that led to this book, but for a decade of convivial friendship. He would also like to make special mention of several networks of researchers and officials studying Afghanistan that came together after 15 August 2021, both face-to-face and online, to canvass the complexities surrounding the decline and fall of Republican Afghanistan: these included Ali Yawar Adili, Waheed Ahmad, Shaharzad Akbar, Farkhonda Akbari, Muzafar Ali, Nasir Andisha, Michael Barry, Nematullah Bizhan, Srinjoy Bose, Wolfgang Danspeckgruber, Abbas Farasoo, Robert P. Finn, Niamatullah Ibrahimi, Haroro J. Ingram, Namatullah Kadrie, Joseph Mohr, Kobra Moradi, Nishank Motwani, Dipali Mukhopadhyay, Rani Mullen, Arif Saba, Mahmoud Saikal, David Savage, Susanne Schmeidl, Timor Sharan, Fred Smith, Barbara Stapleton, Safiullah

ACKNOWLEDGEMENTS

Taye and Wahidullah Waissi, as well as others who would prefer not to be named. The diverse views expressed by these observers have been very helpful in shaping the arguments in this book.

The map in this book is one freely supplied by ontheworldmap. com: see https://ontheworldmap.com/afghanistan/map-of-afghanistan.jpg.

Ahmad Shuja Jamal and William Maley
Brisbane and Canberra,
November 2022

Afghanistan

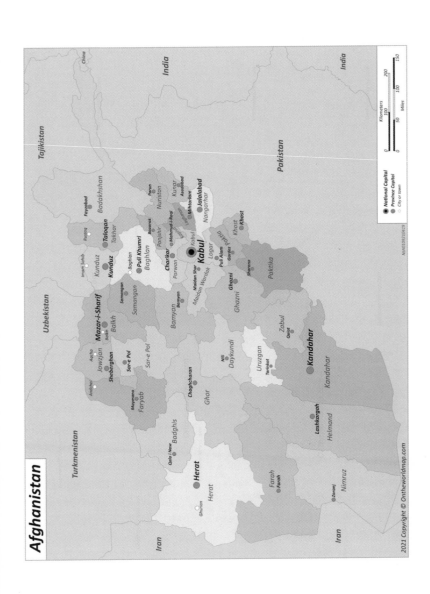

2021 Copyright © Ontheworldmap.com

National Capital
Province Capital
City or town

Kilometers
Miles

PREFACE

On 28 June 1919, statesmen gathered in the Hall of Mirrors at the Palace of Versailles for the signing of a momentous treaty, the product of months of discussion between the victorious powers of the First World War.[1] Article 231 of the Treaty of Versailles affirmed Germany's responsibility for the war, and under threat of invasion, Germany, which had not been part of the negotiations, was forced to sign. Some observers, such as the economist John Maynard Keynes, excoriated the treaty for its lack of magnanimity.[2] Others saw it as too lenient to Germany. French Marshal Ferdinand Foch ominously warned: 'This is not Peace. It is an Armistice for twenty years'.[3]

Just over twenty years later, on 10 May 1940, forces of Nazi Germany smashed their way into Germany's western neighbours—the Netherlands, Belgium and Luxembourg—putting an end to the 'phony war' that had persisted uneasily since the outbreak of the Second World War following the German invasion of Poland on 1 September 1939. Three days later, German forces crossed the river Meuse, and on 15 May, they broke through the French lines at Sedan. As an eminent historian put it, 'Nothing stood between the German armies and the French capital'.[4] The following day, the newly appointed British Prime Minister, Winston Churchill, flew with a small team to Paris for consultations with their French counterparts. Churchill asked the French commander, General Gamelin, 'Where is the strategic reserve?' 'Aucune'—'there is none'—Gamelin replied. Churchill later wrote 'I admit this was one of the greatest surprises I have had in my life'.[5] Six days into the war in the west, the end for the French was in sight. A remarkable operation from 27 May to 4 June evacuated 338,226 soldiers from Dunkirk in northern France and transported them to England; most were from the British Expeditionary Force (BEF), but roughly 110,000 of them were French.[6] But as Churchill himself remarked, wars are not won by evacuations,[7] and on 10 June, the French government left Paris, paving the way for German troops to enter the capital on 14 June. Four dark years were to pass before the liberation of Paris in August 1944.[8] And debate persists to this day as to exactly what factors— military failure, poor leadership, weak institutions, social decay under the Third Republic, sheer complacency—led to the collapse.

Eighty years later, something eerily similar happened in another part of the world, in Afghanistan. In 1937, the French diplomat René Dollot had written 'L'Afghanistan est la Suisse de l'Asie'— 'Afghanistan is the Switzerland of Asia'.[9] No one seemed disposed to make such a claim in 2020 or 2021. In 2001, following the 11 September 2001 attacks by Al-Qaeda on the World Trade Centre and the Pentagon, and the overthrow by the United States of the radical Taliban regime in Afghanistan that had hosted Al-Qaeda, another conference of victors was held, this time in Germany, in the city of Bonn. The Taliban, scorned and scattered, were not invited to participate. The Bonn Conference culminated in an agreement signed on 5 December 2001 between non-Taliban Afghan political actors that set out a pathway towards a new political system.[10] The process was not perfect, but it offered some hope for Afghans after decades of conflict and misery.

Nearly twenty years later, everything unravelled. After years of insurgent attacks by Taliban fighters given sanctuary in neighbouring Pakistan, Afghanistan's long-time backer the United States, under the leadership of the most erratic and unpredictable president in its history, Donald Trump, struck an agreement with the Taliban on 29 February 2020 entitled 'Agreement for Bringing Peace to Afghanistan' (*Mowafeqatnamah-e awardan-e solh ba Afghanistan*).[11] Negotiated and signed by Dr Zalmay Khalilzad, who in September 2018 had been appointed as 'Special Representative for Afghanistan Reconciliation', the fine print revealed it to be an exit agreement for the United States. The Afghan government had been excluded from the negotiations that led to it, and as US forces were drawn down, Taliban attacks on Afghan targets escalated sharply. Peace was nowhere in sight. The end came in July–August 2021. The Taliban, after seizing customs posts at Afghanistan's borders, surged unexpectedly into the north of the country, taking over key cities such as Herat and Mazar-e Sharif. Resistance to the Taliban began to crumble, and at an accelerating pace. With the capital Kabul wide open to attack, President Ashraf Ghani fled the country on 15 August with a few members of his intimate circle, his reputation in ruins.[12] The government of the Islamic Republic of Afghanistan collapsed, and the Taliban occupied Kabul. Scenes of horror emerged as desperate Afghans sought to leave the country by air before the United States terminated its evacuation flights at the end of the month. For Afghans who had been inspired by the vision of a modern, pluralistic and globalised society, life had become dark indeed.

Just as debate has swirled in France and beyond over what factors led to the collapse of Republican France in 1940, a multiplicity of explanations might be offered to shed light on the collapse of Republican Afghanistan in 2021.[13] This book sets out our account of what happened and why.

1

INTRODUCTION

Afghanistan is a landlocked country in West Asia. Within its boundaries are both wide plains and rugged mountains, with the Hindukush, an offshoot of the Himalayas, running from the northeast to the central west. Its present shape and form were not dictated from on high through a settlement between powers, as occurred in Europe with the Peace of Westphalia of 1648, the Congress of Vienna of 1815, or the 1919 Paris Peace Conference. Rather, it owed much to the creeping expansion of powers in the neighbourhood of what is now Afghanistan, most importantly Russia and Britain. Russia, between 1550 and 1700, had 'acquired on the average 35,000 square kilometres—an area equivalent to modern Holland—*every year* for 150 consecutive years',[1] and its influence weighed heavily on the Muslim *khanates* that remained in Central Asia.[2] Britain had entrenched its position in India, especially after the East India Company was replaced as ruler by the British Raj in 1858. It broadly suited the interests of each of these powers to have a 'buffer state' in the region. Anglo-Russian negotiations in 1873 and 1887 largely fixed Afghanistan's northern border,[3] and its eastern boundary with British India was demarcated in 1893 by a British official, Sir Mortimer Durand.[4] But that said, while Afghanistan was subject to colonial influences, it was never colonised, and recent scholarship suggests Afghan players exercised greater agency than has often been realised.[5] Even before the mid-twentieth century, it was a recognised state, a member of the League of Nations from 27 September 1934, and of the United Nations from 19 November 1946.

Afghanistan is sometimes seen as a small country, but the Afghan population, estimated in 2021 to be 38,835,428, is larger than the populations of Canada, Poland, Malaysia, Australia, Syria and many European countries.[6] The bulk of the population is based in villages and small towns, and only the capital Kabul, with an estimated 2021 population of 4,335,770, exceeds 1 million residents.[7] It is also a young population; according to official data from 1 June 2020, some 24,559,262 Afghans, or 74.6 per cent of the total population, were estimated to be under the age of 30.[8] The population is of kaleidoscopic social complexity. While Dari and Pashto are the two most widely spoken languages, multiple languages are used by different communities, reflecting the diverse range of ethnic groups—Pushtuns, Tajiks, Hazaras, Uzbeks and many others—to be found within Afghanistan's borders.[9] While the overwhelming majority of the population is made up of Muslims, there are significant distinctions between members of the Sunni Muslim majority and the substantial Shiite Muslim minority.[10] The complex life-experiences of women in Afghanistan have often differed greatly from the equally complex experiences of their male counterparts,[11] not least because of the persistence of patriarchal norms in many parts of the country. But it is dangerous to over-generalise about social dynamics in Afghanistan, for two reasons. First, people tend to live simultaneously in a multiplicity of social worlds, navigating their complexities as a matter of everyday living. Second, the norms and expectations that are seen as defining 'cultures' are themselves malleable and elastic in the face of factors such as educational opportunity and globalisation.[12] It is perilous to assume that Afghanistan in the twenty-first century is basically the same as it was in the nineteenth or twentieth centuries.

Political theorists have used the metaphor of a social contract to explain the emergence of the instrumentalities of the *state*, but in the real world it is little more than a metaphor. Historically, the state has emerged through a diverse range of processes, including the use of violence to establish a monopoly of centralised force,[13] especially in the hands of what the economist Mancur Olson labelled the 'stationary bandit'.[14] But the emergence of a state and state authority has often been a prolonged process, gradual rather than instantaneous, and involving bargaining, exchange, and patronage as well as pure coercion. While studies of the Afghan state often date it from the times of Ahmad Shah Durrani (1747–72), serious scholarship suggests that this is better seen as one step in a more elaborate process, with critical events coming both before and after Ahmad Shah's reign.[15] Migdal has identified state functions as being to '*penetrate* society, *regulate* social relationships, *extract* resources, and *appropriate* or use resources in determined ways'.[16] He has also sought to distinguish different parts of the state: these he calls the *trenches*, consisting of 'the officials who must execute state directives directly in the face of possibly strong societal resistance'; the *dispersed field offices*, the 'regional and local bodies that rework and organize state policies and directives for local consumption, or even formulate and implement wholly local policies'; the *agency's central offices*, the 'nerve centers where national policies are formulated and enacted and where resources for implementation are marshaled'; and the *commanding heights*, the 'pinnacle of the state' where the 'top executive leadership' is to be found.[17] Afghanistan before an April 1978 communist coup experienced a number of different regime types: monarchy from 1747 to 1973 and a republic from 1973 to 1978. But throughout this period, the state had a somewhat ramshackle character, with varying capacities in different parts of the state.[18]

The analysis of Afghan affairs has often suffered from serious oversimplification, to which a range of tropes have contributed. Recent times have seen the popular press flooded with expressions purporting to sum up Afghanistan in just a few words. 'Graveyard of empires' is one. Another is 'tribal society'.[19] Such expressions, together with the ubiquitous 'forever wars' and 'failed state',[20] do *not* assist in illuminating Afghanistan's complexities. While there is no doubt that networks based on lineage have been and are politically important in some parts of Afghanistan, it is worth recalling Elizabeth Leake's reminder that 'Colonial officials across empires constructed "tribes" to explain local relationships, to create leadership hierarchies, and to establish "stable, enduring, genealogically and culturally coherent units" that were easier to understand and thereby govern'.[21] The deeper lesson here is that Afghanistan is a dynamic space. Its peoples have a much richer history of engagement with the wider world than is often recognised,[22] and internally, relationships wax and wane in importance depending upon a number of factors, ranging from broad sociological developments such as globalisation and urbanisation to very specific calculations that individuals may make in the light of the incentives that they confront, which themselves can change for diverse reasons. As a result, 'essentialising' metaphors that depict a remote, timeless, fixed, unchanging (and often highly romanticised) Afghanistan need to be treated with the greatest degree of caution.

The post-1978 context

On 27 April 1978, a coup d'état mounted by supporters of the Marxist People's Democratic Party of Afghanistan (PDPA) overthrew President Mohammad Daoud, a former Prime Minister who himself had overthrown the monarchy, and his cousin Zahir Shah, in a palace coup in July 1973.[23] It was the 1978 coup that was the ultimate trigger for virtually all the disasters that have befallen Afghanistan since that date. The coup did not reflect any mass demand for revolutionary change; rather it reflected stark divisions within Afghanistan's political elite, divisions which in turn owed much to Afghanistan's character as a 'rentier state', overly dependent on unstable revenue sources such as foreign aid and income from the sale of natural resources.[24] Furthermore, the PDPA was deeply factionalised, with bitter antagonisms separating the *Khalq* ('Masses') faction, led by Nur Mohammad Taraki and Hafizullah Amin, from the *Parcham* ('Banner') faction led by Babrak Karmal.[25] Internecine conflict saw Karmal exiled as Ambassador to Czechoslovakia, where he was targeted for assassination by killers from the *Khalq* faction.[26] Much more seriously, the new regime sought to impose radical policies across a wide range of spheres, and used extreme violence to try to give them effect.[27] This prompted active resistance, and it was this resistance, together with the mounting carnage within the communist elite, including the murder of Taraki at the instigation of the ambitious Amin, that led the Soviet Union to invade Afghanistan in December 1979.[28] The invasion returned Karmal to a position of 'leadership', but it proved a Pyrrhic victory: Karmal's dependence on despised foreign invaders proved fatal to his prospects of securing legitimacy, and the Soviet Union found itself trapped in a quagmire.

The Soviet invasion, far from quelling resistance, led to its massive escalation. Refugees fled in their millions to neighbouring Pakistan,[29] which saw in the Soviet presence in Afghanistan an opportunity to boost its own position as an ally of the United States, a status which had been problematic since the military coup of General Zia-ul-Haq in 1977. One element of the resistance to the Soviets and their Afghan clients was Afghan parties based in the Pakistani city of Peshawar.[30] The Inter-Services Intelligence Directorate of the Pakistan Armed Forces (ISI) particularly favoured a radical Islamist party, the *Hezb-e Islami* of Gulbuddin Hekmatyar,[31] as it had been associated with the ISI since a failed Islamist uprising in Afghanistan in 1975, and seemed unlikely to raise the kind of territorial issues that had long poisoned Afghanistan–Pakistan relations.[32] Hekmatyar tolerated no opposition, and his party was accurately described as 'Islamo-Leninist'.[33] Even more important elements of the resistance were commanders and communities within Afghanistan, for whom the Soviet value system was anathema to what Afghans valued.[34] Known as the *Mujahideen*, these forces received backing from the United States for geopolitical reasons, and the Soviets became bogged down, with the replacement of Karmal in 1986 by a former secret police chief, Dr Najibullah, doing little to save the situation. Ultimately, under a new leader, Mikhail Gorbachev,[35] the Soviet Union in November 1986 took the decision in principle to withdraw from Afghanistan, and the withdrawal was completed by February 1989.[36] In all probability, over a million Afghans had died as a result of the war, and the damage the country experienced was simply enormous, in both human and material terms.

Somewhat unexpectedly, Dr Najibullah's regime survived for some years after the Soviet force withdrawal, but with hindsight it is clear that this was the result of a massive supply of fungible resources by the Soviet Union to sustain the regime and allow Najibullah

5

to buy off potential opponents in different parts of the country. This aid ceased at the end of 1991 when the Soviet Union itself disintegrated, and the communist regime in Kabul then collapsed in April 1992.[37] This ushered in a period of ferocious conflict, in which more moderate resistance parties, which had agreed on some basic transitional arrangements,[38] came under attack from forces of the *Hezb-e Islami*, which aspired to total power and was supported by the ISI. The unravelling of the communist regime had also resulted in the disintegration of the *state*: it lost the regulatory, extractive and redistributive capacities that Migdal identified, and links between the different components of the state fractured or broke altogether. With the main prize therefore being the capital city Kabul, the remaining *symbol* of state authority, fierce battles devastated tracts of the city that fell under the control of different armed factions, and some horrific massacres and atrocities occurred.[39] Finally in 1995, a modicum of unified control was established over Kabul by a noted commander, Ahmad Shah Massoud, in the name of the 'Islamic State of Afghanistan', which occupied Afghanistan's UN seat and was headed by President Burhanuddin Rabbani. But rather than putting an end to conflict, this simply marked the beginning of a new phase.

The critical factor was the emergence of the Taliban movement.[40] The crucial figure here was the Interior Minister of Pakistan, retired Major-General Naseerullah Babar, who, noting the failure of the ISI's preferred proxy Hekmatyar to hold and occupy territory, swung his ministry's support behind a new force, made up of conservative religious students (*Taliban*) from the so-called Deobandi school, some of whose older patrons had in the 1980s been loosely associated with a *Mujahideen* party known as the *Harakat-e Inqilab-e Islami*. Many of the Taliban had come from orphanages in refugee camps, and thus lacked the experience of family socialisation that might have moderated some of their behaviours. Led by an obscure cleric, Mullah Omar, the Taliban were above all a military force,[41] and Babar used to refer to them as 'our boys'.[42] Capitalising on the exhaustion of most other forces, and with strong support from Pakistan, the Taliban seized Kandahar in 1994, Herat in 1995, and finally Kabul in 1996. The regime which they ran from 1996 until their overthrow in November 2001 by the United States was totalitarian and repressive, and also isolated. Their treatment of women attracted scathing international criticism,[43] they were not squeamish about massacring ethnic minorities, notably the 2,000 Hazaras killed in an atrocity in Mazar-e Sharif in August 1998, which one observer described as 'genocidal in its ferocity',[44] and they secured diplomatic recognition only from Pakistan, the United Arab Emirates, and Saudi Arabia. What ultimately led to their downfall was their willingness to supply hospitality to the Saudi terrorist Osama Bin Laden and his Al-Qaeda organisation.[45] When Al-Qaeda launched attacks on US embassies in Kenya and Tanzania on 7 August 1998, this resulted in strong US and United Nations sanctions against the Taliban;[46] when Al-Qaeda attacked the United States directly on 11 September 2001, the result was a US military operation that displaced the Taliban regime.

The rise of the Republic: December 2001

On 7 October 2001, the United States launched a massive attack on Al-Qaeda and the Taliban, under the name of 'Operation Enduring Freedom'. It was a complex and multidimensional military operation that relied on sophisticated air capabilities,[47] but it proved effective in realising the US objective of removing the Taliban regime from power, although Osama Bin Laden succeeded in escaping to Pakistan, where he was finally killed on 2 May 2011 in a US military strike on his hideaway, virtually on the doorstep of the Pakistan Military Academy in Abbottabad.[48] The minute details of Operation Enduring Freedom are less important for the purposes of our discussion than the social dynamics that the operation exposed. What proved especially striking was the way that, in a period of just five days from 9 to 13 November 2001, a slew of towns and cities fell to anti-Taliban forces: Mazar-e Sharif on 9 November, Pul-e Khumri, Nahrin, Bamiyan, Hairatan and Shiberghan on 10 November, Maimana on 11 November, Herat on 12 November, and finally Kabul on 13 November. The lesson was that when dramatic things happen in Afghanistan, they can happen very quickly. The one holdout was the northern city of Kunduz, where a large number of Pakistanis were holed up along with Al-Qaeda members and other radicals. Astonishingly, the United States consented to a Pakistani airlift to evacuate these extremists,[49] and as one specialist recorded, 'The ISI is known to have used the opportunity to fly out senior Al Qaeda members as well as Chechens, Uzbeks, and Afghans considered to be strategic assets'.[50]

The Taliban, while in Kabul, had shown little direct interest in policy or welfare; their focus was on the exercise of power to give effect to their particularly idiosyncratic image of a pure and virtuous society. As a result, the overthrow of the regime confronted both those Afghan forces that had taken over key cities, and the international community more broadly, with a huge political vacuum. There was little or nothing in the way of a functioning state, no remaining constitutional or institutional frameworks on which to build, and a desperate need for a path forward. The United Nations therefore convoked a conference of non-Taliban Afghan political actors that was held in the German city of Bonn from 27 November to 5 December 2001 to lay out such a path. It was chaired by the Special Representative of the Secretary-General, Ambassador Lakhdar Brahimi. The upshot was the agreement signed on 5 December and endorsed by the United Nations Security Council in Resolution 1383 of 6 December 2001.[51] The agreement provided for an 'Interim Administration' with up to 29 departments, to be succeeded, following an 'Emergency Loya Jirga' (Great Assembly), by a 'Transitional Administration' that would hold a 'Constitutional Loya Jirga' to put a new constitution in place. A consensus candidate, Hamed Karzai, was endorsed to head the Interim Administration, which was inaugurated in Kabul on 22 December, with control of departments distributed between the different political forces that had taken part in the Bonn meeting. With hindsight, some have suggested that the Taliban should have been invited to take part in the meeting too, but the other Afghan participants at that stage were in no mood to have anything to do with the Taliban. In any case, the Taliban themselves were in such disarray[52] that it is debatable whether they would have been capable of participating in any meaningful fashion.

In a broad sense, the benchmarks established in the Bonn agreement were met, albeit with some slippage in the timings. The 'Emergency Loya Jirga' took place from 11 to 19 June 2002, and the 'Constitutional Loya Jirga' was held from 14 December 2003 to 4

January 2004. The former king, Zahir Shah, returned to Kabul in 2002 and remained there until his death in 2007 at the age of 93, giving a certain aura of continuity to the new arrangements. How exactly these new arrangements worked out is something that we take up in much more detail in later chapters. Here, however, it is important to note that while all these developments reflected a high level of Afghan agency, they occurred in a context in which the broad approach that was taken to institutional design and political change was also widely endorsed by key players in the international community.

An important consequence was that these processes put in place not just an *organisational* alternative to the Taliban regime, but a dramatically different vision of the character of politics and social life. The Taliban approach, which came to be described as the 'Emirate model', saw political authority grounded in the Taliban's conception of Islam, which was rigid, autocratic, and totalitarian in its implications. The Taliban model fell outside the traditional Islamic notion of *baiy'a,* where people and communities pledge allegiance to the Amir.[53] Even Islamic State has practised a version of this mechanism, which survived from the original Caliphate right after the death of the Prophet Muhammad. It offered a modicum of 'social contract'—albeit hardly of the kind hypothesised by Locke and Rousseau[54]—even if it fell far short of grounding authority in a state–citizen relationship. The Taliban Emirate had neither an entrenched notion of *baiy'a* nor a notion of citizenship, making it strictly neither traditionally Islamic nor republican. Rather than seeing religious texts, and the idea of *Sharia*, as parts of complex traditions open to different analyses and interpretations, the Taliban saw them as codes of conduct that could have one meaning only (namely the meaning that the Taliban supreme leader, designated *Amir ul-Momineen* or 'Lord of the Believers', chose to give them). Mullah Omar openly stated that the holy Koran 'cannot adjust itself to other people's requirements; people should adjust themselves to the requirements of the holy Koran'.[55] In this respect, the Taliban were almost mirror images of the orthodox Marxists of the PDPA, reminding one of Sir Isaiah Berlin's reputed observation that the Communist Party was a cross between a church and an army.[56]

The approach that was to be put in place through the Bonn process offered a stark alternative, and came to be described as the 'Republican model'.[57] This involved much more than simply having a president rather than a monarch or having 'Islamic Republic of Afghanistan' as the new name for the country. It drew on a rich tradition in political thought. With roots going back to the Roman Republic, and even more to the Italian city-states of the Renaissance period,[58] 'republican' political theory has been revived in recent times in the writings of the political philosopher Philip Pettit, who emphasises three crucial elements: first, freedom as 'non-domination', which is a broader notion than freedom as 'non-interference';[59] second, a 'mixed constitution' operating 'on the basis of coordination between different, mutually checking centres of power';[60] and third, for 'each citizen an equal share in a system of popular control over government'.[61] A number of critical points deserve to be highlighted. First, the endorsement of a 'Republican model' does not automatically mean that its requirements are fully realised in the real world; it merely identifies it as the ideal to which to aspire.[62] It is not any the less significant for that reason. Second, the 'Republican model' is not simply 'Western'. There are distinct echoes not just from Renaissance Italy, but from elements of the 'Islamic Mirror of Princes' literature, notably the *Siyasatnama* of Nizam-ul Mulk.[63] Some themes in political thought are much more ubiquitous than is often realised. Third, the gulf between the 'Emirate model'—monist, devoted to the use of unchecked power, and autocratic—and the 'Republican model'—pluralist, sceptical about power, and committed to popular control—is so wide as to be virtually unbridgeable.[64] The authority given to the Taliban supreme leader in the 'Emirate model' closely resembled totalitarian elements of pre-modern, medieval political thought:[65]

> If the test of any theory on government is whether it is capable of leading to a development which is reflected in a constitution, the theocratic-descending theory of government cannot pass the test. If indeed the ruler, be he pope, king, or emperor, formed an estate of his own, was in every respect sovereign, stood above the law, and if, on the other hand, the members

of the community were merely his subjects who had no share in government or the making of the law, but received the law as a 'gift of God' through the mouth of the king, it transcends human ingenuity to devise a constitutional scheme by which the subjects could put fetters on the exercise of the monarchic-sovereign will of the Ruler.

The fall of the Republic: August 2021

On 13 November 2001, the BBC's Kate Clark reported from Kabul that 'Almost all people in Kabul regard the demise of the Taliban as a liberation'.[66] Dislike of the Taliban did not dissipate with the passage of time: in 2019, the annual survey of opinion in Afghanistan conducted by the Asia Foundation—a survey that the historian Carter Malkasian has called 'the most respected survey of the Afghan people'[67]—found that 85.1% of respondents had 'no sympathy at all' for the Taliban.[68] Yet on 15 August 2021, the Taliban re-entered Kabul. The bulk of this book is concerned with how this came to pass, but in order to demonstrate what a seismic shift it represented, it is useful also to say a few words about the Taliban takeover and some of the consequences that flowed from it.

The departure of President Ghani, in the absence of any steps on his part to arrange a formal succession of power in accordance with the 2004 Constitution, inevitably created an escalating level of panic in Kabul amongst both members of the civil service and the wider population, and gave the Taliban a pretext to enter the city under the pretence of establishing order. 'That outcome', it was later reported, 'stunned top U.S. officials, several of whom had been on vacation when the weekend began, having expected the pro-Western government to hang on for weeks, if not months or even years longer'. For Afghans, it was an even more profoundly traumatic experience. Ahmad Nader Nadery, Head of the Independent Administrative and Civil Service Commission and before that a noted civil society activist, who had just flown from the country on official business, remarked 'I just sat there thinking, "I lost my country today" … I saw everything I had fought for, for so many years, crumbling before my eyes'.[69]

From that point onwards, the focus of the United States shifted towards evacuation,[70] based on an agreement struck with the Taliban that any such exercise would be concluded by 31 August. Not everyone welcomed the evacuation: one minor American academic accused the US of 'wallowing in panic and rumours', and even went so far as to assert that the US had committed 'an ethnic cleansing project, taking away the Hindus and the Sikhs who have historically been part of that country'.[71] This suggested little understanding of the nature of 'ethnic cleansing', defined in an authoritative 1994 United Nations report as 'a purposeful policy designed by one ethnic or religious group to remove *by violent and terror-inspiring means* the civilian population of another ethnic or religious group from certain geographic areas'.[72] The evacuation did succeed in extracting some 124,334 persons on 778 flights,[73] some of them citizens or residents of the US and other foreign countries, others Afghans in danger because of their association with the wider republican project in Afghanistan. The evacuation process, like the evacuation from Saigon in April 1975,[74] witnessed multiple individual acts of courage, even heroism. But evacuations in such circumstances are markers of failure, not success, and terrible scenes also accompanied the exercise. In what could easily prove to be one of the most tragically iconic images of the twenty-first century, a desperate young man was photographed falling to his death from the undercarriage of a departing plane to which he had clung in the hope of escaping. He was one of several to perish in that way.[75] And on 26 August, a suicide bomber at the perimeter wall of Kabul Airport killed 13 US service personnel and at least 90 Afghans.[76]

The actions of the Taliban after the completion of the US withdrawal gave little reason for believing that the Taliban in 2021 and beyond would be different in style and policy from the Taliban of 1996–2001—a kind of 'Taliban 2.0'. On the contrary, they rapidly took steps that squashed that optimistic notion, which in any case was much more widespread in Western circles than amongst Afghans.[77] Perhaps the most dramatically symbolic step that they took was the appointment of the head of the so-called 'Haqqani network',[78] Sirajuddin Haqqani, as 'Interior Minister'. This may well have pleased Pakistan—Admiral Michael G. Mullen, when Chairman of the US Joint Chiefs of Staff, once described the Haqqani network as a 'veritable arm of the ISI'[79]—but it highlighted a raft of problems for the new regime. The Haqqani network was a designated terrorist group under the domestic law of the United States, the United Kingdom, and Canada, and even more seriously, Sirajuddin Haqqani himself was a 'specially designated global terrorist', on the 'Most Wanted' list published by the FBI, with a bounty of up to US$10 million on his head for information as to his whereabouts;[80] Afghans had suffered enormous damage as a result of his and his group's terrorism. On 18 October 2021, he hosted an event at the Intercontinental Hotel in Kabul to celebrate the activities of suicide bombers.[81]

Other steps taken by the Taliban were hauntingly reminiscent of their behaviour in the late 1990s.[82] Afghan women encountered prohibitions on leaving their homes without male relatives, as well as in the spheres of education and work. Protections for women were dismantled.[83] Repression of women not only reflected Taliban ideology, but served as a tool for showing that the Taliban were in control.[84] The Taliban cabinet contained not one female member, and the Ministry for Women's Affairs was replaced by a 'Ministry for the Propagation of Virtue and Prevention of Vice'.[85] Civil society activists, and Afghans previously associated with the Ghani government or with Western countries, all too often were forced into hiding, moving from house to house to avoid Taliban who were searching for them.[86] Civilians could be taken away and killed with impunity.[87] Members of the Hazara minority, largely Shiite rather than Sunni Muslims, suffered in multiple ways. Some were simply massacred, prompting the Secretary-General of Amnesty International to warn that 'These targeted killings are proof that ethnic and religious minorities remain at particular risk under Taliban rule in Afghanistan'.[88] The Taliban also engaged in 'ethnic cleansing'—*real* ethnic cleansing—in the provinces of Daikundi, where large numbers of Hazaras lived, and in Uruzgan. Forced evictions occurred without any kind of legal basis or process, highlighting the essentially political character of the exercise.[89] And terrorist attacks on Shia continued. On 8 October 2021, a blast ripped through the Sayedabad Mosque in Kunduz, killing large numbers of Shia,[90] and just a week later, on 15 October,

13

Kandahar's largest Shiite Mosque, the Bibi Fatima Mosque, was bombed, killing over 50.[91] West Kabul also came under attack.[92] For the victims of these atrocities, suggestions that the Taliban takeover had brought 'peace' would have seemed singularly unpersuasive. By late January 2022, over a million Afghans had reportedly taken steps to flee the country.[93]

The structure of this book

Between the overthrow of the Taliban in 2001 and their reoccupation of Kabul in 2021 lie nearly two decades of Afghan history. An understanding of the developments during these two decades is critical to making sense of the decline and fall of Republican Afghanistan. One approach that one might adopt would be strictly chronological, telling the story of the sequence of events that fell between the two crucial dates. Many works of history do just that kind of thing, and do it well. The downside, however, of such an approach is that one can too easily lose sight of the more critical factors that shaped key developments. Thus, the approach that we take in this book is thematic rather than chronological. We have sought in the following chapters to focus in detail on some key matters that impacted on the capacities and performance of the state, and on the attitudes of the public to the way in which power was exercised. Within these thematic chapters, however, we tell a number of stories that are informed by the relevant themes but which also make up part of the wider story of how things went wrong in the course of the transition. If the 'Whig Interpretation of History' involves painting a picture of movement from a dark past to a beautiful future,[94] our story is close to the opposite: like the 1930s in Europe, it is a story of how high hopes were dashed, a story, as Zara Steiner put it, of the Triumph of the Dark.[95]

The following four chapters take up issues that have haunted Afghanistan for much of the period since 2001. Chapter Two is concerned with the problem of political legitimacy. Under this broad heading, we explore a range of issues relating to the structure of the political system, the challenge of insecurity, and problems of corruption and electoral fraud. Chapter Three focuses on aid and development, and shows how the funding of well-intentioned projects and activities in Afghanistan had perverse and dysfunctional consequences. Chapter Four addresses the issue of insurgency and the problems that both Afghanistan and its US and NATO supporters encountered as a result of the availability to the Taliban of sanctuaries in neighbouring Pakistan, a state which purported to be a friend of both the United States and Afghanistan, but acted more like an enemy. Chapter Five takes up the issue of political leadership, outlines some of the skills required to be an effective leader in Afghanistan, and appraises the performance as leaders of Hamed Karzai and Ashraf Ghani, the only two presidents that Republican Afghanistan experienced following the 2001 fall of the Taliban.

At this point, our attention hones in on more recent developments. Chapter Six outlines the way in which an ill-considered and dangerous exercise in diplomacy lit the fuse for an explosion in Afghanistan. Chapter Seven draws on the concept of cascades to show how the specifics of the 29 February 2020 agreement fed into mass psychology in an ultimately destructive fashion, setting the scene for a catastrophic failure of morale, and the prudential repositioning of key actors aware of how life-threatening it could be to find oneself on the losing side. Chapter Eight examines the specifics of the unravelling of the Afghan National Defence and Security Forces and of the commanding heights of the state during the last days of the Islamic Republic of Afghanistan. Chapter Nine draws these themes together in a brief conclusion.

This book does not seek to propound a single grand theory to explain the decline and fall of Republican Afghanistan. Its approach is compositive rather than deductive,[96] recognising how the interaction of a complex array of contingent factors contributed to the final outcome. But that said, from time to time we introduce concepts that are important tools for enhancing our understanding of these factors, with 'legitimacy' and 'leadership' being obvious examples. Terms of this type have typically been used in somewhat different ways by different writers, and as a result, at various points in the book we engage in a certain amount of conceptual clarification to put these terms into historical context and to pin down the specific senses in which we use them.[97] Striving for clarity in this respect offers a means of avoiding the problem of 'conceptual stretching', where 'gains in extensional coverage tend to be matched by losses in connotative precision'.[98] It is also the case that some of the nuances surrounding these terms have been explored by earlier writers, and drawing on their insights allows us to offer a richer discussion of the relevant complexities. Our approach is avowedly eclectic, drawing on different bodies of thought to illuminate different issues.[99] Afghanistan is distinctive, but its experiences are not without precedent, and this is something that drawing on relevant concepts allows us to capture.

The reader will readily discern that the authors have little affection for the 'Emirate model', and far more sympathy for the view of the world captured by the 'Republican model'. Seeing what has happened in recent times, it might seem tempting to give in to despair and turn one's back on Afghanistan and its problems. This would be unfortunate, for Afghanistan's people have ongoing vulnerabilities and needs, even if their world appears to be in ruins and their hopes reduced to dust and ashes at the moment. Nevertheless, our aim in the following chapters is to supply analysis rather than normative judgment, not least because Afghanistan's experiences may hold lessons for other places and other times, as well as for Afghanistan in the future. But that said, it is perilous to aspire to total detachment: as Sir Isaiah Berlin warned, 'Detachment is itself a moral position'.[100] There is one issue arising from recent events that does require some discussion in a more directly normative vein, namely the issue of betrayal. This is something we take up in the Afterword.

2

THE PROBLEM OF POLITICAL LEGITIMACY

A significant problem for Republican Afghanistan was that of political legitimacy. The story, however, is a rather more complicated one than casual discussion might suggest. Political legitimacy did not collapse overnight, and its decline was ragged and patchy rather than linear. Some of the roots of the decline in legitimacy went back to choices made in the early days following the overthrow of the Taliban in 2001, and others derived from the ways in which the political *system* evolved after the new constitution was put in place in 2004. 'We are dealing with a system', Jervis argues, 'when (a) a set of units or elements is interconnected so that changes in some elements or their relations produce changes in other parts of the system, and (b) the entire system exhibits properties and behaviors that are different from those of the parts'.[1] One of the lessons of the Afghanistan case is that systems failure can be just as significant in undermining legitimacy as mistakes for which particular individuals can be held responsible.

The idea of political legitimacy is a venerable one and has generated a vast literature.[2] John Milton in 1667 in *Paradise Lost* wrote 'who overcomes By force, hath overcome but half his foe'.[3] In his famous 1762 book *The Social Contract*, Jean-Jacques Rousseau wrote that the 'strongest is never strong enough to be always master, unless he transforms strength into right, and obedience into duty'.[4] This was echoed in 1775 by Edmund Burke: 'The use of force alone is but *temporary*. It may subdue for a moment; but it does not remove the necessity of subduing again: and a nation is not governed, which is perpetually to be conquered'.[5] The word 'legitimate' can be used to suggest that some actor or system is somehow morally 'right', but we use the term in an empirical sense to refer to an actor or system that broadly enjoys *generalised, normative* support. Mere 'support' is not the same as legitimacy.[6] Support is 'generalised' to the extent that it does not apply simply to a specific action, but to actions in general taken by the actor or resulting from the operation of the system. Support is 'normative' to the extent that it is freely given rather than extracted through coercion or procured as part of an exchange transaction. What we call 'legitimation' refers to actions designed to generate legitimacy. It is legitimacy that transforms mere power into authority. In the real world, legitimacy is a matter of degree rather than a simple 'either/or' dichotomy, and this has led one scholar to coin the notion of 'quasi-legitimacy', referring to support that may be less than fully normative but more than merely prudential.[7]

This is not to say that it is only legitimate actors that can exercise political domination. On the contrary, history is replete with examples of rulers who have survived not because they enjoyed high levels of legitimacy, but because they retained significant, *known*, coercive capacity or because they engaged in pragmatic transactions with other powerholders that worked to the mutual benefit of those in power, even if ordinary people were left outside the magic circle. The classic example of the former was Nazi Germany in the last years of the Second World War. There is clear evidence that generalised normative support for Hitler and the Nazi Party dwindled dramatically following disasters in 1943 such as the Battle of Stalingrad and the Allied bombings that devastated the city of Hamburg,[8] but the regime's coercive capacity was both terrifying and substantially undiminished, and in large measure counted for its endurance until May 1945.[9] The survival of Dr Najibullah in Afghanistan between 1989 and 1992 was a classic example of the latter phenomenon. The lesson, however, from these cases is that non-legitimate modes of domination are a good deal costlier than the exercise of legitimate power, and for this reason it is hardly surprising that regimes typically go to some lengths to try to bolster their own legitimacy. A fully fledged legitimacy crisis can have grave implications for political stability: as Pye famously put it, in 'a genuine legitimacy crisis the challenge is to the basic constitutional dimensions of the system and to the most generalized claims of leadership of those in authority'.[10]

The potential foundations of legitimacy are many and varied. The German sociologist Max Weber drew attention to legitimate domination exercised on traditional, 'legal-rational', and charismatic bases.[11] 'Tradition' is much more malleable than often thought, but can give an air of authority to the exercise of power. Those who come to power through legal means rather than through coups may assert authority on that basis alone. And a charismatic leader may be able to sway a crowd as well as mobilise an inner circle of intensely loyal supporters. The strongest regimes may well be those that have secured some degree of legitimacy on all of these grounds, although if the strongest source of their legitimacy comes from the source that is most resonant in their operating environment, they are generally stronger, even if they may be light on the other sources.[12] But Weber's listing of bases is hardly exhaustive, and rulers may seek to legitimate power in other ways. One is through performance, where generalised normative support flows from the perception that a particular system or constellation of actors has proved capable of 'delivering the goods'.[13] Another is a form of legitimation that was pursued in the Soviet Union, namely 'goal-rational legitimation', based on the desirability of the goals that leaders purported to be pursuing.[14] The Soviet Union also witnessed extensive manipulation of symbols to legitimate the exercise of power[15] as well as, under Stalin, an attempt to synthesise charisma via a monstrous cult of personality of a kind that also surfaced in China under Mao, in Romania under Ceauşescu, and in North Korea under the Kim dynasty.[16] Some normative support may defy ready explanation: as Pascal put it, 'the heart has its reasons that reason does not know'.[17]

One further issue is important to highlight. There can be multiple points of focus for legitimacy and legitimation. The legitimacy of a particular political model, such as the Republican or Emirate model, is not the same as the legitimacy of a formal constitutional structure purporting to give effect to such a model, and neither of these is the same as the legitimacy of a group of rulers or leaders operating in purported fidelity to such a model or within such a structure. Furthermore, within a given country, especially where the administrative instrumentalities of the state have been compromised, there may be multiple actors who enjoy some degree of generalised normative support in at least some parts of the country's territory. Actors who are frequently written off as 'warlords'—a label that needs to be treated with some caution[18]— may have a startling ability to survive.[19] This may be because they have well-developed capacities to extract resources from vulnerable people and use those resources to bolster their own coercive power, but it can also be because they enjoy a degree of normative support from those whom they rule. If this is the case, attempts to displace such strongmen are likely to encounter a backlash. What might be called 'consanguineous legitimacy' arises where, if one's own ethnic group or the powerbrokers of one's 'in-group' are represented in desirable numbers, the system is more legitimate in one's eyes. The more strongmen, ministers, ambassadors and directors of one's own kind that one sees, the more 'service' one will receive, which increases the system's legitimacy. An actor seen locally to be 'one of us', even if somewhat repressive, may secure more normative support than somebody who is seen to be from an out-group, with little interest in the wellbeing or welfare of the population he may be tasked to rule. This has certainly been an issue in Afghanistan,[20] and as we will see later in this book, it proved a complicating factor in the last months of the Republic.

Institutional design and political legitimacy

Issues of legitimacy have long been important in Afghanistan and continue to generate discussion.[21] They also hung in the air at the time of the Bonn conference in November–December 2001, a meeting with significant implications for institutional design, itself a far from straightforward undertaking.[22] While a subsequent commentary suggested that considerations of legitimacy were sacrificed to those of sovereignty in the Bonn agreement,[23] this was not strictly the case. The architects sought to weave together different legitimating tools: the return of former King Zahir Shah to a symbolic role as 'father of the nation', the development of a formal constitutional framework with provision for free and fair elections, and the choice of an inclusive (if not exactly charismatic) consensus leader in the form of Hamed Karzai. What they did not do, however, was reflect sufficiently on the legitimacy implications of choices that were made about the scope and strength of the future state. 'Scope' refers to the activities that the state will undertake, while 'strength' refers to the capacity of the state to undertake them.[24] By providing for up to 29 departments in the new 'Interim Administration', the Bonn Agreement laid the foundations for a swollen state structure beset with rivalries between different agencies. The dangers of this are well known: as Migdal has put it, 'States, more than many other sorts of organizations, may be subject to coming apart at the seams simply because there are so many seams'.[25] The decisions at Bonn resulted in divisive elite politics, with ministries at risk of being used as 'positional goods'[26] by which ministers could use state resources to reward their followers and lock in their followers' ongoing loyalty. This became less the case in later years as ministries' autonomy and decision-making capacities were reduced, but ironically, this was one reason why the government's standing declined.

An additional problem was that the structure of the state for which the 2004 Constitution provided was highly centralised. While a provincial structure was in place, with the creation of Panjsher and Daikundi in 2004 bringing the total number of provinces to 34,[27] the key appointments to state executive office in the provinces were to be made administratively from Kabul rather than via local elections. The Constitution did provide for the election in each province of a 'Provincial Council' (*Shura-i welayati*) in Article 138, but the councils proved to be relatively weak bodies, struggling with limited success against the centralising impulses within the Kabul government.[28] There was also little in the way of fiscal diversification, of a kind that could have empowered local players to respond to local needs; political criteria, rather than considerations of efficiency and equity, played the larger role in shaping the central allocation of resources.[29]

Foreign aid to strengthen local administration failed to come to grips with the problems in play, which were not just technical, but political.[30] John Stuart Mill's warning that 'It is but a small portion of the public business of a country which can be well done, or safely attempted, by the central authorities'[31] did not register strongly with those who crafted the Afghan Constitution or subsequently assumed central leadership roles.[32] Nor did Mill's argument that a sense of proximity between ruler and ruled can enhance both accountability and legitimacy.[33] The disposition to marginalise *customary governance* was particularly unfortunate in Afghanistan. Governance in this sense of the term is actually a reflection of legitimacy. As James N. Rosenau put it:[34]

> governance is a system of rule that works only if it is accepted by the majority (or, at least, by the most powerful of those it affects), whereas governments can function even in the face of widespread opposition to their policies. In this sense, governance is always effective in performing the functions necessary to systemic persistence, else it is not conceived to exist (since instead of referring to ineffective governance, one speaks of anarchy or chaos).

As a careful study has noted, 'Customary governance remains an important option for many Afghans despite decades of war and violence. Most villagers believed that customary governance was *more* responsive after decades of conflict because villages had more autonomy'.[35] All too often, customary governance was displaced by ineffective or corrupt or unresponsive administration. It might have been a different story if *effective* instruments of a modern state had supplanted customary governance, which is not necessarily free of shortcomings. But in the context of high expectations that pervaded the early years of post-Taliban Republican Afghanistan, what displaced customary local arrangements proved sadly lacking.

Compounding this problem of centralisation was the adoption of a strongly presidential form of government. This was something actively supported by the United States, which favoured a president to drive policymaking and as a single point of contact for actors in the wider world.[36] Unfortunately, this overlooked a substantial body of work that pointed to the dangers of such systems, most notably that they permit only one winner.[37] This is a dangerous model in a society with a multiplicity of ethnic groups, and indeed, the push for a presidential system proved extremely controversial when the Afghan Constitution was being drafted, with non-Pushtuns painting it as a Pushtun power grab.[38] A presidential system can threaten political stability in a range of ways. One is if the office of president is overloaded with responsibilities, preventing efficient performance and service delivery. Another is if the person who occupies the office proves to be deficient in emotional intelligence or critical skills with respect to politics and policy. Problems that may be diffused in a parliamentary system can be accentuated in a presidential system, reminding one of the ancient saying that a fish rots from the head down. We will return to some of these issues in Chapter Five.

Of course, none of these features of the state would automatically lead to a crisis or even a diminution of legitimacy. Institutions succeed or fail in significant measure because of the particular context in which they are put to use.[39] In Afghanistan, however, the context proved to be unpromising, and the result was that there were significant unintended consequences of the institutional choices that were made, culminating in the emergence of a distinctive political system that had limited prospects of securing widespread popular support. Much of the problem sprang from the increasing salience of *networks* as mechanisms for political advancement and the distribution of resources. The effects of such networks were far-reaching and destructive.

Timor Sharan, who pioneered the study of Afghan networks, in an article with Srinjoy Bose defines networks as 'a distinct *hybrid hierarchical structure whose members share power and resources through informal and constantly renegotiated deals and pacts*'.[40] In turn, 'network politics' in Sharan's sense refers to a condition 'where the state and political networks have become co-constitutive in state-building',[41] characterised by 'distinct open-hierarchical structures whose members are interdependent on each other's power and resources for political outcomes in an informally structured and continuously renegotiated arrangement'.[42] In such a situation, Sharan notes, it is necessary to take into account 'the daily *performance* of the actors that constitute the state'.[43] Network politics came easily to Hamed Karzai, who had cut his teeth politically in the 1980s in Peshawar, where shifting alliances proved central to the politics of the Afghan resistance parties. After 2001, this led to the emergence of a *neopatrimonial* system in which bureaucratic structures and patron-client relations were intertwined.[44] The system had a distinctively Afghan character. As Sarah Chayes put it, 'Karzai was not, as conventional wisdom had it, doling out patronage. He wasn't distributing money downward to buy off potential political rivals. If anything—with exceptions especially before elections—the reverse was true. Subordinate officials were paying off Karzai or his apparatus. What the top of the system provided in return was, first, unfettered permission to extract resources for personal gain, and second, protection from repercussions'.[45] The salience of networks of this kind is potentially highly damaging for political legitimacy, since very large numbers of people are likely to be excluded from access to the power which involvement in a network can offer. Network politics also tends to undermine the rule of law in a very serious fashion.[46] Perhaps as a result, while as recently as 2019, Afghans surveyed by the Asia Foundation reported themselves as 'very satisfied' (17%) or 'somewhat satisfied' (48%) with 'choosing the president and Parliament by voting, rather than by appointment or selection by some leaders',[47] when it came to confidence in government ministers (that is, individuals likely to be seen as tainted by involvement in network politics), 36% of respondents had 'not much confidence', and 18% had 'no confidence at all'.[48]

Security and legitimacy

Max Weber famously argued that the 'claim of the modern state to monopolize the use of force is as essential to it as its character of compulsory jurisdiction and of continuous operation'.[49] At one level, this is a very obvious point. Any state that is effectively stared down by a multiplicity of armed competitors or challengers, themselves capable of using force to intimidate or coerce the citizenry, is likely to see its generalised, normative support compromised. Yet at the same time, this formulation leaves a number of significant questions hanging in the air. Does *any* state, *ever*, succeed completely in establishing a monopoly over the use of force? If not, to what extent can a state flourish if armaments are distributed amongst the population? Are some *kinds* of force more important to bring under control than others? And what might be the 'tipping points' beyond which the existence of arms in diverse sets of hands might prove to be a clear and present danger to the functioning of the state? Some of these sorts of issues have preoccupied US observers since the armed attack on the Capitol in Washington DC on 6 January 2021, but they have concerned writers on Afghanistan for far longer than that.[50]

The idea of security is a complex one. Traditional concepts of security tended to focus on the security of the territorial state from the risk of armed attack by another, but in recent times there has been significantly more focus on different conceptions of 'human security', where the wellbeing of individuals as well as the survival of the state is brought into focus. Some conceptions of human security have focused on issues such as inequality and material prosperity; others have been directed at the ways in which violence and armed conflict intrude into the lives of ordinary people.[51] Where political legitimacy is concerned, it is this last conception that may be the most useful, since if people feel that their lives are blighted by attacks that the state is incapable of preventing, the credibility of the state is likely to suffer as a result. The issue of security in this sense is also one on which the views of ordinary Afghans have been extensively tapped. In 2019, the Asia Foundation published instructive statistics about the opinions of ordinary Afghans on security. Some 58% of respondents felt that things in Afghanistan were going in the wrong direction, and 54% of these cited 'insecurity' as one of the main reasons.[52] But that said, when respondents were asked to identify the major problems in their 'local area', unemployment (at 31%) outranked 'violence/insecurity/attacks' (at 26%).[53] Furthermore, 62% of respondents who were asked 'does any group currently pose a threat to the security of this local area', answered 'no'; of those who answered 'yes', 69% identified the Taliban as a source of threat.[54]

Afghans also ventured opinions on the instrumentalities of the state tasked with delivering security. In 2019, 58% were of the opinion that the Afghan National Army was getting better at providing security, and 53% strongly agreed that it helped to 'improve security in Afghanistan', with another 36% somewhat agreeing.[55] At the same time, 46% strongly agreed that the Afghan National Army needed foreign support to do its job properly, and a further 38% somewhat agreed.[56] These data on foreign support pointed to a rather clear understanding on the part of ordinary Afghans of the situation that confronted them, and—to anticipate some points we will discuss in more detail in Chapter Seven—highlighted the dangers that could result from a time-based rather than conditions-based extraction of the remaining Western forces and contractors from Afghanistan.

One issue that cropped up frequently in Afghanistan in the two decades following the overthrow of the Taliban in 2001 related to 'warlords' and 'warlordism' as threats to the legitimacy of the state. Modern discussion of warlords emerged in the context of the Chinese civil war,[57] and this in part accounts for its pejorative tone: a number of those who won fame as warlords in Republican China were predatory in the extreme. This made the use of the term in Afghanistan somewhat controversial, since on occasion it was deployed by some actors with the manifest intent of delegitimating others. In Afghanistan, there certainly were predatory players, some of them extremely unappetising, and those with an agenda of centralising the power of the state frequently saw them as enemies to be vanquished, or at least tamed. But the situation was rather more complicated than such a simple dichotomy suggested. Armed strongmen varied both in the degree of their strength and military capacity, and in the extent to which they actually enjoyed generalised, normative support from some fraction of the population. As a result, the relations between 'warlords' and the state proved to be much more nuanced than press reporting captured, something carefully documented in a number of in-depth scholarly works that suggested that positing an ineluctable antagonism between 'warlords' and 'the state' was oversimplified.[58] Some 'warlords' contaminated the standing of the state, but the inclusion of particular 'warlords' could also add to the legitimacy of the state to the extent that they had legitimacy in the eyes of segments of the population. This 'warlord legitimacy' was certainly exploited in election campaigns, and reflected in the distribution of cabinet posts and the doling out of other goods of the state. One key challenge of building a modern state in Afghanistan lay in dealing appropriately with these 'warlords' or 'powerbrokers': as President Ghani's combative approach was to reveal, any state low on formal or procedural legitimacy could ill afford to marginalise them.

One broader implication is that one also should be wary of treating the 'claim of the modern state to monopolize the use of force' as the be-all and end-all of state identity or legitimacy. As Malejacq has put it, 'Afghanistan must in fact be seen as a kind of mini empire in which sources of authority overlap ... and the lines between the sources of authority are often blurred'.[59] This issue was to surge briefly to the fore in the last days of Republican Afghanistan.

Corruption and legitimacy

Corruption is a ubiquitous phenomenon, to be found in rich and poor countries alike.[60] In 1978, the historian Hasan Kakar wrote that 'Afghan civil servants are probably among the lowest paid in the world. It is impossible for them to live decently on their salaries unless they are supplemented by other sources of income. Corruption and embezzlement are accepted facts of Afghan bureaucratic life and are objected to only when excesses are committed'.[61] His article appeared in the very month that the regime of President Daoud was overthrown in a coup, which might lead one to wonder whether members of the general public in Afghanistan were as sanguine about poor administration as this assessment suggested. Defining corruption for analytical purposes has proved to be a rather difficult undertaking, not least because of cultural differences, and variations in perceptions of particular actual behaviours.[62] But for practical purposes, there is much to be said for the definition of corruption as 'the misuse of an office or comparable position of trust for private purposes',[63] with bribery, misappropriation, and nepotism being prime manifestations.[64] Because the practitioners of corrupt activity are typically secretive about what they are doing, it is difficult to measure or calibrate the scale of corruption in a precise fashion. Nonetheless, there may be clear indicators, for example massive unexplained wealth on the part of public officials,[65] which suggests that not all is well.

Because of its nefarious and self-interested character, corruption can easily be viewed simply as an individual moral failing. But there are good reasons for digging deeper when one seeks to expose the roots of corruption. Not all societies display equal levels of corruption; it can be a profound problem in some places and a trivial problem in others. This suggests the need to take two factors into account. One is path dependence—the extent to which past experiences and practices play a role in shaping the present. The other is the existence of specific incentive structures that may encourage corruption, for example by making the potential rewards high, and the risk of detection and prosecution low. Where path dependence is concerned, education appears to be a critical factor: Eric M. Uslaner has argued, on the basis of an impressive comparative analysis, that 'Countries with higher levels of education in the past have less corruption today'. Education, he goes on, 'produces economic equality. The linkage between equality and lower levels of corruption is well-established ... And education promotes specific values that underlie "good government"—or honesty in government. Education provides the foundation for ordinary people to take part in their governments—and to take power away from corrupt leaders'.[66]

Uslaner has also addressed the issue of specific conditions conducive to corruption, arguing that the roots of grand corruption are 'high inequality and low trust'.[67] His conclusion is stark:

> Trying to fix broken windows (street crime, petty corruption) is a worthy goal, but it is taking aim at the wrong target. Of course, arrest the pickpockets and fight people who try to extort money for routine services. But don't fool yourself into thinking that this is simply the first step in ending grand corruption. The gains from grand corruption are too great and it persists even where petty corruption has been eradicated or greatly reduced.[68]

After 2001, with aid monies rushing in to fuel reconstruction, it is fair to say that Afghanistan was in the unhappy position where virtually all the enabling conditions for large-scale corruption had been met. As Jennifer Brick Murtazashvili put it, 'Clearly, the government of

Afghanistan was deeply corrupt. But that corruption was not rooted in Afghan society or culture. Rather it was incentivized by the rules governing society combined with the absurd amount of money being pumped into an economy that could hardly absorb such sums'.[69]

The development of a neopatrimonial system was both a consequence of these incentive structures, and a contributor to corruption's further expansion. Once entrenched networks are in place, it can be very difficult to confront the problem of grand corruption, since those who benefit from it have a greater incentive to defend the retention of the system—even if it is damaging for the wellbeing of the wider society—than the victims of the system may have to achieve its reform. This is a classic manifestation of the so-called logic of collective action.[70] This can be effective not just against local anti-corruption activities, but even against well-resourced and determined international investigators. There is no credible evidence that President Karzai was personally corrupt in a financial sense, but during his presidency, US officials who were very much committed to seeing Afghanistan's transition succeed nonetheless despaired at the way in which corruption flourished in his vicinity. After Karzai's associate Mohammad Zia Salehi—a remarkable survivor in Afghan political circles—was arrested in July 2010 for soliciting a bribe, Karzai moved against the anti-corruption units that had secured the arrest, with his chief of staff stating that Karzai wanted the units to operate 'within an Afghan framework'.[71] The failure of US endeavours to overcome this problem[72] was a cameo of the wider challenge of addressing corruption once it is entwined in the structures of the political system. Such corruption also had grave effects on the operation of agencies in which corruption flourished, a problem which became painfully obvious as the US exit loomed.[73]

The shift from President Karzai to President Ghani brought some ostensible improvement in international assessments of the problem of corruption, although this did little or nothing to alter concerns on the ground. Transparency International in 2020 ranked Afghanistan 165th out of 180 countries assessed for its 'Corruption Perception Index' (CPI), with a score of 19/100, compared to a global average of 43/100. It noted, however, that 'With a score of 19, Afghanistan is a significant improver on the CPI, increasing 11 points since 2012'.[74] Nonetheless, the low ranking highlighted how critical a problem corruption remained in Afghanistan. Courageous staff of Integrity Watch Afghanistan did their best to highlight what was occurring, and expert reports sought to assess the scale of the problem. A 2012 study by the United Nations Office on Drugs and Crime concluded that

> half of Afghan citizens paid a bribe while requesting a public service and the total cost of bribes paid to public officials amounted to US$3.9 billion. This corresponds to an increase of 40 per cent in real terms between 2009 and 2012, while the ratio of bribery cost to GDP remained relatively constant (23 per cent in 2009; 20 per cent in 2012).[75]

President Ghani appeared to treat the problem of corruption much more seriously than his predecessor did, something recognised in a 2021 United Nations report. But the same report also stated that 'A major reason for the international community's sustained concern about corruption has been its negative effect on the legitimacy of the State' and highlighted that 'despite the introduction of several notable reforms there has still been insufficient tangible progress in reducing corruption and that the concerns regarding the impact of corruption on State legitimacy remain valid'.[76]

For ordinary Afghans, the experience of being exploited by corrupt state officials, or 'shaken down' by corrupt police, was not only enraging and humiliating,[77] but profoundly corrosive of respect for the state. No less than 81.5% of respondents in the 2019 Asia Foundation survey saw corruption as a major problem 'for the country', while 67.9% saw it as a problem 'in their daily life'. In the province of Panjsher, 96.8% saw corruption as a major problem in Afghanistan, while a mere 35.6% saw it as a major problem in their daily lives.[78] But in politics, perceptions can be as important as realities, and the perception of corruption can offset or undermine any legitimacy that comes from effective performance in some sphere or spheres of public policy. In the nineteenth century, the renowned American orator John Randolph of Roanoke remarked of an opponent that 'he is a man of splendid abilities but utterly corrupt. Like rotten mackerel by moonlight, he shines and stinks'.[79] The mere smell of corruption may be enough to weaken a government's legitimacy.

Impunity, abuse of power, and legitimacy

The very existence of political elites serves as a reminder that political systems are marked by asymmetries of power, and such asymmetries of power are perpetually at risk of being exploited in an abusive fashion. As the famous historian Lord Acton put it, 'power tends to corrupt and absolute power corrupts absolutely'.[80] When this happens, the consequences for political legitimacy are likely to be serious.[81] Much will depend on the extent of abuse, how localised it might be, and on whether rulers of the state are perceived to be complicit in it, or trying to do something about the problem. But that said, the problem of abuse of power is related to the structures of a political system as well as to the strengths and weaknesses of individual leaders. If a political system is organised in such a way, or develops in such a way, as to facilitate the abuse of power by the strongest players, then even well-intentioned leaders may find that the problem is an intractable one. If this proves to be the case, it may be tempting for leaders to try to co-opt abusive powerholders rather than challenge them.

The problem of impunity arises when a system functions in such a way as to hold some people accountable for crime or malfeasance, but not others. This has been much discussed in the Afghanistan context, but often in respect of the continued exercise of political power after 2001 by individuals credibly implicated in mass atrocity crimes such as the 11 February 1993 Afshar massacre.[82] The impunity that such individuals enjoyed cast a shadow over the political process: as one observer put it,

> Afghans interviewed recognised that holding an election before impunity has been curbed, guns removed and warlords disempowered will only mean that discredited and reviled leaders will be 'legitimised' in elections that are held under the threat of guns … Impunity must be tackled first if a genuinely legitimate outcome is desired in the elections in Afghanistan.[83]

31

But as time went by, impunity enjoyed by the well-connected for *ongoing* abuses also became a source of frustration. The 2019 Asia Foundation survey asked 'If you were a victim of violence or any criminal act, how much confidence would you have that the government law-enforcement organizations and judicial systems would punish the guilty party?', and 29% of Afghans responded 'not very much' and 14% responded 'no confidence at all'.[84]

In part because of the ever-present temptation to co-opt rather than confront abusive players, one mechanism for addressing the threat of the abuse of power is promotion of the rule of law. The rule of law is a metalegal principle—a principle *about* the operation and functioning of law—and while debate has surrounded its exact dimensions,[85] there is much to be said for the formulation offered by the late Joseph Raz:

> (1) All laws should be prospective, open, and clear (2) Laws should be relatively stable (3) The making of particular laws (particular legal orders) should be guided by open, stable, clear, and general rules (4) The independence of the judiciary must be guaranteed (5) The principles of natural justice must be observed (6) The courts should have review powers over the implementation of the other principles (7) The courts should be easily accessible (8) The discretion of the crime-preventing agencies should not be allowed to pervert the law.[86]

In Afghanistan after 2001, it was the independence and accessibility of the courts, and the character of the crime-preventing agencies, that proved most problematic. Delays in the functioning of state courts were legion, and doubtless helped account for the preference that some Afghans expressed for traditional, local conflict resolution mechanisms.[87] Judges had few protections if exposed to pressures from the powerful or well-connected, and given the ubiquity of 'land grabs', issues of land ownership proved especially difficult for state courts to handle fairly.[88] Crime-prevention agencies were also corrupted by the selling of key police positions in exchange for cash,[89] or by the appointment of nominees of the very people who should have been under investigation. Ultimately, the rule of law prevails when the conditions set out by Raz are reinforced by complex, interdependent, judicial, executive, and administrative cultures.[90] With limited progress in these spheres after 2001,[91] impunity and abuse of power were poised to flourish.

In some important instances, the government chose to undermine accountability. For example, in March 2007, parliament passed a 'National Reconciliation, General Amnesty and National Stability Law', which provided blanket absolution for human rights abuses of the past. This protected many sitting members of parliament against whom credible accusations of human rights violations existed. Then-President Karzai did not sign the bill but let the fifteen-day presidential veto period lapse, allowing it to become law after it was published with minimal publicity in the official gazette in 2008.[92] This law rendered moot the provision in the electoral law barring those convicted of crimes against humanity from running for president or parliament because it eliminated the prospect of anyone being prosecuted for the crimes of the past several decades.

Presidential elections and legitimacy

One recognised source of political legitimacy is popular election. It provides the institutional mechanism by which ordinary people can change their rulers without bloodshed.[93] To function effectively as a mechanism of legitimation, elections must take place within a framework defined by rules governing candidature, campaigning, voting and scrutiny, and must be free and fair rather than fake. 'Freedom', argued Jørgen Elklit and Palle Svensson in a classic study, 'entails the right and the opportunity to choose one thing over another', which requires freedom of movement, assembly, association, and speech, as well as freedom from intimidation, and universal adult franchise. 'Fairness', they argued, means impartiality and 'involves both *regularity* (the unbiased application of rules) and *reasonableness* (the not-too-unequal distribution of relevant resources among competitors)'. Criteria for fairness include independent electoral authorities, impartial voter education, fair media access, secure polling stations and ballot boxes, and appropriate, transparent, and reviewable scrutiny procedures.[94] Secrecy of the ballot is especially important.[95] Unfortunately, while elections can function as tools of legitimation, they can also be corrupted in diverse ways,[96] and when this happens, their value as a tool of legitimation is likely to decline precipitously. A promising start came in the presidential election of 9 October 2004, where the United Nations provided crucial technical support and expertise,[97] and Afghans turned out in large numbers to vote. Karzai was elected in the first round of voting with 55.4% of the vote. Unfortunately, things thereafter took a rapid turn for the worse.[98]

A first crisis came in 2009. President Karzai was eligible for re-election for a second term, but confidence in the country's trajectory had certainly dropped since 2004, making it likely that the 2009 election would be much more competitive than the 2004 poll. This had the effect of creating incentives for fraudulent activity on the part of Karzai's network, since in a neopatrimonial system it does not pay to lose an election. What eventuated was a fully fledged political crisis. To begin with, the election was *constitutionally* required to be held by 22 May, but for its own reasons the US pressed to defer it to 20 August. As then US Secretary of Defense Dr Robert Gates later put it, 'No one, including me, was indelicate enough to mention that the new administration, dedicated to building "the rule of law" in Afghanistan, had just decided to violate the Afghan constitution and connive with Karzai on keeping him in power illegally for several months'.[99] The election itself was marred by industrial-scale fraud, predominantly in the form of ballot-box stuffing,[100] fraud so blatant that while sophisticated statistical techniques are available to identify the likelihood of fraud,[101] they were hardly required in this case, although they confirmed what multiple witnesses had seen.[102] The 'Independent Election Commission' (*Komision-e mustaqel-e entekhabat* or 'IEC') initially announced a vote tally of 54.1% for Karzai, but this was then overturned by the separate 'Electoral Complaints Commission' (*Komision-e shekayat-e entekhabati*), on which impartial international experts constituted a majority. Of the 5.66 million votes that had (allegedly) been cast, over 1.3 million were invalidated on account of fraud, and over 75% of these favoured Karzai.[103] As a result, his tally fell below the 50% threshold required to avoid a run-off election against his main challenger, former Foreign Minister Dr Abdullah. This did not, however, solve the problem: the Chair of the Independent Election Commission, Dr Azizullah Lodin, an ardent Karzai supporter, pre-empted the run-off when he said 'Karzai is going to win'.[104] Unsurprisingly, Dr Abdullah then withdrew from a process that had become somewhat farcical.

The consequences of this sequence of events proved to be disastrous. Karzai, who rightly concluded that the US (or at least its Special Representative for Afghanistan and Pakistan, Richard Holbrooke) wanted to see the back of him,[105] was livid. He directed his anger at the Electoral Complaints Commission, moving in the name of 'Afghanisation' to eliminate its international majority. For the wider world, this should have been a 'red line', but that proved not to be the case. The Special Representative of the United Nations Secretary-General, Kai Eide of Norway, agreed that 'our transition agenda should include full Afghan responsibility for future elections',[106] and was reported as telling his diplomatic counterparts that 'the UN had no intention of opposing Afghanization as a principle'.[107] This virtually green-lighted further exercises in electoral fraud, and compromised the central mechanism for government legitimation that had been built into the 2004 Constitution. There is no evidence that ordinary Afghans were unprepared for democracy: they showed every sign of broadly supporting a system whereby they could change their rulers when necessary. The electoral process was undermined by elite players, and when it came to the crunch, the international community failed to protect it.

At the 2014 presidential election, for which Karzai was not a candidate, the chickens metaphorically came home to roost. A first round of voting, held on 5 April, went relatively smoothly on the day, with the atmosphere in Kabul particularly positive. The count put Dr Abdullah ahead with 44.72% of the vote, a substantial lead over Dr Ashraf Ghani, Karzai's former finance minister, with 31.37%.[108] But the run-off, on 14 June, proved to be a shambles. Barely two hours after the close of the polls, the IEC chair, Yusuf Nuristani, claimed that 7 million had voted, which it was impossible for him at that point to have known.[109] Initial turnout figures for the run-off suggested an astounding surge in turnout in Pushtun majority provinces likely to support Dr Ghani, and a forensic examination of the figures suggested high levels of fraud.[110] The final published results gave Ghani 55.27% and Abdullah 44.73%,[111] but by then the specifics of the election had been overtaken by other events. First, on 22 June, Abdullah's camp released phone intercepts in which the Chief Electoral Officer, Ziaulhaq Amarkhil, allegedly plotted fraud. As a report at the time put it, 'In 15 minutes of sometimes slightly surreal conversation, two men urge an official to fire election staff with suspect loyalties and replace them with known supporters, ramp up plans for vote buying and ballot stuffing, and close down polling stations in areas thought to be unsympathetic'.[112] Amarkhil was forced to resign.[113] Second, with tensions running extremely high, US Secretary of State John Kerry brokered a deal for a 'National Unity Government' in which Ghani would become president and Abdullah 'Chief Executive Officer'.[114] A direct result of these events was a collapse in popular confidence in the IEC. According to the Asia Foundation's survey, confidence in the IEC plunged from 66.4% in 2014 to 36.4% in 2015.[115]

The shadow cast by the 2014 election was a long one, and the 28 September 2019 presidential election proved deeply unsatisfactory. It was delayed twice, and the United States, for the sake of its 'peace process', pushed hard (although unsuccessfully) to have it deferred altogether, seemingly indifferent to the fact that it was required by the Afghan Constitution of 2004. Perhaps the most striking feature of the result was a massive fall in turnout: according to the final results, only 1,823,858 valid votes were cast, a mere 18.9% of the registered enrolment of 9,665,745. Ghani scraped in with only 923,592 votes (or 50.64%) compared with the 720,841 (or 39.52%) cast for Dr Abdullah.[116] Once again, much about the process was suspicious: in particular, the closure of polling places in areas likely to support Abdullah could easily be seen as a classic example of 'voter suppression'.[117] But from the point of view of legitimacy, it was the low turnout that sent the gravest signal. If, in a country with a population larger than that of Canada, a president holds office on the strength of fewer than a million votes, that president's authority in the event of a crisis may prove to be severely attenuated.

The weaknesses of the Wolesi Jirga

The 2004 Constitution did not provide simply for a presidency; it also provided for a two-chamber parliament, with a popularly elected lower house, the *Wolesi Jirga*, and an upper house, the *Meshrano Jirga*, comprising a mixture of presidential appointees and indirectly elected members. Parliamentary bodies have venerable histories in many different countries, with varying models having evolved over time as absolutism gave way to pluralising or democratising impulses or demands. The phenomenon of the bicameral (two-chamber) parliament is a common one, with an upper house often being seen as a 'house of review', with weaker democratic credentials than the lower house, and a more constrained mandate of checking any excesses that may have slipped through the deliberations of its more democratic counterpart. Depending upon specific constitutional formulae, parliamentary chambers may play different roles. In systems of so-called 'responsible government', a country's government is drawn from that party or coalition that can command the support of a majority in the lower house. In presidential systems, by contrast, the executive government enjoys an existence distinct from the legislature, although the legislature may still play a vital role in approving appointments, budgets, and statutes. Furthermore, while in some parliaments one witnesses a high degree of party loyalty and discipline on the part of the members, in others the members function much more as independents, and this can have very significant ramifications for the way that the parliament actually works. Whereas presidential systems can have a 'winner-takes-all' character, parliamentary systems can permit a multiplicity of political actors to have a place in the sun.[118]

The *Wolesi Jirga* consisted of 250 seats, with 68 reserved for women. This was a very notable development, which provided a platform for Afghan women to voice their social and political concerns. A grave problem, however, arose from the choice of the electoral system that was used to choose the members. Known as the single non-transferable vote, or 'SNTV', it had some extremely perverse consequences. Under this system, Afghans voted by province, and within the province, seats were allocated to candidates simply on the basis of the total votes that they secured. This had the effect of severing any direct link between the prevalence of particular values or orientations within the electorate, and the allocation of seats. Thus, if in a province with ten seats, a popular, moderate candidate secured 90% of the vote, he or she would secure only one seat, and the remaining nine seats would be divided between candidates, possibly quite extremist in their views, who in total had secured only 10% of the vote. As a result, in the 2005 elections, some very suspect individuals found their way into the *Wolesi Jirga*.[119] And in the 2018 election, the first-elected candidate in Kabul, Haji Ajmal Rahmani, won only 11,158 votes—a mere 2% of the total in the province—and only 23.5% of voters in Kabul voted for a candidate who actually won a seat.[120]

The SNTV system is famously unfriendly to political parties, since only if they have extraordinarily disciplined supporters can they avoid having large numbers of votes 'wasted' through being allocated to the parties' most prominent candidates. This may be one reason why the system appealed to Karzai, who had no party of his own, and was notoriously suspicious of parties and party activity. Yet parties are extremely important in democratic politics, for as well as fostering expression and (two-way) communication, they crucially perform what Sartori called a 'channelling' function for the mass public: 'The larger the number of participants, the more need for a regularized traffic system'.[121] Of course, this may come in different forms: in the eighteenth century, David Hume distinguished between parties of *interest*, of *principle*, and of *affection*.[122] Karzai's animus seemed to be against the last of these, perhaps as a result of his having witnessed the personalistic politics of Peshawar in the 1980s. But he may have been naïve in believing that marginalising parties would be an effective device for marginalising personal competitors. The blocking of *overt* activity by political parties runs the risk of fostering *covert* activity by factions and networks, which is indeed what Afghanistan experienced, and which put much of its politics well beyond the realm of any formal accountability. Ethnicity was (predictably) mobilised to try to shape coherent voting blocs within the *Wolesi Jirga*,[123] and noisy grandstanding became common in the chamber, as members needed to build up their 'name recognition' in the hope of securing re-election.

More seriously, the structure of the *Wolesi Jirga*, and the SNTV electoral system, had significant effects on how lower house members set out to discharge their functions. With re-election such a lottery, members had a strong incentive to focus not on abstract ideas of what might be good for Afghanistan, but rather on functioning as brokers between the state and their local constituents. This was a role that had been played by members of the *Wolesi Jirga* between 1965 and 1973,[124] and while it was quite understandable that members of the new *Wolesi Jirga* first elected in 2005 would act similarly, it opened the door for unsavoury networks that were entwined with the state also to penetrate the halls of the parliament.

A final severe problem proved to be the scale of the gulf between the executive and the legislature. In significant respects, the SNTV system weakened the parliament and there is some evidence that it appealed to the US for this very reason: Astri Suhrke has argued that an 'election system likely to shield the executive from the parliament was consistent with US interests in a strong presidential system' that would 'streamline the relationship with its main interlocutor in the country—the president'.[125] But as things turned out, even a relatively weak *Wolesi Jirga* had the potential to confront the executive in a menacing if indirect fashion. The Constitution required that appointments of ministers be ratified by the *Wolesi Jirga*, and the rather regular withholding of ratification prompted President Ghani in particular to appoint a significant number of 'acting ministers' who did not require ratification. This often resulted in relatively weak leadership in crucial ministries, at the very moment when it was critical that all components of the political system work concertedly to resist the looming threat of Taliban attack.

Conclusion: The decline of political legitimacy

Surveying the points that we have made about political legitimacy in this chapter, there are a number of conclusions worth highlighting that are pertinent to the wider decline and fall of Republican Afghanistan. The story, however, is a rather complex one, and points to the need for a nuanced rather than simplified approach to the issue.

One important point to note at the outset is that most of the foundations for legitimacy problems were laid early in the life of Republican Afghanistan, often with the active or tacit approval, if not at the instigation, of Afghanistan's Western allies. Moreover, the development of a neopatrimonial system was very much a creature of Hamed Karzai's terms in office and formed part of the rather toxic legacy that President Ghani inherited in 2014. Once networks are entrenched, they are very difficult to pick apart. This, somewhat surprisingly, was also an area in which the United States played a role: Donald H. Rumsfeld, Secretary of Defense under President George W. Bush, argued that Karzai 'should learn to use patronage and political incentives'.[126] The danger with such an approach was that while it provided an illusion of stability and inclusiveness in the short run—something we take up in more detail in Chapter Five—it laid the foundations for the gradual erosion of political legitimacy in the medium to long term.

Second, it should not be forgotten that the Afghan state succeeded in coping with the challenge posed by the withdrawal of the bulk of foreign forces from Afghanistan by the end of 2014. Some were sceptical that it would be able to do so, but it rose to the challenge, and a crisis of legitimacy did not ensue. Several factors accounted for this success. One was that the withdrawal was carried out hand-in-hand with the Afghan government and with the US's NATO and other allies, rather than as the result of an exit deal struck with the enemy. Another was that the withdrawal of foreign forces was not total; some foreign military personnel and contractors remained, small in number compared with numbers at the height of President Obama's 'surge' but nonetheless reassuring Afghans by providing niche capabilities to the Afghan National Army. Furthermore, the Afghan government survived even though the mortality rates in its armed forces remained high, especially compared with those of the United States, which saw only 64 'hostile deaths' in Afghanistan between the end of 2014 and the fall of Kabul in mid-August 2021.[127] Speaking at the World Economic Forum in Davos in January 2019, President Ghani gave a figure of 45,000 security personnel killed since 2014.[128] Given these figures, it is remarkable that the Afghan government was able to *avoid* a legitimacy crisis for so long.

One explanation is simply that while much went wrong over two decades in Afghanistan, this was not the whole story. Different components of the state were viewed differently.[129] One need not accept every exaggerated claim about progress in Afghanistan—of which there were unfortunately many[130]—in order to recognise that the country changed radically during this period, and in notable respects for the better. This was partly due to the 'bubble effect' of the international presence, an effect that dissipated substantially after 2014, but it was also because Afghanistan was exposed to the forces of globalisation in a way that for the first time in the country's history began to create a significant middle class. Many young people benefitted from this, and if not exactly thanking the government directly, nonetheless recognised that this was very much a product of a republican *system* that would be at risk if the 'Emirate' model were to reappear. In 2015, 57.5% of Asia Foundation survey respondents saw the country as moving in the wrong direction, but of these, only 11.4% listed 'bad government' as the first or second reasons.[131] As noted earlier, in 2019, 58% saw the country as moving in the wrong direction, with only 6% pointing to 'bad government' as first or second reasons.[132] These reasons need to be treated with some caution, as other reasons offered could potentially reflect adversely on the government as well, but they suggest that at the level of the mass population, as opposed to the engaged political elite in Kabul, the situation in 2019 seemed somewhat similar to that in 2015. By 2021, Ghani had lost much of his popularity, but that did not mean the Republican *system* was in crisis. And in 2020, the International Institute for Democracy and Electoral Assistance (International IDEA) categorised Afghanistan as a 'hybrid' rather than 'authoritarian' regime type, with inclusive suffrage, media integrity, and freedom of association and assembly being areas of strength,[133] and its score on gender equality at an 'all-time high'.[134] All of these were to regress dramatically with the Taliban takeover.

What this suggests is that there may be dangers in reading history backwards. Timur Kuran, among others, has warned of the need 'to guard against the biases that outcome knowledge introduces into historical analysis'.[135] Because the government *did* eventually collapse, it is tempting to see the collapse as the inevitable coming-to-a-head of a legitimacy crisis that had been long in the making. Our analysis points to a more complicated picture. A regime, government, or system may experience diminishing generalised, normative support without that bringing it to the point of imminent crisis. This was a large part of the story of France's defeat in 1940. As the historian Julian Jackson put it:[136]

> Even those who believe there was something fundamentally wrong with France in 1940 are hard put to show how this related to the short six weeks of fighting. They can argue only that France was like the victim of a violent murder who was subsequently found to have been suffering from an incurable disease, but they cannot show that the disease was the cause of the death in the form it took place. The defeat of France was first and foremost a military defeat—so rapid and so total that these other factors did not have time to come into play.

To put it another way, the internal problems of France in 1940 were serious, but they were neither necessary nor sufficient for the defeat that France experienced. Similarly, problems of political legitimacy were significant and long-standing in Afghanistan, and help explain its *decline* from the high point of optimism in the early twenty-first century. But they were not sufficient to explain its *fall*.

3

PATHOLOGIES OF AID AND DEVELOPMENT

When the Taliban were overthrown in 2001, the new post-Bonn leadership of Afghanistan arrived to find the cupboard bare. Over the previous five years, the Taliban had failed to develop more than a rudimentary system of public management and budgeting,[1] and ordinary Afghans, to survive, were dependent upon support from personal networks, and from the circular flow of income in a dysfunctional market economy that lacked both a modern banking system and mechanisms for the mobilisation of savings to support productive investment. As a result, the new leadership found itself heavily dependent upon international aid, not only for the purposes of establishing and sustaining state instrumentalities but also to fund developmental projects in various parts of the country. As we show in this chapter, the direct achievements of international systems were somewhat patchy, with a range of paradoxical impacts. The most durable effect was the exposure of a new generation of Afghans to the forces of globalisation. The failures associated in particular with US aid were searingly documented in a range of reports from the US Special Inspector-General for Afghanistan Reconstruction (SIGAR) and in studies that showed how certain forms of aid either undermined the state or empowered networks. At the same time, it would be going too far to suggest that these failings were a critical factor in the fall of Republican Afghanistan. Development projects in many parts of the world have been plagued by similar problems,[2] but the result has rarely been government or state collapse.

From 2001, it was very clear that the task of reconstruction in Afghanistan was going to be enormously complicated. As one of the authors wrote at the time:[3]

> To put the country back on its feet, it is necessary to accomplish the interconnected tasks of reconstituting the state, rebuilding trust at elite and mass levels, overcoming the threat of predatory warlordism, redeveloping a shattered infrastructure and meeting the urgent needs of the most vulnerable Afghans without disrupting market mechanisms and norms of reciprocity which have sustained a large proportion of the population through decades of turmoil. All these objectives must be pursued in a climate of uncertainty as to the exact amount of aid that will be made available in the long run, and in the face of rising expectations on the part of ordinary Afghan men and women, a very large number of whom are deeply traumatized as result of their experiences of war.

From these basic points, several challenges immediately arose. One was the challenge of *sequencing*. Effective aid delivery is not simply a matter of developing a project idea and then putting it into effect; great attention may be required to the exact order in which tasks must be executed if the project is to succeed. Proper sequencing in turn may require the development of planning systems to give sequencing the attention it deserves. At a higher level, another challenge was that of *coordination*. When resources are scarce, it is important that their use be carefully coordinated in order to avoid duplication and waste. This in turn requires a distinct system for the coordination of activities, above and beyond the planning systems just mentioned. A third challenge was that of *financial management*, to enable aid funds to be tracked and to ensure that they were not siphoned off through corrupt practices. And a fourth challenge, casting a shadow over all the others, related to whether reconstruction should be carried out in a *centralised* fashion or using devolved centres of authority. As we saw in the previous chapter, the highly centralised political structure put in place by the 2004 constitution to a degree resolved this question in favour of centralisation; but the consequences were not happy ones, not just in terms of political legitimacy as we have already discussed but also in terms of the effectiveness, efficiency, and value for money of reconstruction projects. That said, it would be foolish to deny that Afghanistan, during the two decades before the August 2021 collapse, experienced dramatic change, some of it very positive, as a result of development and reconstruction activities. But given the high expectations that accompanied the establishment of the Republican system, it is something of a tragedy that more was not achieved and that much that was achieved proved so readily reversible once the Taliban returned, inaugurating a humanitarian crisis.

The forms and significance of aid

Aid to Afghanistan after 2001 came in a number of different forms. One particularly important form was focused on the reconstitution of the security sector. This embraced the obvious areas of armed forces and policing but also the less obvious areas of the disarmament, demobilisation, and reintegration of combatants ('DDR'). All these were areas of great complexity. One element, but only one, involved training of new personnel, but beyond this lay a wide range of issues: the development of training capabilities; the development of curricula to determine what trainees should be trained to do; the development of management systems and structures, and logistical support; and the preparation of key staff for higher leadership and policy development roles. All these occurred in an environment in which a significant number of armed groups existed whose leaders had no particular interest in fading into obscurity. In the short run, of course, it was international forces deployed as part of the post-9/11 intervention that predominantly occupied the security space, but their immediate objective was not so much providing durable security for Afghans as confronting remnants of Osama bin Laden's organisation. Perhaps the greatest challenge of all was that of inculcating a high level of organisational solidarity within new security structures as well as a culture of loyalty to the new and untested civil authorities, when for decades armed groups in Afghanistan had typically been loyal to other kinds of powerholder.

A second form of aid was development assistance. In contrast to humanitarian assistance, which is designed to alleviate emergency shortages of food, water and shelter that are essential for life, development assistance is focused on lifting standards of living to levels that match acceptable norms, which can be defined locally (one example from Afghanistan being 'genteel poverty'[4]) or internationally, in the form of standards such as the Millennium Development Goals or Sustainable Development Goals, promulgated by the United Nations in 2000 and 2015.[5] Afghanistan in 2001 fell far below any of these standards, something only to be expected given the decades of disruption and destruction that it had encountered since the coup of April 1978. Its 'Human Development Index' in 2000 was 0.350; life expectancy at birth was only 55.8 years, and gross national income (GDP) per capita on a purchasing power parity basis was US$904.[6] With no functioning banking system to mobilise savings that existed domestically, the need for foreign aid to confront development problems was immediate and obvious.

A third form of aid relates to the budget of the state. States can fund their spending in a number of different ways. One way, historically the most popular, is through the levying of taxation, namely compulsory imposts that the law requires be paid into state coffers. Classically, taxes are categorised as direct (such as income tax) or indirect (such as taxes on transactions like the import or the sale of goods). Different taxes have different effects, and there is a vast literature on public finance that seeks to explore what these effects might be and what systems of taxation might be optimal in particular circumstances. States can also fund their spending from borrowings, and this may be appropriate if the monies involved are spent on infrastructure or capital works which will benefit future generations as well as simply current taxpayers; in this way the cost can be spread more equitably between different beneficiaries. In addition, many states have historically resorted to printing money as a way of funding their expenditure, but this runs the risk of 'inflation'—that is, a general increase in price levels—as too much money chases too few goods. Finally, states can be funded by external donors, a common practice in Afghan history which resurfaced with a vengeance after 2001.[7]

Two consequences flow from dependence on external donors as key sources of revenue for a state's budget. The first relates to the power relations between the donor and the recipient. Inevitably, the donor will enjoy significant leverage, simply because of the knowledge or apprehension on the part of the recipient that the donor has the discretion to withdraw or withhold funds in the future. Even the threat of withholding funds can wreak havoc with the budget strategy of the recipient. On the one hand, the leverage that the donor enjoys can be general, allowing it to shape the broad policy orientations of the recipient across a wide range of policy settings. On the other hand, the leverage may be much more specific, reflecting a disposition on the part of donors to micromanage the project development and implementation strategies of the recipient state. The more this happens, the less scope the recipient has to engage in truly discretionary spending, and this may have wider political consequences. This need not, of course, reflect any particular malevolence on the part of the donor. On the contrary, the budgetary processes of donor states may themselves be so structured that funds disbursed to the recipient have to be tied to particular purposes or projects.[8] Managing this 'sovereignty gap' can be a considerable challenge.[9]

A second consequence of dependence upon external donors for state revenue is what might be called a 'dependency curse', most dramatically on display in the case of what are known as 'rentier states', where an unhealthy volume of state revenue comes from unstable sources such as foreign aid or the sale of natural resources, the prices of which can fluctuate wildly. Afghanistan has been a rentier state for much of its recent history,[10] and a strong case can be built that this was a major contributing factor to some of the disasters that befell Afghanistan from the 1970s onwards.[11] A critical danger in a rentier state is the erosion of any real sense of accountability on the part of rulers towards their own citizens: if the bulk of state revenues are externally supplied, much more effort is likely to be put into keeping the donors happy than ensuring that the wishes of the locals are understood and respected.

Security sector assistance

To assess the worth of security sector aid, it is important to put such aid in the context of the specific threats that a given recipient might face. This will often be critical in determining the appropriateness of the aid that is actually supplied. If too much is invested in preparing for remote contingencies, at the expense of investment in addressing immediate threats, there is a risk that forces will run into significant difficulties no matter how well funded they may have been. It is also important to recognise that there may be certain kinds of military threat that require non-military responses, for example through the application of diplomatic pressure. To highlight the obvious example, when the Taliban retreated to the sanctuaries that they enjoyed in Pakistan, it was simply not possible for the Afghan armed forces to follow them in hot pursuit; even the United States agonised over the 2 May 2011 incursion that eliminated Osama bin Laden. On this issue, Afghanistan depended on its allies to pressure Pakistan effectively over the sanctuaries issue. The failure of the United States to do so created an ongoing problem for both Afghanistan and its allies that no investment in the Afghan security sector on its own was capable of overcoming.

In addition, security sector assistance needed to be equally attuned to the complexities of Afghan society, which was in no sense a *tabula rasa*. In a society in which the educational system had been disrupted for decades, in which a multiplicity of languages were spoken, and in which loyalties over time had shifted from the state to other authority figures and powerholders, reconstituting an army and police force was far more than simply a technical issue; it involved navigating an exceptionally complex set of power structures in which measures that might in the abstract appear useful for the society as a whole could be detrimental to the interests of particular actors with enough accumulated power to function as spoilers. This was especially the case when it came to the demobilisation, disarmament, and reintegration of combatants, and it was hardly surprising that this process proved to be fraught with difficulties. An additional problem was that the main narrative with the potential to bind different elements of the new security sector together, namely wariness about Pakistan,[12] was a narrative that the US did not want to employ given its dependence on Pakistan for the delivery of materiel to the Afghan theatre of operations.

Aid to the 'Afghanistan National Defence and Security Forces', or ANDSF, was largely a US responsibility, although Germany played a 'lead nation' role with respect to policing. In particular, procurement was entirely a US responsibility, an area of endeavour for which Afghanistan never developed a strong capacity. The budget was deeply opaque: the Office of the National Security Council in Afghanistan tried for over two and a half years to obtain a complete picture of how much the ANDSF were receiving by way of aid from the US, but failed to get a consistent figure. The Ministry of Interior did not have a reliable breakdown of its budget until the very end of the Republic's life. A 2021 study from the Stockholm International Peace Research Institute concluded that from 2001 to 2020, US disbursements of security-related reconstruction spending totalled '$81.6 billion in constant 2019 dollars',[13] overwhelmingly delivered through a dedicated 'Afghanistan Security Forces Fund'. Yet despite this financial largesse, problems remained rife. A 2019 'Lessons Learned' report from the office of the US Special Inspector General for Afghanistan Reconstruction (SIGAR) offered some sobering conclusions relating to US Security Sector Assistance (SSA) that deserves to be quoted at length:[14]

> The lack of a comprehensive and consistent long-term plan to train, advise, assist, and equip a partner nation's military and security forces results in misalignment of advisors and ad hoc decision-making … Conducting SSA activities while the United States is engaged in major combat operations fractures the traditional way the United States develops partner forces and creates a disjointed command-and-control relationship between the U.S. military and civilian leadership … U.S. financing of partner nation security forces may be a continued requirement even as their capabilities improve … Equipping partner forces requires determining the capabilities the United States will train and advise on for the long term, versus those capabilities the United States will assist with in the short term to help the host nation reduce or remove a particular threat. Failure to determine

this will result in equipping a partner nation with capabilities it may not need or be able to sustain.

In diverse ways, each of these failings played a role in contributing to the collapse of 2021.

Assistance in the development of policing capability faced a somewhat different set of challenges. From the outset, there was a dissonance between the legal duties of the police and their actual duties: the law specified that 'detecting' crimes was the duty of the police (with the Attorney-General's Office being the prosecutor), but for much of the Republic's life, the police functioned as the first line of defence against the Taliban and other terrorist groups. This resulted in significant investment of resources in counter-terrorism rather than community policing, and tremendous loss of lives amongst the police, distracting them from their actual work. Policing works best as a community-based activity, highly dependent upon both the development of trust between citizens and policing agents, and on the integration of a range of related functions, such as the operation of a reliable and trustworthy judiciary, and the establishment of an appropriate penal system. Aid in these spheres was fragmented, with Germany playing a lead role in police development but Italy playing the lead role in the development of the judiciary.[15] A deeper problem, however, was incoherence in the assistance effort, as an insightful Afghan commentary captured:[16]

Since it became a state in the 18th century, Afghanistan has never had an effective national police force ... When the United States and NATO created the International Security Assistance Force (ISAF) in 2001, a variety of police training efforts began, but the new policing institutions were all shaped by the assumptions and values of the countries providing the trainers: European police trainers had good goals but few resources to implement them; the American effort relied primarily on contractors who advocated a culture of militarization rather than civilian policing. Deep-seated Afghan cultural habits of political patronage continued to undermine the policing institutions brought in from outside the country. As a result of these competing cultures, the

Afghan National Police is a hodgepodge of various entities and organizations, none of which are very effective.

The Afghanistan police were routinely excoriated by critics,[17] but they also suffered huge casualties as the Taliban targeted them for attack. This made policing an increasingly unattractive career option, a perception which no amount of foreign assistance could easily shift.

The issue of sustainability of the ANDSF remained hanging right up to the end of the Republic. According to the Stockholm International Peace Research Institute, from 2004 to 2020, the Afghan government's military expenditure totalled '$3.6 billion in constant 2019 dollars, equivalent to only 4.6 per cent of all US military aid disbursed to Afghanistan'.[18] In an early commentary, the US scholar Barnett R. Rubin observed that 'If the state cannot sustain the recurrent cost of its security forces, its stability will always be at risk. Nor can any state long survive the funding of its army and police by foreign powers'.[19] The crisis that came to a head in August 2021 highlighted a further dilemma: the sudden *dis*continuation of military aid from foreign powers can be even more devastating.

Provincial Reconstruction Teams

One distinctive form of aid that was delivered to Afghanistan was channelled through what came to be known as 'Provincial Reconstruction Teams', or PRTs. In the aftermath of the December 2001 Bonn Agreement, the Security Council of the United Nations had approved the deployment in Afghanistan of what came to be known as the International Security Assistance Force (ISAF), and the near-universal recommendation from people with knowledge of Afghanistan's complexities was that it be deployed as quickly as possible to different parts of the country in order to fill any security vacuum. Unfortunately, this was blocked by the administration of US President George W. Bush, which was already making plans for what was to become its disastrous invasion of Iraq, and did not want to see crucial airlift assets tied up in Afghanistan in support of ISAF. The deployment of mixed civilian-military PRTs was very much a second-best option, but it provided the basis for aid to be delivered in

Afghanistan not just by the United States, but by its NATO partners and other allies. The deployment of PRTs was marked by a high degree of improvisation; while the first PRT was deployed in Gardez in January 2003, it was not until April 2008 at the Bucharest NATO summit that a 'Comprehensive Strategic Political-Military Plan' for Afghanistan was finally adopted.[20] PRTs functioned in different parts of the country for more than a decade but were finally closed down as part of the 'transition' (*inteqal*) process that saw the vast bulk of foreign forces withdrawn from Afghanistan by the end of 2014. As Kilcullen and Mills put it, the:

> fact that each PRT covered a province, and each was sponsored by a troop-contributing nation, meant that the varying abilities and enthusiasm of national leadership came with the turf. It also meant that nations tended to focus on high-profile aid programmes within their provinces, bolstering their credentials as contributing members of the coalition, rather than on longer-term, lower-visibility issues of greater importance.[21]

In practice, there was no single PRT 'model' but rather a diversity of approaches reflecting the interaction of local conditions with the specificities and particularities of the PRT-contributing state.[22] US PRTs, for example, tended to be very well resourced; the Lithuanian and Romanian PRTs had far fewer resources on which to draw. The military cultures of different contributing countries also proved relevant, with the US heavily involved in parallel kinetic operations, in sharp contrast to the New Zealanders in the more serene environment of Bamiyan. Rapid personnel turnover proved a complication across the board, as key military figures were often rotated out of theatre just as they were beginning to understand the complexities of the operating environment. Under the circumstances, it was extremely tempting for PRT leaders to seek out local strongmen with whom to partner, but this of course often had local political consequences that the PRT leaders were slow to understand. These in turn had the potential to complicate or compromise the effective delivery of assistance.[23]

A particular problem related to the location of PRTs. Their deployment appeared much more focused on providing the possibility of a 'peace dividend' in the wake of successful kinetic operations than rewarding those communities that had made serious efforts on their own to create an enabling environment for reconstruction and development. At the same time, and pulling in the opposite direction, the domestic politics of contributing states often inclined the governments of those states to try to avoid casualties (one of the authors recalls asking a very senior Australian defence official in 2005 when a decision might be made on an Australian PRT contribution; he received the reply: 'Soon, hopefully, since otherwise all the easy places will have been taken'). An effect of this was that on the whole there was less engagement with Afghan communities during the course of PRT work than one might have wished. Furthermore, the hope for a peace dividend in troubled places proved elusive; a detailed study by Sexton suggested that aid contributions had positive effects in areas that were already stable, but not so in contested areas.[24] Money, infused in sufficient amounts, can have the same (unintended) effect as introducing armed men in an area: it can destabilise the area's political-economic equilibrium and create conditions for protection rackets (à la the famous description of a Talib allowing a bridge to be built as long as the contractor paid him and he could blow it up after completion). When effectively used, a PRT could of course play a constructive role. One of the best examples of this was in the province of Bamiyan, where a small New Zealand PRT, extremely sensitive to the complexities of the province, made positive contributions without in any way seeking to displace the office of the provincial governor;[25] its success was widely noted,[26] and became almost a paradigm of what could be achieved with the right settings.

What the PRT approach could not do was stabilise Afghanistan on a 'province-by-province' basis. With ambient threats emanating from the Taliban's sanctuaries in Pakistan, the so-called 'ink spot' model whereby success in stabilising one area would spread to others was highly optimistic, if not simply an example of wishful thinking. The sad reality that it is almost always cheaper and easier to be a wrecker than a builder was very much on display in Afghanistan, where the Taliban had no hesitation in using child suicide bombers to attack aid workers attempting to contribute to reconstruction in areas where the Taliban saw the achievement of peace and stability as a threat to their own interests.[27] Indeed, as long as the sanctuaries problem remained unaddressed, the delivery of significant quantities of aid to needy localities and populations ran the risk of attracting the unwanted attention of the Taliban, for whom there could be political value in demonstrating a capacity to strike at symbolically important projects to which supporters of Afghanistan's transition had concluded it would be worthwhile to contribute resources. Development assistance can find itself unwittingly caught in the middle of a very vicious circle.

Funding the Afghan state

For two decades from 2001, the Afghan state was heavily dependent upon international contributions to fund its activities, typically supplied through channels such as the 'Afghanistan Reconstruction Trust Fund' (ARTF) and the 'Law and Order Trust Fund for Afghanistan' (LOTFA). It had made some progress in increasing domestic revenue collection, but this was undercut by increasing insecurity and the COVID-19 outbreak: the World Bank reported in April 2021 that 'Domestic revenue collapsed to 11.4 percent of GDP in 2020 after reaching a record high of 14.1 percent in 2019'.[28] The state budget approved on 22 February 2021 anticipated total revenue of US$5.47 billion, of which US$2.66 billion, or 48.6 per cent, was to come from foreign aid, including loans.[29] When the Taliban seized Kabul in August 2021 and international contributions ceased to flow, the state largely collapsed. No state can readily survive both the loss of the bulk of its income and the loss of key personnel, as occurred when members of Afghanistan's educated younger generation, horrified at the return of an anti-modernist tyranny, came to see exit as the only viable option if they were to have meaningful lives in the future. This collapse, however, demonstrated how fragile the fiscal basis of the state had been between 2001 and 2021.

Furthermore, in Chapter One, we noted both the range of functions that the state may discharge and the different components of a state that need to be taken into account. One implication is that it is not especially helpful to speak in the abstract about the funding of the state. The very complexity of the state means that even with what might appear to be access to a considerable volume of resources, key parts of a state might nonetheless be under-resourced. This can be manifested in the form of some ministries being overfunded and others underfunded; or in some provinces receiving more state funds than others even when one controls for population and needs; or in disproportionate emphasis on the funding of 'showcase' central offices at the expense of the dispersed field offices and trenches. In Chapter Two, we also noted the importance of the issues of scope and strength of the state in institutional design. These issues had ramifications for the fiscal needs of the state. If the state has a large number of functional components, it is likely that each will require a certain minimum volume of funds in order to operate effectively. A poorly designed state often involves unnecessary duplication, 'reinvention of the wheel', and scarce time devoted to lobbying efforts to ensure that a unit's cut of the annual budget does not shrink. There is a great deal to be said, in terms of both legitimacy and efficiency, in favour of a state that does a small number of things reasonably well rather than a state that attempts to do a great deal but with a relatively high likelihood that some endeavours will be costly failures. Afghanistan from the outset had a bloated state, in its form more the product of the unintended consequences of bargaining processes at Bonn than of careful reflection on what kind of scope would be appropriate for the state to have. This heightened the dependence of the new state on external aid.

This in turn had implications for what areas of state activity received funding priority. There were two elements here that came into play. One was that some forms of state activity were likely to be more valued by donors than others. For example, given the widely publicised repression of women by the Taliban before 2001, state activities to advance the position of Afghan women were understandably welcomed by the donor community. The result was that funds were often earmarked for purposes or projects that reflected donor rather than recipient priorities.[30] The other element was slightly more subtle, and reflected the ways that donors too could rely on networks. Some new ministers in the Afghan government were well known to policymakers in the West, and, especially if they spoke fluent English, they were optimally positioned to draw on those links in order to be favoured with aid flows. Those who lacked such links were not nearly so well positioned. For example, as Bizhan reported, 'In 2005, when Ali Ahmad Jalali, the Interior Minister, resigned, the US, Canadian, and UK aid agencies all withdrew their funding from the Afghanistan Stabilization Programme (ASP), led by the Ministry of Interior'.[31]

One other, and distinctly dispiriting, example of funding of the Afghan state came in the form of the rescue package that had to be put together in the wake of the collapse of the Kabul Bank in September 2010. Commercial banks, which make profits by lending depositors' funds to investors at commercial rates, typically do not have on hand sufficient cash to meet all depositors' demands at once: they are therefore vulnerable if a crisis of confidence leads to a sudden 'run' on the bank. The Kabul Bank, it turned out, had been lending monies not just for productive investment, but to underpin the often extravagant lifestyles of friends of the management, a number of whom were very well connected politically. President Karzai's brother was a notable beneficiary, and some rather shameless efforts were made by Karzai's circle to pin the blame for the collapse on the under-resourced local regulators, who had been the victims of conscious duplicity.[32] The High Office of Oversight and Anti-Corruption, chaired by the same Karzai loyalist who had been chair of the Independent Election Commission in 2009, refused to cooperate in an investigation of the fraud carried out by the Independent Joint Anti-Corruption Monitoring and Evaluation Committee.[33] State intervention, followed by a large-scale bailout to the tune of $825 million (much of it ultimately supplied by the US), proved necessary.[34]

'Off-budget' funding

One of the more pernicious forms of 'aid' was so-called 'off-budget funding'. As Astri Suhrke put it, 'Two-thirds of all aid money was spent directly by donors through sub-contractors of their choice. Afghan authorities had no control over these funds and did not have full information about their magnitude and purpose. This so-called "external budget" dwarfed the government budget'.[35] Some 'off-budget' aid flowed through PRTs; other aid was delivered by agencies or firms—international, Afghan, or both—working directly for donors. It proved extraordinarily difficult for the Afghan government to keep track of what was happening, and this in turn had ramifications for the coherence of both the 'Afghan National Development Strategy', which had been developed to inform a major international conference in London in 2006, and the related 'Afghanistan Compact' that covered 'Security', 'Governance, Rule of Law and Human Rights', 'Economic and Social Development', 'Education', 'Health', 'Agriculture and Rural Development', 'Social Protection', and 'Economic Governance and Private Sector Development'.[36] This lack of transparency only grew worse over time. As Bizhan put it, after 2005:

> the rise of Taliban activities, such as suicide bombings, intimidations and targeting of the government, NGOs and aid agencies employees, further weakened off-budget transparency, as contractors and donors would prefer to keep their information as confidential as possible to safeguard the safety of their staff. This situation became an excuse for concealing contractual arrangements in insecure provinces and bred corruption, damaging the perception of aid and the government in society.[37]

The prevalence of 'off-budget' funding emerged in part as a response to the institutional vacuum that existed when the Taliban were overthrown in 2001. Re-establishing even a basic financial management capability for the Afghan state inevitably took time, and in the meantime 'off-budget' funding was a convenient mechanism for rapidly addressing some of Afghanistan's more obvious problems. A further contributing factor, however, was the growing disposition—worldwide—of government aid agencies to outsource project delivery to private commercial contractors and NGOs. Over time, this had led to a 'hollowing out' of donor state capacity in the sphere of aid delivery. In some cases, this led donors to sign 'head contracts' with contractors legally domiciled in the donor's territory, which encouraged further subcontracting with Afghanistan-based actors that carried the responsibility for the actual delivery of projects.

This came at the expense of transparency, of effective monitoring and evaluation, and—in many cases—of donor credibility, although ironically it was often the Afghan government that was in the front-line to be blamed by critics when 'off-budget' projects failed to meet people's expectations. A scathing 2006 report identified multiple cases of mismanagement and waste,[38] findings which a number of subsequent analyses replicated. As a recent analysis put it, 'The large amounts of money being spent on the war effort and on rebuilding Afghanistan after years of conflict strained the U.S. government's ability to vet contractors and ensure the money was spent as intended'.[39]

A particular problem with 'off-budget' funding in Afghanistan was its focus on short-term rather than long-term needs. At worst, this led to an emphasis on notoriously perilous 'quick impact projects', or QIPs, designed and implemented with an eye to a political dividend rather than sustainability or durable community development. In 2002–3, less than 25% of US agency spending focused on long-term reconstruction issues.[40] In particular, the 'fast tracking' of projects with a view to the approaching 2004 presidential election in Afghanistan led to corner-cutting and shoddy outcomes in projects funded by the US Agency for International Development.[41] Even more seriously, 'off-budget' funding provided ample fuel to launch corruption on a large scale.[42] One of the main difficulties that arose with project implementation in the early years of the Republic related to the complexity of the bureaucratic landscape that contractors were required to navigate. It did not take contractors long to realise that one way of lubricating the bureaucratic process was to use local 'fixers' to ensure that necessary bureaucratic approvals were obtained, whether by lawful or illicit means.

The exact scale of 'off-budget' funding is almost impossible to calculate, simply as a result of its kaleidoscopic character. In a 2020 study, Haque and Roberts concluded that 'off-budget' programmes 'accounted for nearly 70 percent of all donor contributions in 2018 ($5.8 billion of the $8.6 billion total)', but warned that 'Data on off-budget aid to Afghanistan (especially on off-budget security grants) is fragmented, incomplete, and often inconsistent' and that 'Estimates are subject to an appreciable margin of error'.[43] Even assuming a wide margin, however, it is very clear that only a small proportion of aid contributed to Afghanistan was available to the Afghan government for discretionary spending. Since only a fraction of 'on-budget' funds were available for development purposes—according to Shapour, in Afghanistan's 2021 budget 'for every one dollar spent on development, the government spent two dollars keeping the state running'[44]—the government remained extremely constrained in what it could do to better the lives of ordinary people.

One further consequence of the way that aid was disbursed related to the distribution of human capital between the state and other actors. This was foreshadowed early in the life of the Republic in a World Bank study, which, noting that most aid was not channelled through the government treasury, observed that

> this has resulted in a 'second civil service' consisting of NGOs, consultants, advisors, and employees of UN and other international agencies, including expatriate consultants and Afghans attracted by relatively high salaries. Not only has this second civil service taken some of the best talent from the Government, but with the relatively small share of resources at the Government's disposal, it is a constant challenge for the Government to stay 'in charge' of the development agenda.[45]

The scale of this problem arguably went down after 2014, but it remained something of a challenge until the Republic's final days.

Management issues

A range of further issues relating to the funding of development also surfaced during the life of the Republic. One was the challenge of living within limited means. The scale of Afghanistan's needs in 2001 was simply awesome. Across a vast range of critical spheres, but especially health, education and training, and the maintenance of infrastructure, Afghanistan had suffered from decades of neglect, or active damage. It is easy to be dazzled by reports of the sums that were delivered in aid to Afghanistan after 2001, but when these are put in the context of profound poverty caused by unmet needs, they become less impressive. In these circumstances, competition for scarce funds was likely always to be intense, between different agencies of the state, between different parts of the country, and between various networks that had emerged in the context of the neopatrimonial system that took shape during the Karzai presidency. This scarcity of resources was one reason why conspicuous consumption on the part of the well-off or well-connected did not go down well with the broader Afghan population, but even without the self-indulgence that some members of the new elites blatantly displayed, many needs or wants would still have gone unmet, simply because of the inevitable effects of unavoidable prioritisation in the use of scarce resources.

Added to this were problems arising from the general tension between the executive and the legislature. As we noted in Chapter Two, one of the effects of the SNTV voting system was to focus the attention of legislators on the extraction of resources from the state for the benefit of the particular provinces in which they would be seeking re-election. This in turn set the scene for a great deal of tension during the budget process, since Article 90 of the 2004 Constitution identified 'approval of the state budget' (taswib-e budjah-i dawlati) as one of the powers with which the legislature was invested. This kind of tension is not unknown in democratic systems: there were major crises over just such issues in the United Kingdom from 1909 to 1911, and in Australia in 1975,[46] and they have become almost commonplace in the US. It is one thing to face such a crisis in peacetime, but it is another thing altogether to struggle with such problems when the state is under existential insurgent attack. From December 2020 to February 2021, there was a great deal of to-ing and fro-ing between the executive and the legislature in Afghanistan over the exact content of the budget,[47] at a time when the looming military threat from the Taliban was undoubtedly a matter of greater immediate concern.

An additional problem, which many developing countries have confronted, was related to the integrity of the process of revenue collection. Some forms of revenue collection are relatively difficult to subvert, but others are easily manipulated. Collection of customs duties at border posts can be especially problematic: it was a source of major friction when Ashraf Ghani was Finance Minister from 2002 to 2004, and Ismail Khan, the strongman in Herat, was collecting and spending funds that Ghani and President Karzai wished to see remitted to Kabul. Ghani, as one historian has put it, 'led the charge to neuter Ismail Khan, and to force him to submit his taxes to Kabul'.[48] Ghani succeeded, but at a rather high price, as became apparent in August 2021 when Herat fell to the Taliban. At least where Ismail Khan was concerned, a significant proportion of revenue collected at the border seemed to have been fed back into development projects within the province.[49] In other cases, the system of customs revenue collection was thoroughly corrupted, with the immediate practitioners of corruption often under pressure to pay kickbacks to officials higher up in the system. In a graphic account, Afghanistan's last finance minister, Khalid Payenda, outlined some of the challenges he faced in confronting these problems before he finally resigned on 10 August 2021.[50]

Centralisation also proved a significant obstacle to development. One particular initiative did run against this trend, namely the National Solidarity Program (NSP), behind which Finance Minister Ghani was the driving force. The NSP was administered by the Ministry of Rural Rehabilitation and Development and operated from 2003 to 2017. Funded by donors, the NSP saw around US$1.5 billion disbursed through the channel of 85,918 completed sub-projects that were identified and managed by some 35,075 'Community Development Councils' (CDCs).[51] The NSP had positive effects on access to services and opportunities for women but no obvious effects on social cohesion.[52] But it was the exception that proved the rule. A recent study of the allocation of discretionary development budgets (DDBs) told a very different story, that

> the allocation of DDBs in Afghanistan does not focus on achieving the normative criteria of participatory, transparent, predictable, and equitable budgeting. Instead, Afghanistan's central government considers certain political criteria to buy political capital. These political criteria consist of political affiliation— ethnic affiliation and alignment with the central government's policies—political importance, and strength and weakness of local actors.[53]

Afghanistan of course was by no means the only country in which political criteria rather than measures of good public financial practice came to dominate resource allocation, but the danger of such approaches is that they can leave the central authorities substantially bereft of friends if things begin to deteriorate.

One final issue to note related to the cultivation of opium, the principal commodity within the 'illicit' component of the Afghan economy. The Taliban certainly benefitted from opium cultivation, although by no means to the extent that is often suggested.[54] The greater impact, however, of opium came through its adverse effects on perceptions of the state. The history of opium cultivation in Afghanistan is complex,[55] as have been the factors driving cultivation in different parts of the country. International approaches to dealing with the narcotics issue fluctuated wildly over time and often had unintended consequences both for power relations within provinces and for the wider disposition of rural dwellers to value the intrusions of the central state into their day-to-day lives. The 'Helmand Food Zone Programme', touted as a major counter-narcotics initiative, ended up feeding the patronage networks of the provincial governor, as well as producing a raft of other damaging effects.[56] And a campaign of aerial attacks launched from November 2017 on suspected drug laboratories ('Operation Iron Tempest') reportedly 'had a negligible effect on the Taliban's finances, exacted little toll on drug trafficking organisations, and served to alienate the rural population in and around the areas where airstrikes were deployed'.[57] The state tended to carry the political costs of these approaches, even if it had not played a major role in instigating them.

Conclusion: The complex effects of aid

Two decades of aid and development left Afghanistan a very different country from what it was in 2001, not so much because of political change or foreign aid per se, but rather as a result of the way in which the confluence of these two factors exposed Afghanistan to forces of globalisation, which it had never before encountered on such a scale. In that respect, the fall of the Republic confronted the Taliban with a very different population from the one that its leaders would have remembered from the late 1990s. A significant number of the key 'products' of a globalised world were evacuated in the second half of August 2021, but millions more remain, with memories and experiences that the Taliban lack the capacity to eradicate or expunge. This is not so much a matter of an energised, organised 'civil society', since many organised activists were targeted by the Taliban; it is more a matter of society more broadly having been transformed by a range of subtle forces with lingering effects.

The Afghanistan experience also illustrates the extreme complexity of development processes, marked in the post-2001 environment by a multiplicity of actors, objectives, and models for development. It is clear that the problem of donor fragmentation was never effectively overcome, and, added to the challenges of what was an Afghan state structure in its infancy, it set the scene for discordant endeavours that would not be effectively integrated or evaluated. It is tempting to see this problem as purely technical, but deeper scrutiny suggests that it was also a reflection of asymmetries of power, combined with complex politics not just in Afghanistan, but in the various capitals and international organisations where contributions to Afghanistan were being contemplated. In this respect, the experience in Afghanistan was not so different from that which many developing countries have encountered, and which was anticipated decades ago by Sir Robert Jackson in the introduction to his famous 'Capacity Study' for the United Nations.[58] The Afghanistan case also illustrates the destructive effects that a neopatrimonial system can have on aid delivery, directing the flow of aid monies along pathways shaped by networks rather than rational policy design.[59]

That said, one of the unhappiest consequences of the way that aid was delivered to Afghanistan was simply waste. The Office of the US Special Inspector General for Afghanistan Reconstruction (SIGAR), which was established by the National Defense Authorization Act for fiscal year 2008 and reported quarterly to the US Congress, documented this problem in detail. Much had to do with a poor understanding of the operating environment. In May 2018, SIGAR concluded that:

The elite capture of relationships with, and aid and contracts from, the coalition created new grievances and exacerbated old ones as some tribes and other groups benefited from the war, while others were alienated and driven toward the insurgency … Under immense pressure to quickly stabilize insecure districts, U.S. government agencies spent far too much money, far too quickly, in a country woefully unprepared to absorb it. Money spent was often the metric of success. As a result, programming sometimes exacerbated conflicts, enabled corruption, and bolstered support for insurgents.[60]

At worst, it aided the Taliban directly: a US Agency for International Development official quoted by the journalist Douglas A. Wissing concluded that '50 percent of the Taliban funding is skimmed from US military logistics and development contracts, as well as payoffs from US-funded cell phone companies, banks, utilities, and other Afghan private enterprises. Most of the rest comes from the US-condoned opium trade'.[61]

In focusing on waste and poor administration, however, it is easy to lose sight of what was achieved. As noted earlier, in 2000, Afghanistan's 'Human Development Index' was 0.350; by 2019 it had risen to 0.511. In 2000, life expectancy at birth was only 55.8 years; by 2019 it had risen to 64.8 years. In 2000, gross national income per capita on a purchasing power parity basis was US$904; by 2019 it had risen to $2229.[62] These figures tell only part of a much more complex story, which in its entirety would need to take into account issues of inequality, gender disparity, and opportunities for future advancement. Nonetheless, it is also important to avoid stereotypical conclusions about these issues. For example, in some circles it has become virtually *de rigueur* to suggest that women in urban areas are detached from the concerns of rural women. Yet a careful and important study by the Afghanistan Analysts Network found that conversations with rural women 'clearly challenge the idea that women in rural areas are satisfied by what is often portrayed as "normal" by the Taleban or other Afghan conservatives', and that the 'priorities of rural women are not that different from those put forward by the more well-connected women activists and the concerns activists raise are deeply-felt and urgent'.[63] It is also easy to lose sight of the *imposed* challenges with which the Afghan government was struggling. Some issues of huge concern—such as internal displacement[64]—were a product at least in part of insurgent attacks for which the Taliban were responsible, not the Afghan state.

All in all, the picture that flows from this discussion is a mixed one. Much was achieved between 2001 and 2021; much more could in all probability have been achieved with better coordination and a better appreciation on the part of donors of the complexities of the operating environment; some aspects of aid policy contributed to corruption and undermined the standing and functioning of the state. But one would be hard-pressed to argue that these failings were the crucial contributors to the collapse in August 2021.

4

PROBLEMS OF INSURGENCY

The statement that Republican Afghanistan was confronted by a problem of Taliban insurgency simultaneously tells us a great deal, and not very much. It identifies the critical threat that ultimately led to the decline and fall of the Republic, but on its own says little about the specific character of the threat: its roots, its dynamics, and its dimensions. Yet probing these complexities is central to an understanding of how things unravelled in Afghanistan. At the very least, it is necessary at a more abstract level to appreciate the kind of existential military challenge that the Afghan state faced and then to appraise the specific characteristics and activities of the Taliban, and of the Afghan and international forces that were arrayed against them. Finding a vocabulary to characterise the armed conflict within Afghanistan after 2001 is not, however, without its difficulties. We have opted for the term 'insurgency' to capture the reality that attacks on the Afghan population and state were more than simply sporadic and involved political rather than merely criminal objectives. In some writings, the term insurgency is linked to 'the "spirit" of traditional peasant "rebellion"',[1] but we do not seek to imply any such things by our use of the term; indeed, it is debatable whether a reductionist notion of 'the peasantry' is of much use in making sense of Afghanistan's diverse social relations.

Nor does our use of the term suggest that insurgency is purely internal in its genesis.

The notion of 'insurgency' is preferable to a range of other terms that one might seek to deploy. The idea of 'revolution' is of little value in characterising the Taliban's military campaign. If one takes as a point of departure Theda Skocpol's notion of social revolutions as 'rapid, basic transformations of a society's state and class structures ... accompanied and in part carried through by class-based revolts from below',[2] the disconnect becomes obvious: 'class-based revolts' were no more on display than the 'mass mobilisation potential' highlighted by Goldstone.[3] Mass popular revolutions are in fact exceedingly rare, and Afghanistan did not experience one in 2021. Similarly, to see the Taliban's activity after 2001 as a form of 'rebellion' is to mischaracterise its genesis.[4] A rebellion at the outset is essentially a localised uprising; it may spread—as did the Pugachev Rebellion in Imperial Russia in 1773–5 and the Boxer Rebellion in China in 1900[5]—or it may not. Furthermore, while in some of the Taliban's actions one can find resonances with the recorded behaviours of 'rebel' groups in other contexts,[6] the differences are also profound, especially because of the Taliban's transnational character, which we discuss in more detail later in this chapter. This transnational character equally militates against seeing the conflict in Afghanistan as simply a 'civil war', localised and bounded by the borders or frontiers of a single state.[7] That said, however, some important work on the complexity of micro-level action in civil war, which is often quite detached from macro-level conflict, is potentially of value in making sense of actions in the context of a transnational conflict as well. As Kalyvas puts it, 'for the many people who are not naturally bloodthirsty and abhor direct involvement in violence, civil war offers irresistible opportunities to harm everyday enemies'.[8] A transnational insurgency can supply very similar opportunities, and this was certainly one reason why foreign forces often found local Afghan politics deeply inscrutable, especially in parts of Afghanistan where there were long-standing feuds between different networks, animated by powerful norms of revenge.[9]

A transnational insurgency can acquire its transnational character by virtue of the participation of a diverse range of nonstate transnational players, but it can also be the product of conscious state policy. This can amount to aggression as defined in the Statute of the International Criminal Court, which, after identifying certain forms of aggressive act, also includes as aggression 'The sending by or on behalf of a State of armed bands, groups, irregulars or mercenaries, which carry out acts of armed force against another State of such gravity as to amount to the acts listed above, or its substantial involvement therein'.[10] This is often characterised as 'proxy war';[11] it can also amount to a 'creeping invasion'. This occurs:

> when a middle power uses force against the territorial integrity or political independence of another state, but covertly and through surrogates, denying all the while that it is doing any such thing; and this use of force is on a sufficient scale to imperil the exercise of state power, by the state under threat, on a significant part of its territory, and is designed and intended to do so.[12]

The character and objectives of the Taliban

As we noted in Chapter One, the Taliban movement emerged as a military actor in 1994 with support from Pakistan's Interior Minister. But it is important also to note some of the sociological features of the Taliban. While it is commonplace to observe that within the Taliban different power centres crystallised—for example the 'Quetta Shura' and the 'Peshawar Shura'[13]—it is also the case that what one might loosely call a 'class structure' was to be found within the Taliban movement as well. Some of the Taliban were products of developing sectarianism in Pakistan in the 1990s. As Zaman put it, 'Though led by Afghans of the Pashtun ethnicity—the numerically dominant of the country's numerous ethnic groups—this movement had strong ties with Pakistan and was, in fact, rooted in the Deobandi madrasas, especially of Pakistan's North-West Frontier and Balochistan provinces'.[14] From these madrasas, Afghan refugee students absorbed a rigid, inflexible curriculum that offered very little of the subtlety to be found in the approach to Islam taken in the famous madrasa in nineteenth-century British India from which the Deobandi school originated.[15] As it rose, however, the movement sucked in a number of other elements so that at the ground level, it often appeared a brutish militia of angry street thugs, not unlike the brownshirted *Sturmabteilung* ('Stormtroopers') in 1930s Germany. To a significant degree, they were the product of the dislocation that the war of the 1980s created. This was poignantly captured by the journalist Ahmed Rashid:[16]

> These boys were what the war had thrown up like the sea's surrender on the beach of history. They had no memories of the past, no plans for the future while the present was everything. They were literally the orphans of the war, the rootless and the restless, the jobless and the economically deprived with little self-knowledge. They admired war because it was the only occupation they could possibly adapt to. Their simple belief in the messianic, puritan Islam which had been drummed into them by simple village mullahs was the only prop they could hold onto and which gave their lives some meaning. Untrained for anything, even the traditional occupations of their forefathers such as farming, herding or the making of handicrafts, they were what Karl Marx would have termed Afghanistan's lumpen proletariat.

While the concept of the lumpenproletariat is not much discussed these days,[17] in the *Manifesto of the Communist Party* Marx and Engels characterised it as 'this passively rotting mass thrown off by the lowest layers of old society'[18] (*diese passive Verfaulung der untersten Schichten der alten Gesellschaft*). They also saw the lumpenproletariat as profoundly manipulable by players with their own interests, prepared by its 'conditions of life' for 'the part of a bribed tool of reactionary intrigue'.[19] This certainly proved to be the case where these elements of the Taliban were concerned.

One highly distinctive feature of the Taliban movement was its underlying *mélange* of values. This was easily downplayed: as one researcher put it, 'As the Taliban challenge intensified, it became common among military and political leaders in the countries involved in the international war operation to speak about non-ideological, easy-to-convert, "ten-dollar-a-day" Taliban'.[20] Much discussion focused on the Taliban's eccentric and highly conservative interpretations of Islam, but other dimensions were arguably more important. One was a preoccupation with moral purity, which can be an exceedingly potent basis for repressive behaviour,[21] albeit often in the context of profound levels of hypocrisy, as well as double standards.[22] Another was a complete refusal to share power with other players at the macro level, something that episodes of pragmatic negotiation or cooperation at local levels[23] or soothing words from Taliban officials[24] did not in any meaningful way compromise. A third was an essentially totalitarian mindset, using 'totalitarian' not to refer to a particular syndrome or model of political system,[25] but as 'a more general term signifying patterns of thought and action that tend to total social control'.[26] These attributes set the scene for tyranny, defined by Chirot as 'the systematic abuse of power by those in positions of authority'.[27] A fourth was a broad lack of interest in the welfare of ordinary people: as recently as November 2021, the Taliban 'Prime Minister' Mullah Hassan reportedly brushed aside the threat of famine as 'a test from God, after people rebelled against him',[28] adding that 'the Taliban had not promised to provide for the people and that citizens needed to cry out to God to end the famine and drought',[29] and that 'God will provide food for the people'.[30] Even Taliban footsoldiers all too often seemed devoid of basic human sympathy. When a massive earthquake struck Paktika on 23 June 2022, a Talib responded to the suffering of destitute villagers in the following way: '"This was an act of God and they need to accept it," he continued, explaining that people in the villages around him should pray for help. "When God is angry with people he sends events like this. It's a test."'[31]

A further issue relates to the structure of the Taliban movement. Movements, as opposed to formal organisations, are often extremely amorphous, with the idea of 'membership' being at best loose and on occasion meaningless. It is possible, however, for some elements within a 'movement' to be relatively hierarchical and institutionalised while others remain diffuse. There are good reasons for seeing the Taliban as a movement of this kind. In his study of Helmand, Mike Martin characterised the Taliban there as a 'super-decentralised, patronage-based organisation',[32] a characterisation that the evidence he adduced well justified. In some other places, the Taliban took a rather different form. For example, the 28 September 2015 attack on

Kunduz was carried out by what David Kilcullen called 'professional full-time fighters, put through rigorous training by experienced instructors in the camps in Pakistan, with uniforms, vehicles, heavy weapons, encrypted radios, and a formal command structure'.[33] Indeed, it is hardly far-fetched to argue that in 2021, the Republican system fell to two types of Taliban: on the one hand, the kinds of Taliban that Martin documented in Helmand and that were present in other Pushtun-dominated provinces[34] and on the other hand a highly organised and strategically focused spearhead orchestrated from Pakistan and based on the radical 'Haqqani network',[35] which had long been close to Pakistan's ISI. This is entirely consistent with Thomas Ruttig's insightful depiction of the Taliban as a 'network of networks'.[36]

In amorphous movements, the very concept of 'leadership' can be highly problematic, and this is especially the case when movements are secretive to the point of impenetrability. The Taliban in the twenty-first century became much more sophisticated users of propaganda than before 2001,[37] but this did not mean that their internal power structures were better understood by Western observers. The most dramatic manifestation of this came with the death of the Taliban's founding leader, Mullah Omar, on 23 April 2013. Omar's death was successfully kept secret for more than two years,[38] and even a highly respected analyst was to write in 2014 that 'Mullah Omar remains the Taliban supreme leader and the source of all authority in the movement'.[39] The death of Omar's successor, Mullah Akhtar Mansour, was rather more public—he was killed in May 2016 in a US drone strike in which Pakistan, wary of possible freelancing by the new Taliban leader, may have been complicit.[40] It was hardly surprising that his successor, Mulla Hibatullah Akhundzada, kept such a low profile that rumours swirled that he too was dead. Where this impenetrability mattered most was in the context of attempts to engage the Taliban in negotiation; it is very difficult to negotiate meaningfully if one lacks a clear understanding of the power dynamics within the force with which one is dealing.[41]

The Taliban were also an extremely violent group. They committed numerous human rights abuses during their occupation of Kunduz in September–October 2015.[42] Furthermore, they had no qualms about mounting gruesome mass-casualty attacks on targets of no military significance, such as the Serena and Intercontinental hotels in Kabul, a popular restaurant, and the American University of Afghanistan,[43] and detonating car bombs in crowded public places.[44] Anthony Richards has argued that 'terrorism is a method that entails the use of violence or force or the threat of violence or force with the primary purpose of generating a psychological impact beyond the immediate victims or object of attack for a political motive'.[45] While Western governments on the whole shrank from labelling the Taliban a terrorist group, from a definitional point of view, the Taliban ticked all the boxes. And they also retained links with indisputably transnational terrorist groups: a June 2021 report from the UN Analytical Support and Sanctions Monitoring Team concluded that 'the Taliban and Al-Qaida remain closely aligned and show no indication of breaking ties'.[46] It was hardly a surprise that when al-Qaeda leader Ayman al-Zawahiri was killed in a US drone strike on 31 July 2022, he was living in downtown Kabul.[47]

Pakistan as a source of instability

During a visit to Kabul in August 2007, President Pervez Musharraf of Pakistan stated that 'There is no doubt Afghan militants are supported from Pakistani soil. The problem that you have in your region is because support is provided from our side'.[48] In a November 2009 cable to Washington, the US Ambassador to Afghanistan, retired Lieutenant-General Karl Eikenberry, warned that:

> More troops won't end the insurgency as long as Pakistan sanctuaries remain. Pakistan will remain the single greatest source of Afghan instability so long as the border sanctuaries remain, and Pakistan regards its strategic interests as best served by a weak neighbor … Until this sanctuary problem is fully addressed, the gains from sending additional forces may be fleeting.[49]

In 2015, Theo Farrell and Michael Semple wrote that the Taliban leadership was 'acutely aware that its military campaign is dependent upon retaining access to Pakistani territory'.[50] Republican Afghanistan

73

on its own had virtually no capacity to deal with this problem. It was in no position to invade Pakistan, or even to mount much diplomatic pressure in response. All interested governments and serious analysts knew what was happening, but for their own reasons, Western powers shied away from confronting the problem, seemingly hoping that it would go away. The United States was in a particular bind, namely that its dependence upon Pakistani cooperation for the transport of materiel to US forces in Afghanistan hamstrung its capacity to address the very problem that was putting those forces at risk of attack. Pakistan's perfidy was one of the fundamental contributors to the decline and fall of Republican Afghanistan.

For historical reasons, relations between Afghanistan and Pakistan had been tense for much of the period following the partition of the subcontinent in 1947. The drawing of the 'Durand Line' in 1893 had had the effect of dividing members of the Pushtun ethnic group between Afghanistan and British India, and when partition came into view, Afghanistan revived a demand that Pushtuns of the North-West Frontier be given the opportunity to reunite with their brethren in Afghanistan. This idea went nowhere, but Afghanistan was the one state to vote against the admission of the new state of Pakistan to membership of the United Nations, and ironically, for much of the next three decades, Muslim-majority Afghanistan had more cordial relations with Hindu-majority India than with Muslim-majority Pakistan. Diplomatic relations between Afghanistan and Pakistan were actually severed for several years in the early 1960s, amid superheated rhetorical exchanges over what the Afghan side called 'Pushtunistan'.[51] The Pushtunistan dispute fuelled a deep suspicion in Pakistan of secular Afghan nationalism.

The Pushtunistan dispute also played into a deep-rooted fear in Pakistan about the territorial integrity of the Pakistani state. The loss of 'East Pakistan' through the emergence of Bangladesh as an independent state in 1971 greatly aggravated this problem[52] and was one of the contributors to mounting political disarray within Pakistan in the 1970s. This culminated in a military coup by General Zia-ul-Haq in 1977. Pakistan had experienced earlier episodes of military rule—from 1958 to 1962 and 1969 to 1972—but Zia's rule, brought to an end only when he was killed in a plane crash in August

1988, was both the longest and the most profound in its effects, since he embarked on a vigorous program of 'Islamisation' within Pakistan[53] that also saw him support Islamist rather than secular nationalist groups from within the Afghan resistance following the Soviet invasion of Afghanistan in December 1979.[54] When Soviet forces were withdrawn from Afghanistan in 1989, some Pakistani officials were disposed to see it as Pakistan's victory, which Pakistan was entitled to exploit by having the determining say in who should subsequently dominate Afghanistan. This, needless to say, did not go down well with Afghans.

A major part of the explanation for Pakistan's desire to dominate Afghanistan was geopolitical, flowing from the tensions that had marked relations between India and Pakistan almost continuously since partition. There was a Cold War dimension to this—successive Indian governments were quite close to the Soviet Union, while Pakistan sought to nurture its relationship with United States[55]—but the more immediate contributor was the ongoing dispute over the contested territory of Kashmir,[56] combined with the existential sense of insecurity felt by Pakistan, positioned next to its larger Indian neighbour with which it had fought wars in 1948, 1965 and 1971, not to mention their clashes over Kargil in 1999. Indeed, one of the authors personally recalls a Pakistan Chief of Army Staff, during the course of a dinner conversation, describing himself as being 'obsessed with India'. This obsession with India had extremely unfortunate ramifications for Afghanistan, which Pakistan saw either as a state to be dominated in order to provide strategic depth in the event of an Indo-Pakistan conflict, or as a state to be dominated simply for the purpose of denying India a foothold to Pakistan's west. There are strong grounds for believing that the involvement of external players with independent goals significantly complicates efforts to resolve internal conflicts.[57] The critical Pakistani tool for the exercise of such domination was the Inter-Services Intelligence directorate (ISI) of the Pakistan Armed Forces.[58] During the 1980s, when Pakistan was a generous host for Afghan refugees, the ISI was integrally involved in channelling assistance to resistance groups that were implanted within the refugee population, with radical groups such as the *Hezb-e Islami* of Gulbuddin Hekmatyar being distinctly favoured.[59]

It was predominantly an intimate relationship with the ISI that gave the Taliban their transnational character. As we noted earlier, it was the Interior Minister of Pakistan, General Babar, who dubbed the Taliban 'our boys', and the former Foreign Secretary of Pakistan recorded that 'When asked at a press conference if the Taliban had been created by Pakistan, Naseerullah Babar reportedly nodded with a certain satisfaction'.[60] But thereafter, the operational management of the Taliban was very much in ISI hands, through its 'Directorate S'.[61] When, not surprisingly, a Pakistani spin-off from the Afghan Taliban emerged in 2007—the *Tehrik-i-Taliban*, or TTP—this created a certain challenge for Pakistani leaders, who witnessed, among other things, the murder by the Pakistan Taliban of a long-time ISI agent who had worked closely with the Afghan Taliban.[62] This led to the drawing of a somewhat tortured distinction between 'good' and 'bad' Taliban, and although in 2014 Prime Minister Nawaz Sharif repudiated the distinction,[63] it did not lead to any diminution in support for the Afghan Taliban.

Sanctuaries and their significance

The importance for insurgents of having sanctuaries outside the borders of the country in which they are seeking to operate cannot be overestimated. As one careful analysis has put it,

> While states enjoy a relative advantage in the internal use of force, their power is largely confined to their own security jurisdiction, or sovereign territory. If rebel groups can use other territories as a base of operations, thereby escaping the jurisdiction and repressive capabilities of the state, they can significantly lower their own costs of fighting and gain bargaining leverage.[64]

In light of this, the author noted that 'U.S. counterinsurgency operations in Afghanistan and Iraq have been hampered by the ability of opposition groups to slip across porous borders'.[65] That Pakistan provided such sanctuary was not surprising, as Pakistan had the experience in the 1980s of hosting Afghan *Mujahideen* parties (although the Taliban, unlike the *Mujahideen*, had no credible legal claim to be pursuing a war of national liberation, since the 2001

Bonn Agreement had been explicitly endorsed by the UN Security Council[66]) as well as the Taliban from 1994 to 1996. The critical point is that Pakistan had no need to start from scratch in nurturing the Taliban after 2001: the mechanisms for doing so were already firmly in place to be put to use by the ISI and its minions. They were activated as early as December 2001.[67]

Nor should one think that there was anything particularly secretive about the Taliban's activities. The title 'Quetta Shura' given to a key Taliban leadership council was itself instructive: Quetta is not a remote mountain village but the capital of one of the major provinces of Pakistan, namely Baluchistan.[68] The Taliban's presence in Quetta was actually quite brazen. As Ahmed Rashid noted, 'Thousands of long-haired, kohl-eyed, black-turbaned Taliban roamed the streets. New madrassas were built to house a new young generation, who banned television, the taking of photographs, and the flying of kites, replicating Kandahar in the early 1990s. Local people, including the police and journalists, were too frightened to enter the suburb'. Nearby, 'young militants were brought in for several weeks of religious training before being sent to the front line by Taliban recruiters, who often arrived with ISI officers'.[69] Carlotta Gall of *The New York Times* was beaten up by Pakistani intelligence agents when investigating the Quetta sanctuary.[70] Pakistani intelligence also moved against Taliban figures who showed signs of independence; one such figure, Mullah Baradar, a Popalzai Durrani Pushtun with links to Afghan President Karzai's brother, was arrested in 2010,[71] most likely with a view not only to putting a halt to his activities but also to signalling to other Taliban leaders not to engage in freelancing. This tight control helps explain why many Afghan Taliban felt no particular love for Pakistan, and relations became strained once the Taliban takeover in Kabul reduced their dependence on Pakistan and ISI[72]—even though it was the ISI's closest collaborators, the Haqqani network, which emerged as dominant after the takeover.

Sanctuaries of the kind that the Taliban enjoyed in Pakistan are militarily significant because they provide safe venues for the preparation of attacks and reduce critical vulnerabilities. The former is important in the areas of training and accumulation and storage of weaponry. In particular, a network of sanctuaries allows industrial-scale activity in the production of explosives. For example, a report in 2011 concluded that Afghan insurgents planted a staggering 14,661 Improvised Explosive Devices (IEDs) during 2010.[73] It is inconceivable that IEDs in such quantities could have been produced and distributed effectively in the contested environment of Afghanistan at that time without external assistance, especially through the supply of ammonium nitrate.[74] In terms of critical vulnerabilities, there could hardly have been a better environment for the Taliban than that which Pakistan supplied. In some cases—for example during the Vietnam War—sanctuaries and supply-lines in neighbouring countries came under attack.[75] The US struck at the Ho Chi Minh Trail in Cambodia and Laos, one of the reasons why to this day Laos has a major problem of unexploded ordnance. Arguably, the effect of these attacks was not to disrupt the activities of the Vietcong so much as to destabilise South Vietnam's neighbours, but Pakistan, by virtue of its 'dual track' approach to Afghanistan,[76] had little to fear of this kind. A US dependent upon Pakistan permitting the transit of US provisions to US forces in Afghanistan found itself caught in a nasty trap of its own making.

Despite latent tensions in the relationship, the Taliban greatly valued the sanctuaries that Pakistan provided, and as long as the Taliban's activities coincided with Pakistan's interests, the ISI was happy for them to continue. Pakistan became particularly supportive after 2005. A senior Taliban leader remarked that around then, 'Pakistan removed all the restrictions and we told all Taliban members that Pakistan does not want to arrest us, they want to support us'.[77] The ability of Taliban to retreat to the sanctuaries meant that collateral damage from combating their insurgent and terrorist activities was borne by Afghans, something which understandably caused the gravest concern for President Karzai. Nonetheless, he was in a somewhat lonely position. As Partlow recorded:

> In June 2008, Karzai had threatened, at a press conference, to send his troops into Pakistan. 'If these people in Pakistan give themselves the right to come and fight in Afghanistan, as was continuing for the last thirty years, so Afghanistan has the

right to cross the border and destroy terrorist nests, spying, extremism, and killing, in order to defend itself, its schools, its people, and its life,' Karzai said. The American diplomats at the time took their normal stance and warned Karzai against publicly criticizing Pakistan.[78]

Pro-Pakistan US diplomats and officials often sought to deride the evidence of Pakistani support for the Afghan Taliban as circumstantial or to argue that if support was being supplied, it was not being supplied by the Pakistani state. Their easy resort to these arguments helps explain why the US's handling of the Afghanistan situation was ultimately to prove so disastrous, and there are a number of reasons why. First, the fact that evidence is circumstantial does not mean that it is unconvincing or tainted. As H.D. Thoreau observed in 1850, when it was suspected that some milk supplies were being adulterated, 'some circumstantial evidence is very strong, as when you find a trout in the milk'.[79] Second, there is a difference between circumstantial evidence and anecdotal evidence, and of the latter there is plenty drawing attention to Pakistani support for the Taliban.[80] It is worth remembering the shrewd observation that the plural of anecdote is data.[81] But third, and arguably most seriously, the view that support for the Taliban might not have been coming directly from the Pakistani state missed a crucial point about state responsibility. In 1949, the International Court of Justice addressed this directly in the *Corfu Channel* case, where it affirmed 'every State's obligation not to allow knowingly its territory to be used for acts contrary to the rights of other States'.[82] In the light of President Musharraf's August 2007 remarks quoted earlier, it is clear that Pakistan knew that its territory was being used in this way. This broad principle had been specifically reinforced by UN Security Council Resolution 1333 of 19 December 2000, which required states to prevent 'the direct or indirect sale, supply and transfer to the territory of Afghanistan under Taliban control ... by their nationals *or from their territories*, of technical advice, assistance or training relating to the military activities of the armed personnel under the control of the Taliban'.[83] Everyone knew to whom this mandatory provision referred.

Taliban revenue and resources

Appraising how the Taliban insurgency was sustained financially is actually quite a complicated task. One difficulty is measuring the exact value of the 'in-kind' assistance that the Taliban received via the sanctuaries in Pakistan. Because of the secretiveness surrounding the exercise, it is virtually impossible to attach a meaningful value, beyond making the obvious point that such 'in-kind' assistance relieved the Taliban of a range of costs that they would otherwise have had to find some way of meeting, perhaps with considerable difficulty because of UN sanctions. In Resolution 1267 of 15 October 1999, the Security Council had imposed a broad requirement for states to freeze 'funds and other financial resources' belonging to the Taliban or available for their use.[84] When a non-state actor is confronted with such constraints, 'in-kind' support looms more prominently as a tool for sustaining its operations.

The most widely discussed and controversial source of actual revenue for the Taliban came from the exploitation of opium and narcotics. Some of the discussion of opium production in Afghanistan was overly florid, creating the impression that opium dominated the Afghan economy. This was not the case. The Afghanistan Opium Survey for 2020 reported the total farm-gate value of opium production as US$350 million, with potential opium production of 6,300 tonnes. Just one province, Helmand, accounted for 115,597 hectares of cultivation, or 51.6 per cent of the nationwide total of 224,000 hectares.[85] By comparison, cereal crop production for 2020 was estimated at 6,252,000 tonnes.[86] Opium was important in value rather than volume. A 2021 UN report estimated the 'gross output of the Afghan illicit opiate economy' (as opposed to simply the farm-gate value of opium production) as US$1.8 to 2.7 billion, and stated that the 'total value of opiates, including domestic consumption and exports, stood at between 9 to 14 per cent of Afghanistan's GDP'.[87] This created a nice pool of funds which the Taliban could seek to tap, and there is virtual unanimity that they sought to do so. What has proved much more contentious is the exact scale of the benefits that they derived from 'taxing' the opium trade. As we noted in the previous chapter, these benefits have often been overstated.

Mansfield's analysis brings this out. It points to 'revenues from the tax on opiates that would amount to $19 million in 2020'.[88] His conclusions are worth quoting in detail:[89]

> In Afghanistan, inaccurate estimates of the Taliban's finances and the depiction of the movement as a narco-insurgency have not been helpful. Misconceptions hurt the ability of Western diplomatic and military officials to understand the insurgency: its resources, motives, supporters and political ambitions. Flawed narratives drove policies that alienated the rural population, such as forced eradication of opium and the bombing of heroin labs, which led to farmers giving help to the Taliban, believing the insurgents could defend them against the counternarcotics policies of the Afghan government and its foreign backers.

One consequence of the fixation on Taliban income from taxing opium was a neglect of the importance of Pakistan's 'in-kind' assistance that we discussed earlier. Another was neglect of other kinds of income source on which the Taliban drew. These included the Taliban's own refining of opiates, beyond mere taxation of opium, and an increasing involvement in much more lucrative methamphetamine production which gave their revenues a significant boost.[90] Furthermore, even in the 1990s, there had been a close relationship between the Taliban and 'trucking mafias' in Pakistan,[91] which had alerted the Taliban to the economic significance of transport. In more recent times, so-called 'taxes' (or more accurately, extortion[92]) from the transport of goods proved lucrative, amounting to 'an estimated $83.4 million a year on the trade in fuel and transit goods in 2019 from Iran alone'.[93] Furthermore, a recent in-depth study by Mansfield and the Organisation for Sustainable Development and Research highlighted the importance of 'chokepoints' in controlling economic life. Their research revealed:

> a substantial undeclared economy, in which imports and exports reported by the Afghan authorities are less than half the amounts and values that cross the international borders, resulting in hundreds of millions of dollars in lost revenues to the Afghan state and a steady stream of funding for both the insurgent and state-affiliated actors in the provinces.[94]

The implications of this research for the position of the Afghan state were sobering:[95]

> This research shows that where the administration in Kabul loses financially, corrupt officials and the Taliban gain. The latter two have a deep knowledge of the amount of goods that enter and exit Afghanistan due to their presence on the ground. Control over chokepoints provide a comparative advantage to the Taliban and corrupt officials, whether at the points of production in the case of talc stone, at strategic locations in transit such as checkpoints at critical junctures on the main highway for fuel and transit goods, at official and unofficial border crossings, or at the point of sale. What Kabul doesn't see Kabul doesn't receive.

A lesson from this analysis is that in a basically zero-sum situation, the success of an insurgent movement in extracting internal revenues to boost its military performance can come at a direct cost to the capacity of the state to fund its resistance to insurgency. The relatively low level of spending in Afghan budgets on the military suggests that this problem did not loom as prominently as it should have in the thinking of Afghan leaders, since the existence of external support for the Afghan state may have dulled their awareness of how dangerous the Taliban's internal revenue raising could be in the long run.

Furthermore, the costs to the state were not simply financial, but also symbolic. Insurgents may well feel that they have much to gain from performing what might be seen as 'state-like' roles, since the ability to 'extract taxes' would normally be seen as a distinctive function of the state. Much has been written about states maintaining a monopoly on the exercise of legitimate violence, but just as much could usefully be written about the implications of states maintaining a monopoly on the routinised extraction of resources from the population. When states fail to do so, the distinction between different actors populating the political space can become blurred in the eyes of local players, and this can be very dangerous if other factors come into play to destabilise the functional capacities of the state on a day-to-day basis, including the effective use of armed force by the state.

The Afghan National Defence and Security Forces

For many years, and particularly from the end of 2014 onwards, the Afghan National Defence and Security Forces were at the front line of combatting the Taliban attackers. A study from the Watson Institute for International Studies in September 2021 estimated that between October 2001 and August 2021, the national military and police in Afghanistan suffered 69,095 direct war deaths. This was nearly thirty times greater than the number of direct war deaths suffered by the US military in Afghanistan in the same period (2,324), and more than nine times greater than the total number of direct war deaths in Afghanistan of the US military, US Defense Department civilians, US contractors, and other allied troops (7,391).[96] Given these figures, US President Biden's 16 August 2021 statement that 'American troops cannot and should not be fighting in a war and dying in a war that Afghan forces are not willing to fight for themselves'[97] reflected an astounding ignorance of, or callous indifference to, the sacrifices over decades of Afghan security personnel, and the losses suffered by their families. It is no wonder that Kilcullen and Mills, in discussing politicians such as Biden, concluded that 'The moral stench of this betrayal will cling to them forever, and so it should'.[98]

How the ANDSF unravelled in 2021 is an issue that we take up in more detail in Chapters Seven and Eight. For the moment, however, it is sufficient—but also important—to note that the specific structures and practices of the ANDSF were very much the product of security sector reform (SSR) measures that had been largely put in place by Afghanistan's allies in much earlier times. The critical point here is that the key components of the Afghan military were not designed to be 'free-standing'; on the contrary, they were very much premised on an assumption of interoperability between Afghan forces and the forces of Afghanistan's key allies, above all the United States. Initially, the plans for the Afghan National Army (ANA) were relatively modest: President Karzai in December 2002 announced a target of 70,000.[99] It also performed relatively well. As one observer put it,

> Despite the many problems that the ANA has faced, it is widely viewed as a 'success story' in the SSR process, particularly

83

when compared with the state of reform in the police and the judiciary. The ANA has displayed a high degree of discipline, professionalism and combat effectiveness and, due to the institution of ethnic quotas, is largely representative of the country's ethnic composition.[100]

It was vulnerable, however, as a result of its dependence on services provided by its allies. These included air cover and medical evacuation capabilities, intelligence, and logistics, which were abundantly available until the bulk of foreign forces were withdrawn by the end of 2014. Thereafter, its vulnerabilities began to mount.[101]

A further factor pertinent to military performance is leadership. In the early years, there was relative stability in the professional leadership of the military, with General Bismillah Khan Mohammadi as Army Chief of Staff from 2003 to 2010 and Abdul Rahim Wardak as Defence Minister from 2004 to 2012. Of these, the former was more dynamic; the latter had been involved in the 1980s with one of the least militarily engaged *Mujahideen* parties, was not famous for his energy, and in the later part of his term was dogged by reports that his son's firm had profited massively from US contracts.[102] Mohammadi was to return to defence leadership when he was appointed Defence Minister in June 2021, but by then the position was a poisoned chalice. After the initial terms of Mohammadi and Wardak, both of the key leadership positions they had held experienced considerable turnover, and Mohammadi's predecessor as Defence Minister from 2018 to 2021, Asadullah Khalid, was not only frequently absent because of medical problems following a 2012 assassination attempt but also had a suspect human rights record.[103] In the absence of clear strategic guidance from a country's leadership, rapid leadership turnover within specific bureaucratic and military organisations can create genuine uncertainty about the direction that an organisation is to take. The reference to 'bureaucratic' structures is important because it is easily overlooked that to sustain an army in the field, it is necessary to have a middle management system to ensure that it is properly provisioned, that salaries are paid on time, and that a range of other support services are in place. Failure in any of these spheres has the potential to compromise the ability of an army to stare down the threat posed by insurgents.

One reason that this was important was the frontline vulnerability of Afghan soldiers, which the statistics that we quoted earlier on direct war deaths make clear. Combat deaths are tragic for the families and comrades of those who perish, but they are not necessarily fatal to military efficiency. A great deal depends on whether losses of frontline personnel—through either death or injury—lead broadly to a crisis of morale, or an intensified commitment to confront the enemy: either is possible. But much depends on the scale of losses and whether they are unsustainable or are seen to be unsustainable. The latter may also depend on how many soldiers are real and how many are 'ghosts'[104] and on exactly where the burden of losses falls: whether those being lost are relatively easy to replace or whether they are highly trained personnel with specialised niche capabilities. Kilcullen and Mills argue that 'the post-2015 posture might have been sustainable for the coalition, but it was far too costly in human terms to be sustainable for the Afghans'.[105] They further argue that one key reason related to the perverse effects of cultivating elite 'Special Forces' is that:[106]

Capable troops, particularly non-commissioned officers, who would otherwise have been junior leaders forming the backbone of conventional combat units, are instead selected for service as individual fighters in elite units. Their skills, talent and motivation are thus lost to the larger force, which suffers a steady brain-drain from its conventional component to its elite component.

Once in elite units, the force's best groups are thrown into high-intensity battles. They are used to rescue desperate situations or committed to dangerous and difficult tasks beyond the capabilities of ordinary troops, so that they typically suffer much higher losses than their conventional counterparts. Over time, this selection-destruction cycle progressively selects the most talented members of the larger force and kills them off, lowering the combat effectiveness of the organisation as a whole.

This was especially a problem given the large number of potential targets for Taliban attack: it was not surprising that political leaders saw special forces as the tool for recovering lost territory of symbolic significance.

One further point relating to the capabilities of the Afghan National Army deserves elaboration. It is easy to slip into a mode of thinking that highlights the advanced character of US technological capabilities and assumes their relevance to the Afghanistan theatre of operations. Such an approach is suspect on two grounds. The first is that it is dangerous to seek to foster high-technology capabilities in a low-technology space; it is always important to reflect not just on the capabilities of particular technologies but on how those capabilities will or will not be maintained given the levels of technological sophistication of the country to which they may be transferred. High-tech equipment effectively serviced by skilled contractors may be a battlefield asset; without skilled contractors to service the equipment, it may prove to be a costly white elephant. The second is that technologies may have different uses. In a thoughtful essay, Ankerson and Martin have made the important point with respect to Afghanistan that 'much of the technology was aimed at reducing the risk of casualties rather than achieving outright victory. Western forces invested heavily in weapons that could remove soldiers from harm's way—air power, drones—or technology that could speed up the delivery of immediate medical treatment'.[107] They further argue that the ANDSF were not 'in a position to create or even operate advanced systems on their own. Western nations were reluctant to equip Afghans with cutting-edge weapons, fearing that they would not be maintained or might even end up in the hands of the Taliban'.[108] In terms of military technology, the Afghans were caught between a rock and a hard place.

The US and its military activities

The United States was of course the major military player within Afghanistan for much of the period between 2001 and 2021, but it was always a player acting in pursuit of its own interests. On many occasions these coincided with the interests of the Afghan government, but not always. Furthermore, to a significant degree US activity was devoid of clear strategic focus for much of this period, and manifested a disjointed incrementalism of a kind that in a different context Charles Lindblom labelled 'the science of muddling through'.[109] This was partly a consequence of changing circumstances on the ground, especially as the US struggled to adjust to the revving-up by the Taliban of their military activities from around 2005. But it was also because the US was seeking simultaneously to pursue several different missions in Afghanistan, one essentially a counter-terrorism exercise directed against any signs of a recrudescent al-Qaeda, and the other a stabilisation exercise via PRTs, involving not just the US, but NATO and non-NATO allies acting under the umbrella of ISAF. It was only at the NATO summit in Bucharest in April 2008 that a clearer 'ISAF Strategic Vision' was articulated, based on four principles: a firm and shared long-term commitment; support for enhanced Afghan leadership and responsibility; a comprehensive approach by the international community, bringing together civilian and military efforts; and increased cooperation and engagement with Afghanistan's neighbours, especially Pakistan.[110] This was a step forward compared to the preceding incoherence, but it proved much easier to give voice to these principles than effect. As Farrell put it, 'The NATO plan was mostly aspirational and short on essential detail, in no small part because certain states were opposed to key aspects of any realistic plan'.[111] And by 2008, the US invasion of Iraq—an invasion endorsed by then-Senator Biden[112]— had proved a massive and disastrous distraction for Afghanistan. In December 2007, the chair of the US Joint Chiefs of Staff, Admiral Mullen, remarked that 'In Afghanistan we do what we can. In Iraq we do what we must'.[113] US Defense Secretary Robert Gates later wrote that 'our later challenges in Afghanistan, especially the return of the Taliban in force by the time I became defense secretary, were, I believe, significantly compounded by the invasion of Iraq'.[114]

The 2009 change of US administration from that of George W. Bush to that of Barack Obama led to a reconsideration of the US's approach to the situation in Afghanistan. Obama outlined his strategy in a speech on 1 December 2009, in which he announced the decision to send an additional 30,000 troops to Afghanistan. His new approach, building on counterinsurgency (COIN) doctrines,[115] had three objectives: 'We must deny al Qaeda a safe haven. We must reverse the Taliban's momentum and deny it the ability to overthrow the government. And we must strengthen the capacity of Afghanistan's security forces and government so that they can take lead responsibility for Afghanistan's future'. It also had three core elements: 'a military effort to create the conditions for a transition; a civilian surge that reinforces positive action; and an effective partnership with Pakistan'. Unfortunately, he undermined all this with one further statement: 'After 18 months, our troops will begin to come home'.[116] His aim was seemingly to prompt Karzai to 'make hard decisions about his own government's responsibilities',[117] but the public articulation of a time limit virtually invited the Taliban and the ISI simply to wait out the 18-month duration of the 'surge' (Barnett Rubin, an experienced academic working for the office of the US Special Representative for Afghanistan and Pakistan, was 'stupefied' to hear of the time limit[118]). In this respect, the US strategy replicated at a macro level a problem with the practical implementation of counterinsurgency doctrine at the micro level that had already become obvious. As Jalali put it:

> For many years the practice of clearing insurgent-infested areas and then leaving the place disenchanted even the strongest supporters of the government and its foreign partners. Abandoning areas taken back from the insurgents made the population vulnerable to the threat of returning Taliban. The shattered credibility thwarted full-hearted local support in future operations since the population did not trust that the troops would stay on, thinking that either the insurgents or the warlords would move in. This inspired the population to sit on the fence.[119]

Furthermore, Obama's strategy was fatally weak in coming to terms with the problem of Pakistan; indeed, increasing the number of US troops in Afghanistan had the perverse effect of enhancing Pakistan's leverage over the US by augmenting its capacity to disrupt supplies to US forces in the field.

At one level, the Obama announcement nominally allowed for somewhat more flexibility than it was generally understood to be offering, in that he stated that troops would simply 'begin' to come home after 18 months. In December 2009, General Stanley McChrystal testified to the US House of Representatives Committee on Armed Services as follows: 'I don't view July 2011 as a deadline. I view that as a point at which time the President has directed we will begin to reduce combat forces, but we will decide the pace and scope of that based upon conditions at that time. So I don't believe that is a deadline at all'.[120] But by 2014, the Commander of US Forces in Afghanistan, General Joseph F. Dunford, used subtly different language, referring to the US presence as 'largely' conditions-based. This embodied a recognition that the draw-down of US forces was ultimately a political rather than simply military issue—and this is how it was understood in Afghanistan and its neighbourhood. In the same testimony, Dunford also offered a remarkably prescient warning:

> My assessment is that, if we are not there after 2014, the Afghan security forces will immediately begin to deteriorate and, largely, that is because of … the systems, the processes, these institutions that allow them to sustain themselves. Things like spare parts, fuel, oversight of contracts, ammunition distribution … When the Afghan security forces begin to deteriorate over time, the Afghan environment as a whole will begin to deteriorate. And my assessment is that what we will see is, in fact, a fracture in the Army over time and, as importantly, deteriorating security conditions. And I think the only question after 2014 is the pace of deterioration of both the Afghan security forces and the environment as a whole.[121]

The Obama strategy proved to be the trigger for a process of substantial disengagement from direct combat involvement on the part of the US and its allies. The 2010 NATO Summit in Lisbon produced a declaration making provision for a process of *inteqal*, or 'transition'. It involved five phases, which were announced by President Karzai on 22 March 2011, 27 November 2011, 13 May 2012, 31 December 2012, and 18 June 2013. The details of this staging were determined by a 'Joint Afghan-NATO *Inteqal* Board' (JANIB), and all the PRTs were phased out. At one level, there was considerable apprehension within Afghanistan as to whether the Republican system would survive the extraction of the vast bulk of international supporters. As we mentioned in Chapter Two, several factors help explain why it did. The process of downsizing was not carried out unilaterally but in a way that appeared to emphasise Afghan as well as international ownership of what was happening. And the withdrawal of international forces was not total: it was not a manifest abandonment of the Afghan people and the Republican system. Instead, relatively small, relatively inexpensive, but absolutely critical niche capabilities were left in place to sustain the operations of the ANDSF. We shall discuss these capabilities further in Chapters Seven and Eight.

One little-noticed aspect of the US approach to the Taliban insurgency was how grounded it was in a highly distinctive conception of the character of war, and in particular in the notion that wars should be expected to terminate in 'victory', with a winner and a loser—what one might call the 'Appomattox', 'Compiègne', or 'Tokyo Bay' model of war. As Martel has put it, 'victory on the scale represented by unconditional surrender remains as central to the American ethos of war as the ideals of freedom and prosperity are to its politics and economics'.[122] Regrettably, thus conceived, the struggle in Afghanistan was almost always likely to be 'endless', in the sense of there being no prospect of any such surrender. This is not a particularly surprising insight: work by Mary Kaldor on 'new wars' driven by a logic grounded in distinctive actors, goals, methods, and forms of finance suggests that old-style wars are becoming less and less common.[123] Nonetheless, as Cian O'Driscoll has put it, 'While it is true that the standard account of victory, which involves one army prevailing over another in a climactic encounter, has little pertinence to the military realities of modern war, it still guides our understanding of warfare'.[124] An antiquated conception of what 'victory' means can set the scene for an erosion of support for the *status quo*, even if it is objectively quite sustainable. Victory is much more a matter of perception than is often appreciated.[125] A 2019 RAND study captured the nature of the problem: 'That there is no military solution to the war in Afghanistan has become a commonplace.

But this is, at best, only half true. Winning may not be an available option, but losing certainly is. A precipitous departure, no matter how rationalized, will mean choosing to lose'.[126] A preoccupation with an unachievable conception of 'victory' can distract attention from the central reality that *not losing* can be a legitimate focus of statecraft and military strategy, since the possibility of parametric shifts in the operating environment can never be discounted. This was essentially the approach adopted by British Prime Minister Churchill between the fall of France in June 1940 and the attack on Pearl Harbor in December 1941, which drew the United States into the Second World War. During this period, Churchill would not have been able to articulate a credible strategy for the United Kingdom and its few remaining allies to defeat Nazi Germany on their own, but he had the wisdom to appreciate, as some of his colleagues (notably Viscount Halifax) did not,[127] that it was better to concentrate on not losing than to go down a path of negotiation with the enemy which had every prospect of leading to perdition.

Civilian casualties and drone strikes

Civilian casualties were amongst the most tragic consequences of the insurgency in Afghanistan. Protection of civilians during times of war is addressed in international law, notably in Additional Protocol I to the Geneva Conventions of 12 August 1949. Afghanistan became a party to this Additional Protocol on 10 November 2009. Article 51.2 provides that 'The civilian population as such, as well as individual civilians, shall not be the object of attack. Acts or threats of violence the primary purpose of which is to spread terror among the civilian population are prohibited'. Article 51.4 explicitly provides that 'Indiscriminate attacks are prohibited'.[128] Incidental harm, where civilians are at risk by virtue of proximity to a legitimate military target, is governed by a principle of proportionality.[129]

The following table sets out UN data on civilian deaths between the completion of the withdrawal of the bulk of foreign forces at the end of 2014 and 30 June 2021, on the eve of the collapse of the Republic.[130]

Recorded number of civilian deaths by parties to the conflict 2015–21

	2015	2016	2017	2018	2019	2020	2021 (to 30 June)	Total
Caused by AGEs:	2,324	2,138	2,303	2,243	1,668	1,885	1,041	13,602
Caused by PGFs:	628	905	745	1,185	1,473	841	422	6,199
Other:	613	467	390	376	262	309	196	2,613
Total:	3,565	3,510	3,438	3,804	3,403	3,035	1,659	22,414

AGEs = anti-government elements; PGFs = pro-government forces

A consistent pattern revealed by these figures is that *anti-government* elements were responsible for the majority of civilian deaths: 60.7 per cent were attributable to these elements, as opposed to 27.7 per cent attributable to pro-government forces. Improvised explosive devices, a notably indiscriminate weapon, accounted for many of the fatalities caused by anti-government elements, and in July 2021, the United Nations Assistance Mission in Afghanistan (UNAMA) recorded that:

> During the first six months of 2021, and in comparison with the same period last year, UNAMA documented a nearly threefold increase in civilian casualties resulting from the use of non-suicide improvised explosive devices (IEDs) by Anti-Government Elements. This was the most civilian casualties caused by non-suicide IEDs in the first six months of a year since UNAMA began systematic documentation of civilian casualties in Afghanistan in 2009.[131]

Civilian casualties can have complex effects,[132] and impact on different elements of a population in different ways. Not all areas within a country are necessarily combat zones, and those who dwell in more serene areas may be largely untouched by the effects of civilian casualties elsewhere. For others, closer to front lines, the fear of becoming entangled in the battlefield may be pervasive and dominate people's lives. In the political realm, civilian casualties certainly inflamed relations between President Karzai and the US, and in military terms, their effects were not trivial. A 2010 analysis of statistics on civilian casualties at that time concluded that 'the data are consistent with the claim that civilian casualties are affecting future violence through increased recruitment into insurgent groups after a civilian casualty incident'.[133] A further study, published in 2013, suggested that civilian casualties at the hands of external forces were more poorly received than those at the hands of the Taliban,[134] but it is not clear whether this finding continued to hold with respect to the post-2014 period following the withdrawal of the bulk of foreign forces.

One particular source of civilian casualties that has generated some attention is drone strikes by the US. Drones are 'armed and networked unmanned aerial vehicles',[135] and they have the advantage for the operator of minimising the risk of harm to its own personnel. They were greatly feared by the Taliban (although the Taliban sought to use drones of their own[136]) because of the risk they posed to key leaders. Despite their fearsome reputation, statistics suggest that they caused only a small fraction of civilian casualties: while comprehensive data are lacking, Jacob and Mathieson, drawing together several different data sources, conclude that between 2015 and 2020, the number of civilians killed in Afghanistan in US drone strikes was between 333 and 878, or between 8.03 and 8.76 per cent of total deaths in US drone strikes.[137] Where they perhaps impacted more starkly was in generating a sense of apprehension that haunted people's everyday lives.[138] Advocates of drone warfare have on occasion argued that it allows for higher levels of discrimination in combat, since extensive surveillance can precede a strike, but this claim should not be taken too far. A US drone strike on 29 August 2021, prompted by the suicide bombing in the vicinity of Kabul airport that we mentioned in Chapter One, killed ten entirely innocent people, seven of them children, on the basis of what was later admitted to be a mistaken conclusion that they were involved in terrorist activity.[139] Drone warfare is ultimately no more immune from error than any other kind of kinetic activity.

Loosely associated with the idea of civilian casualties is another phenomenon, also of a highly troubling character: war crimes committed by international forces. One US example was a 'months long shooting spree against Afghan civilians' by soldiers 'who had a fondness for hash and alcohol'.[140] In November 2020, the Office of the Inspector-General of the Australian Defence Force released a searing report documenting disturbing, and in some cases horrific, abuses by members of the Australian 'Special Operations Task Group' in Afghanistan. The inquiry found that there was:

> credible information that junior soldiers were required by their patrol commanders to shoot a prisoner, in order to achieve the soldier's first kill, in a practice that was known as 'blooding'. This would happen after the target compound had been secured, and local nationals had been secured as 'persons under control'. Typically, the patrol commander would take a person under control and the junior member, who would then be directed to kill the person under control. 'Throwdowns' would be placed with the body, and a 'cover story' was created for the purposes of operational reporting and to deflect scrutiny. This was reinforced with a code of silence.[141]

And the BBC exposed chilling evidence of British violations.[142] This kind of behaviour was almost certainly the exception rather than the rule, but such exceptions can have devastating effects on attempts to counter the activities of insurgents.

Conclusion: The US failure to address the problem of Pakistan

The failure on the part of the US to address the problem of Pakistan was the key factor that lay at the heart of the insurgency in Afghanistan. In 2001, the Bush Administration had dealt both forcefully and effectively with the problem: according to President Musharraf, a firm demarche delivered by US Deputy Secretary of State Richard Armitage informed Pakistan that if it sided with the terrorists, it should 'be prepared to be bombed back to the Stone Age'.[143] The effects of this warning were both immediate and positive, but unfortunately, the US failed to realise the importance of signalling to

Islamabad that it would be on long-term probation. The result was a shift, far too swiftly, to the use of positive inducements rather than the threat of negative consequences in order to try to shape Pakistani behaviour. In particular, the US provided US$10 billion in aid to Pakistan in the five years following the 9/11 attacks, with very little to show for it.[144] President Karzai was understandably infuriated by US naïveté, and years later won some sympathy from US officials, notably former Defense Secretary Robert Gates: "'Every time we had a huge fight with Karzai or he blew up in public, in every single instance he had been talking to us for months in private about that problem," Gates said. "We didn't pay attention … Many of these things we could have prevented had we just been listening better."'[145]

The extent to which ISI had been involved in duplicity was massively demonstrated on 2 May 2011 when Osama bin Laden was killed in a US raid on his compound in Abbottabad, virtually at the front door of the Pakistan Military Academy. The author of a history of ISI put it very bluntly: the 'claim that Bin Laden lived with his family for five years in Abbottabad without coming into contact with the security services of this garrison town seemed absurd'.[146] For years, Pakistani officials had confidently asserted that Bin Laden was in Afghanistan. As Ahmed Rashid wrote, 'Now, in the eyes of the world, Pakistan's leaders had turned out to be liars or worse'.[147] This was a key reason why Pakistan received no advance notice of the raid. As President Obama put it, 'it was an open secret that certain elements inside the country's military, and especially its intelligence services, maintain links to the Taliban and perhaps even al-Qaeda, sometimes using them as strategic assets to ensure that the Afghan government remained weak and unable to align itself with Pakistan's number one rival, India'.[148] Only one US president was prepared publicly to castigate Pakistan for its actions. In a speech on 21 August 2017, President Trump stated that:

> For its part, Pakistan often gives safe haven to agents of chaos, violence, and terror … The next pillar of our new strategy is to change the approach and how to deal with Pakistan. We can no longer be silent about Pakistan's safe havens for terrorist organizations, the Taliban, and other groups that pose a threat to

the region and beyond ... We have been paying Pakistan billions and billions of dollars at the same time they are housing the very terrorists that we are fighting. But that will have to change, and that will change immediately.[149]

In January 2018, the US suspended most military aid to Pakistan,[150] although Pakistan, despite its angry response, had almost certainly factored in the likelihood of such a cut by the time it occurred. But as things turned out, it was Trump, not Pakistan, that was to change course.

There was no shortage of arguments for doing little or nothing about Pakistan, most of them fed to the US at one time or another by Pakistani officials, and sometimes swallowed whole. One line of argument simply asserted that Pakistan was more important for the United States than Afghanistan. Another highlighted logistic dependence, although this was much less significant after 2014. Another maintained that any meaningful pressure on Pakistan ran the risk of precipitating an internal collapse, and the emergence of a fundamentalist regime with nuclear weapons. Another was that pressure on Pakistan would simply drive it further into the arms of China. Yet another maintained that dominating Afghanistan through proxies was such a central Pakistani interest that nothing that the US could do would ever change its behaviour. A more sophisticated argument was that significant pressure would be required to prompt Pakistan to change its behaviour.[151] Amongst specialists on Pakistan, there was less disposition than in policy circles to take these claims at face value.[152] Some researchers highlighted the costs that the US was paying as a result of its failure to address the problem. Others focused on the forms that stronger diplomatic action could take. In 2017, Husain Haqqani, a former Ambassador of Pakistan to the United States, authored a paper with Lisa Curtis, a former US diplomat with extensive experience in South Asia, identifying a range of measures that could be taken. Their critical recommendation was that the US should 'Present to Pakistan a list of calibrated actions for ending its support to the Afghan Taliban and the Haqqani Network, and make clear that failure to make substantial progress on these steps could eventually result in Pakistan's designation as a State Sponsor of Terrorism'.[153]

This did not happen. Instead, the problem of Pakistan's support for the Taliban was left to fester, as Trump and his envoy Khalilzad, once a critic of Pakistan's activities,[154] pivoted to a position of treating Pakistan instead as a partner in procuring a US-Taliban agreement. The English essayist G.K. Chesterton famously wrote that 'The Christian ideal has not been tried and found wanting. It has been found difficult; and left untried'.[155] Much the same could be said of a policy of forcefully addressing Pakistan's support for the Taliban. In testimony before the US Congress in September 2021, the Chairman of the US Joint Chiefs of Staff, General Mark A. Milley, cited never 'effectively dealing with Pakistan' as a critical error.[156] But by then, it was too late.

5

POLITICAL LEADERSHIP

'Beware of the beggar who becomes king'. So runs an old Afghan proverb. 'Uneasy lies the head that wears a crown'.[1] So said Shakespeare's King Henry IV. These words capture the way that political leadership can be at once both a temptation and a curse. It certainly proved to be so in Republican Afghanistan. For many Afghans, the decline and fall of Republican Afghanistan will likely appear to be predominantly the result of failed leadership, and President Ghani's abrupt exit by helicopter, just days after he had pledged to stay the course, had a ruinous effect on his reputation. But that said, focusing solely on individuals can obscure several other factors that are also important in assessing political leadership. One is the wider frameworks—constitutional, political, bureaucratic, and international—within which a given individual is operating. Another is the burden of 'path dependence'—the legacy of policy settings and expectations that a new leader can inherit from an old leader. In this chapter, we discuss leadership in a general sense, but then move to discuss in a contextualised fashion how both Hamed Karzai and Ashraf Ghani performed as leaders. Essentially, the neopatrimonial system that took shape under Karzai was ill matched to Ghani's personality and policy approach, and when combined with the highly centralised presidential system, set the scene for overconcentration of decision-making in the presidential palace and fracturing within the Afghan political elite at the very time when it was important that different components of the Afghan state, and different political forces opposed to a Taliban takeover, work cooperatively with each other.

The meaning of leadership

In the 2004 Constitution of Afghanistan, the expression used to describe the president is *Rais-e Jomhur* or 'leader of the Republic'. But what exactly might we mean by 'leader'? The phenomenon of leadership is certainly pervasive. As the political scientist Jean Blondel has argued:

> Leadership is as old as mankind. It is universal, and inescapable. It exists everywhere—in small organisations and in large ones, in businesses and in churches, in trade unions and in charitable bodies, in tribes and in universities. It exists in informal bodies, in street gangs and in mass demonstrations ... For leadership to exist, of course, there has to be a group: but where ever a group exists, there is always a form of leadership.[2]

Drawing on the work of Robert C. Tucker,[3] Blondel identifies three crucial elements of leadership: 'diagnosis' of 'what has to be redressed', 'prescription of the course of action', and—critically—'mobilisation' of those 'who will be involved in ensuring that the action does take place'. On this final point, Blondel argues that 'Mobilization has to be conceived broadly: it covers the mobilization of subordinates, immediate or distant (within the bureaucracy, for instance), and of the population as a whole, or at any rate the fraction of the population that is relevant to the course of action'.[4] This point was echoed more recently by Nannerl Keohane, who argued that the core of leadership is 'providing solutions to common problems or offering ideas about how to accomplish collective purposes, *and mobilising the energies of others to follow these courses of action*'.[5] From this it is apparent that leadership can require a number of different skills, not all of which will necessarily be possessed by an aspirant to a leadership position. This point is usefully elaborated in a recent study which argues that 'leadership is essentially a process of social identity management', and identifies 'four key facets of identity leadership'. These are: (1) 'Leaders as *identity prototypes* who are representative, and are seen to be representative, of the groups that they seek to influence'; (2) 'Leaders as *identity champions* who advance, and are seen to advance, the interests of those groups'; (3) 'Leaders as *identity entrepreneurs* who create and shape group identity'; and (4) 'Leaders as *identity impresarios* who shape reality in the image of group identity'.[6] As Henry Kissinger recently put it, 'good leaders elicit in their people a wish to walk alongside them'.[7]

Leadership can be exercised at many different points within a political system. Almost invariably, it is leadership within the top political elite that attracts the most attention and scrutiny. National political elites are collections of individuals who regularly exercise significant power across a range of issues and aspire to control central state institutions and agencies. In certain circumstances, ruling elites can find themselves under challenge from counter-elites, who may end up replacing them through a process of elite circulation; free and fair elections can be one mechanism by which this replacement occurs. Consensually unified elites foster political stability in a way that fragmented elites do not.[8] National elites can be quite complex in their structure, and as Archie Brown has reminded us, 'Within a democratic government—and even in some authoritarian regimes—*there are people of substance within the leadership group who should not be regarded as "followers" of the top leader*'.[9] Managing relations with such figures can be a key leadership challenge, and proved to be so in Republican Afghanistan. But in any but the simplest of political systems, there are likely to be local elites and local leaders as well. These can come in very different shapes and sizes. In some cases, they may be formally plenipotentiaries of the central state, such as the provincial governors and district administrators in Republican Afghanistan. This need not mean, however, that they are not political players. Dipali Mukhopadhyay remarked that 'Governors also occupied the center of gravity of a complex political matrix in which personalized, patronage-based relationships reigned supreme'.[10] Furthermore, strong local personages were on occasion either appointed as governors or were more than able to dominate the person who formally held the position. Whether or not such figures could be characterised as warlords, they were often in a position to function as local leaders.

Institutional frameworks can be crucial in directing potentially destructive individual impulses into constructive channels, something recognised in the eighteenth century by Giambattista Vico and Bernard Mandeville[11] and more recently in political science literature.[12] In some circumstances, the exercise of leadership is highly institutionalised, with an individual's ability to exercise leadership being crucially dependent upon continued occupancy of a formal position. This potentially gives rise to a situation in which, to paraphrase an Australian politician, one can be a rooster one day and a feather-duster the next. This is a particular pathology of a strongly presidential system, and it can create a situation in which the incentive for an incumbent leader to seek to hang on to office by hook or by crook is very strong, something even the United States witnessed in late 2020 and early 2021. But the incentive to hang on to office can also exist in a neopatrimonial system of the kind that developed in Afghanistan, and the leader may find some support for doing so. This is because the departure of a leader can detrimentally affect the interests of those linked to that leader through networks or specific patron-client relationships. In a neopatrimonial system, constraints on the exercise of power during a leader's term may be quite weak. Here, there can be overlap with what Guillermo O'Donnell called 'delegative democracy', resting 'on the premise that whoever wins election to the presidency is thereby entitled to govern as he or she sees fit, constrained only by the hard facts of existing power relations and by a constitutionally limited term of office'.[13]

No matter what the wider institutional framework, patterns of leadership are likely to vary dramatically according to the personal attributes of a given leader. A whole range of factors can come into play, such as energy levels, clarity of vision, and intellectual capacity. High voltage can be combined with low wattage, or vice versa. The health of a particular leader may be of critical significance in making sense of an individual's performance. Medical conditions or even medications can be far from trivial influences on patterns of behaviour.[14] Another important variable is how curious an individual leader may be. Winston Churchill's relentless questioning of his military advisors doubtless infuriated them from time to time, but a recent study shows how much this Socratic approach contributed to his effective leadership during the Second World War.[15] He was far less comfortable with reticent or taciturn generals such as Sir John Dill and Sir Archibald Wavell than with combative generals such as Sir Alan Brooke. He was also capable of changing his mind when the arguments justified his doing so: a wartime Australian Prime Minister, who knew Churchill for thirty years, recalled from personal experience that 'even when Winston refused to listen, he listened'.[16] Of course, the leadership styles of particular leaders can also reflect the impact of wider cultural norms and expectations in the societies in which those leaders emerge and operate: the style of US presidents and presidential candidates is typically quite different, for example, from the style of a Prime Minister of Japan, for whom a reputation for flamboyance could be a liability rather than an asset from a political perspective. The personality traits of leaders can also change over time as a result of ageing, experiences, changing beliefs, and the effects of power.[17]

There is by now a substantial scholarly literature, dating back to Harold D. Lasswell's 1930 book *Psychopathology and Politics*, that seeks to use psychoanalytic techniques to enhance understanding of political leaders. Some of the categories that Lasswell employed—notably 'agitators', 'administrators', and 'theorists'[18]—have stimulated significant further research.[19] But that said, no single scheme of categorisation has come to dominate the field. There are a range of interesting works, notably by the psychiatrist Jerrold M. Post,[20] that seek to make sense of real-world leaders by drawing on insights from psychiatry and psychology, which are concerned not simply with psychoses, but with different forms of personality disorder, such as the narcissistic and the antisocial or sociopathic. Post pioneered the development of 'political personality profiles', combining a psychobiography and a personality study. Furthermore, in one famous study, the political scientist James David Barber sought to categorise US presidents according to how much energy the president invested in the presidency (*activity-passivity*) and how the president felt about what he did (*positive-negative*). As he

103

put it, 'Active-positive Presidents want most to achieve results. Active-negatives aim to get and keep power. Passive-positives are after love. Passive-negatives emphasize their civic virtue'.[21] Insights from these literatures can be useful and instructive, but they have three limitations. One is that not every leader will fit easily into a schematic category; in 1941, Sir Hastings Ismay warned the incoming British commander in the Middle East, Sir Claude Auchinleck, that Prime Minister Churchill 'was different from anyone we had ever met before, or were ever likely to meet again'.[22] The second is that considerable care is required in using techniques of psychological analysis to make sense of the behaviour of specific individuals;[23] there is always a risk that unless one knows the individual personally, one will be analysing popular *images* of the individual rather than anything real. The third is that in explaining events such as the decline and fall of Republican Afghanistan, it is the question of how leadership behaviour and actions account for outcomes, rather than the question of what personality traits might have accounted for such leadership behaviour and actions, that will matter the most.

The skills and requirements of leadership in Afghanistan

Different kinds of leadership skill may be more important in some countries and contexts than in others. It is therefore useful to identify at the outset what might have been some of the more important requirements in Republican Afghanistan. This will allow a more nuanced discussion of both the particular types of leadership, broadly defined, that surfaced after 2001, and the particular strengths and weaknesses of the two presidents who sought to lead the country.

One skill—or gift—that has historically been much discussed is *the ability to inspire*. It is not the magic key to success. Bores can rise to the apex of a political system, but usually by being persistent, or unthreatening, or both. And conversely, inspiring political leaders can sometimes flame out quickly, like a meteor hitting the atmosphere. Nonetheless, an aspiring leader with a gift to inspire followers can have a considerable advantage. Max Weber explored this gift in his discussion of its extreme form, charismatic leadership. 'The term "charisma"', he wrote, 'will be applied to a certain quality of an individual personality by virtue of which he is considered extraordinary and treated as endowed with supernatural, superhuman, or at least specifically exceptional powers or qualities'.[24] This is very general, and for some, too general.[25] Nonetheless, use of the concept of charisma in the exploration of leader–follower relationships has proved fruitful for leaders as different as Adolf Hitler and Donald Trump.[26] Fortunately, a leader can inspire without being charismatic in a grim sense. Both Hamed Karzai and Ashraf Ghani proved capable of inspiring loyalty and support on occasion. But the qualification 'on occasion' is important. The ability to inspire beyond a narrow circle can dissipate if disappointment spreads about a leader's performance. This happened to Mussolini in Fascist Italy,[27] and arguably both Karzai and Ghani fell victim to this as well. In a crisis, the ability to inspire may really matter.

So may a second critical skill, captured in the definitions of leadership that we discussed earlier: *the ability to mobilise*. Put simply, in Republican Afghanistan, no leader could do everything on his own. Fear can be a durable device for mobilisation, as Stalin proved in the USSR, but even Stalin found it necessary to work with a team of associates who proved remarkably stable through the duration of his regime.[28] Furthermore, fear can have paralysing effects on the performance of a leadership team and the wider population: it tends to promote conformity, and a situation in which decision-makers are told only what they want to hear rather than what they need to know. For this reason, 'strong leaders' are often not nearly as strong as they would like to think, and more collegial forms of leadership, in systems marked by the rule of law and an engaged citizenry, may prove more effective, and, paradoxically, 'stronger' as a result.[29] That said, the value of an ability to mobilise is not limited simply to a leader's immediate associates. Effective mobilisation may depend critically upon a leader's capacity to prioritise, to define responsibilities in the light of such priorities, and to ensure both that resources are provided to discharge those responsibilities and that performance in discharge of those responsibilities is properly appraised. In the abstract, the notion of 'mobilisation' can be overly vague; it is critical always to ask 'mobilisation to what end'? In the years 2001 to 2004, when Hamed Karzai was technically Chairman of an 'Interim Administration' first and then a 'Transitional Administration', there were others on hand to assist with these tasks, in the form both of international officials and of Ashraf Ghani as a notably dynamic finance minister. After the 2004 election, Karzai himself was expected to take over these tasks.

Discharging such executive tasks is, of course, a highly political exercise, requiring diverse political skills, notably *the ability to balance competing interests and players*. A leader may be tempted to rule by decree, but may easily come unstuck in the face of everyday forms of resistance. This is where other skills come into play, notably the ability to bargain, cajole, and persuade. Indeed, in a famous book on the American presidency, Richard E. Neustadt argued that the power of the presidency was 'the power to persuade'.[30] Leaders with domineering personalities who are convinced that they know best may easily come to think that all they need to do is lay out their case, and others will follow. That is rarely the case. Different players will have interests and objectives of their own: the old maxim 'where you stand depends on where you sit' comes to mind. This was certainly the case in Republican Afghanistan, where a number of the actors whose cooperation might be required for policies to be given effect were 'strongmen' with interests and power bases of their own to protect.

Related to the skills of balancing competing interests and players is *the ability to assemble and manage a personal staff* capable of giving effect to a leader's wishes. This is equally important whether one is talking about the president of Afghanistan, a minister in the government, a provincial governor or district administrator, or a strongman operating outside a formal institutional framework. Even in highly personalised and loosely structured conquest empires such as the Timurid empire in Central Asia in the fourteenth century, there was a need for such staffs. But there can be a trade-off between administrative and political objectives when such staffs are being assembled. As a historian of the Timurid empire put it:

> Temür had not only to govern his extensive realm, he also had to reward and to control his ruling class. His elite had to be repaid for their support, and the granting of offices in his administration was an important element of this reward. An office presented to

its holder not only a set of duties and an opportunity for income, but also a certain amount and type of power.[31]

Exactly the same challenge confronted Afghanistan's Republican presidents after 2001, and considerations of administrative competence on occasion came a distant second to political factors when key personnel appointments were being made.

Given the sheer scale of the problems that confronted Afghanistan's post-2001 leadership, one additional critical skill was *the ability to develop policies and see that they were implemented*. This skill goes well beyond the setting of priorities: it involves the development and successful execution of specific measures to respond to the problems that it is a priority to address. The policymaking process in any country is a realm of considerable complexity,[32] and it was immensely so in Afghanistan after 2001 given the scale of state collapse that was inherited by the new Republic. Institutional structures were weak or non-existent; baseline data to assist prioritisation and policy development were similarly absent; huge uncertainties surrounded the possible consequences—intended and unintended—of different alternative policies; and there was a dire shortage of skills at both mass and elite levels to confront policy challenges. Perhaps unsurprisingly, Afghanistan's first leader after 2001 seemed more comfortable with the symbolic rather than the policy dimensions of his role.

Forms of leadership in Afghanistan

In Republican Afghanistan, a number of different forms of leadership were on display. To start with, the president of Afghanistan came to provide a form of *symbolic* leadership as head of state. To some degree this was shared until 2007 with former King Zahir Shah, who returned to Afghanistan in 2002 and remained in his homeland until his death. This was formally recognised in Article 158 of the 2004 Constitution which accorded Zahir Shah the 'title of Father of the Nation' (*laqab-e baba-i mellat*). The title was not, however, hereditary, and with Zahir Shah's passing, it fell into abeyance, and the president became the principal focus of symbolic leadership. An additional factor that facilitated the president playing this role was the absence of symbolic competition, notably from a hierarchical religious establishment. Afghanistan is a Sunni-majority country, and Sunni Islam lacks a 'clergy' in any strong sense of the term. This could be contrasted with the situation in Shiite-majority Iraq after the 2003 US invasion, where Grand Ayatollah Ali al-Sistani was widely recognised as a source of authoritative moral leadership, although in keeping with older Shiite traditions, he eschewed involvement in day-to-day politics despite playing a significant political role.[33]

In an executive sense, the president discharged functions of *institutional* leadership enumerated in Article 64 of the Constitution. Pursuant to this article, the president was *inter alia* responsible for determination of the fundamental policies of the state with the approval of the National Assembly; command-in-chief of the armed forces; appointment, dismissal and acceptance of the resignation of ministers and a wide range of public officials; and the signature of laws and legislative decrees. Other articles, however, qualified some of these powers, notably Article 71 that provided that ministers should be 'introduced for approval to the National Assembly'. This was to prove a source of endless tension between the palace and the parliament, not least over the question of whether a 'no-confidence' vote could require a minister's removal, and set the scene for presidential attempts to circumvent the requirements of Article 71 through the appointment of 'Acting Ministers' and 'State Ministers' whose names were not put forward for parliamentary approval. A particularly significant power was the ability to appoint provincial governors and district administrators, and although an 'Independent Directorate of Local Governance' (*Idara-e mustaqel-e organha-i mahalli*) was established by presidential decree on 30 August 2007 to enhance the quality of local administration, it was only one player in shaping local personnel appointments.

The importance of local leadership in Republican Afghanistan is easily overlooked, but it should not be. The insurgency, after all, was largely prosecuted in a myriad of specific localities, and local leadership could contribute to determining how effectively the insurgency was combated. An assessment by Englehart and Grant suggested that governors with local ties often performed more effectively than those with technocratic skills.[34] In this context, it is also important to note how much variation exists—geographically, politically, and socially—between different parts of Afghanistan. Any attempt to analyse Afghanistan on the strength of a simple 'urban-rural' distinction is likely to mislead;[35] in contradistinction to such an approach, Englehart drew attention to notable differences in 'strongman' governance between northern and southern parts of Afghanistan, writing that in the north, 'military formations were typically descended from government forces', whereas in the south, 'the strongmen's forces tended to be based on tribal affiliations, especially after the Soviet withdrawal in 1989. All politics in the south—whether within the Communist Party, among the *Mujahideen*, or between the civil war militias—remained inflected with tribal feuds and longstanding competition between leading local families'.[36] Prominent local leaders were also much more vulnerable to assassination than highly protected national leaders: examples that come to mind included President Karzai's brother Ahmad Wali Karzai in Kandahar, killed in July 2011;[37] Faridullah, the district administrator of Alisheng in Laghman, killed in August 2012;[38] police chief Matiullah Khan from Uruzgan, killed in March 2015;[39] and police chief Abdul Raziq of Kandahar, killed in October 2018.[40]

In studies of political leadership, one can find useful distinctions between different kinds of leadership based on what it is that a leader actually attempts to do, namely *transactional*, *redefining*, and *transformational* leadership. Of course, to some extent what a leader can attempt to do will depend upon the wider structure of the political system. A national leader who is also the leader of a political party may operate differently from a leader who confronts no such constraint. But bearing this in mind, the distinctions are still useful, all the while remembering that these are not exclusive categories and a given individual may display dimensions of all three.

Transactional leadership, according to James MacGregor Burns, 'occurs when one person takes the initiative in making contact with others for the purpose of an exchange of valued things'.[41] It characteristically comes into play in the context of opinion, groups, parties, legislatures, and the executive,[42] and is the kind of leadership associated with wheeler-dealers who bargain with other players in order to achieve their objectives. This is not limited to the domestic politics of a state: it can figure prominently in international negotiations as well. Some transactional leaders may be more interested in holding power than exercising it to achieve some higher end. One is reminded of a remark allegedly made by Giovanni de Medici upon becoming Pope Leo X in 1513: 'Since God had given us the papacy, let us enjoy it'. Karzai's leadership was for the most part transactional. *Redefining leadership*, as explained by Archie Brown, is exercised by leaders who 'challenge previous assumptions, who redefine what is thought to be politically possible, and who introduce radical policy change';[43] this category includes leaders such as US President Franklin D. Roosevelt, British Prime Minister Margaret Thatcher, and German Chancellor Konrad Adenauer. Ashraf Ghani's leadership had distinct redefining dimensions. Finally, Brown points to the importance of *transformational leadership*, where the leader 'plays a decisive role in introducing *systemic change*, whether of the political or economic system of his or her country or (more rarely) of the international system'.[44] Examples mentioned by Brown include President Charles de Gaulle of France, Soviet leader Mikhail Gorbachev (on whose career Brown remains the pre-eminent specialist[45]), Chinese paramount leader Deng Xiaoping, and Nelson Mandela of South Africa. Ghani may have had transformational inclinations, but certainly did not succeed in putting them into effect.

Karzai as a leader

At the Bonn conference in 2001, Hamed Karzai emerged as a consensus candidate to chair the new Interim Administration, but he was not the favourite for the position when the conference began; the most likely consensus candidate at that point was Abdul Sattar Sirat, who had served as Justice Minister from 1969 to 1973 during the reign of Zahir Shah, and who was associated with the former king through the so-called 'Rome group'. Sirat's candidacy, however, came unstuck, with his personal attributes and his Uzbek ethnic background being variously cited to explain what went wrong. Karzai, born in 1957, came from a well-known Popalzai Durrani Pushtun family; his father Abdul Ahad Karzai, who was assassinated by Taliban gunmen in Quetta in July 1999, had served in the *Wolesi*

Jirga during the Zahir Shah period. Hamed Karzai studied in Shimla in India, obtaining an MA degree from the University of Himachal Pradesh, and was trained to teach.[46] In the 1980s and early 1990s, he was associated with a small, Peshawar-based 'moderate' *Mujahideen* party led by Sebghatullah Mojaddidi, and after the collapse of the Communist regime in 1992, he briefly served as Deputy Foreign Minister before quitting the capital after receiving threats from a future associate, Mohammad Qasim Fahim. When the Taliban seized Kabul in 1996, they nominated Karzai to represent them at the United Nations, but he wisely did not take up the position. In general, those who encountered him found him polite but somewhat inscrutable— although he made no secret of his suspicions of Pakistan. He lacked the kind of national profile, Jihadist credentials or popular following that some of those gathered in Bonn boasted. In 2001, he seemed to non-Pushtun players to be the kind of figure from a Pushtun background with whom they could work congenially. But there were some rocky moments for Karzai between the Bonn conference and the 2004 election that gave him a popular mandate, notably at a June 2002 Emergency *Loya Jirga* where Dr Zalmay Khalilzad forcefully headed off a move to restore Zahir Shah to a more than symbolic political role. As a well-informed observer put it, 'By blatantly interfering with the Afghan leadership selection process on behalf of Hamid Karzai, the United States fumbled a rare opportunity to let Afghans themselves choose a leader who would not be seen as imposed by outsiders … The American interference in the process enlarged Karzai's image as an American puppet'.[47] Ironically, the Americans found him anything but a puppet.

A critical point to note about this career path is that Karzai was scarcely ever involved in policy development and implementation. Politics in Peshawar during the 1980s was politics *without the state*. It was a politics of networking and alliance building, quintessentially transactional in character, rather than a politics focused on solving economic and social problems that dominated the lives of ordinary people. This meant that when it came to policy, Karzai was highly dependent on others to perform vital tasks. Ghani played such a role as finance minister, and Khalilzad, as US Ambassador from 2003 to 2005, became involved in policy too, although according to

Ambassador Peter Tomsen, Khalilzad's 'invasive style reinforced the pattern of American pre-eminence and Afghan dependency'.[48] This did not mean that Karzai was completely divorced from the policy sphere, but rather that his role came into play in less direct ways than if he had had a strong policy agenda to drive. An insightful reflection on his policy style, shared with one of the authors by a number of close observers, was that if and when he was presented by others with a range of policy alternatives, he could ask penetrating and useful questions about the ramifications of those alternatives, but he did not have the skill of developing such policy alternatives himself.

Where he did excel was in the realm of politicking. He had the patience in the Afghan context to spend a great deal of time with those who might otherwise have caused trouble, although he had less patience in dealing with those Americans who showed little interest in listening to his warnings. The neopatrimonial system that developed under Karzai significantly reflected his own political predilections and experience, using patronage and networking as a way of securing his position and—in his view—promoting stability. This he probably did manage to do in the short term, but the ramifications were to haunt Republican Afghanistan in the longer run. As Englehart observed when Karzai was still president:

> Karzai's great talent as a politician is also his greatest weakness as a state builder. By deploying the same kind of patronage politics in the north that he uses in the south, he has made great progress in bringing the region under his control, but at the cost of undermining the institutions nurtured by the warlords. The warlords had interests in transcending segmented divisions and longstanding feuds to secure large, prosperous base areas to support their militias. Karzai conversely has incentives to exploit these divisions in order to penetrate the north and build networks of political support.[49]

His transactional style also elevated relatively small regional players to the status of larger, national figures. Atta Muhammad Noor, General Abdul Raziq, Sayed Mustafa Kazemi, General Daud and similar figures, whose spheres of influence were at best regional, came to play national roles, much like Karzai himself. By working with such figures, he may have hoped to counterbalance weightier players such as Abdul Rashid Dostum, Ustad Sayyaf, Dr Abdullah, and Karim Khalili. Karzai's personal lifestyle was far from opulent—in contrast to those of quite a number of the members of Afghanistan's new national elite—and no one ever credibly accused him of personal corruption. But at the same time, a number of individuals who were close to him had much more troubling reputations, and his brother Ahmad Wali Karzai, the Kandahar strongman assassinated in July 2011, was the target of persistent rumours of involvement in the opium trade.[50]

Karzai's tragedy, in a way, was that as time went by, his undoubted skills became less and less relevant to solving Afghanistan's problems, and his weaknesses became more and more relevant. His great strength was a genuine belief in the importance of inclusivity and bringing the country together, and this served him well during his term as Chairman of the Interim and Transitional Administrations and his first term as elected president. But as time passed, he was confronted more and more with expectations that he would be a dynamic policy figure, and this simply took him beyond his comfort zone. It was one reason why the United States lost confidence in him. A leaked cable from US Ambassador Eikenberry in April 2009 stated that Karzai's 'inability to grasp the most rudimentary principles of state-building and his deep-seated insecurity as a leader combine to make any admission of fault unlikely, in turn confounding our best efforts to find in Karzai a responsible partner'.[51] The outcome of the 2009 election only compounded the problem. With a weakened mandate, Karzai was even more poorly positioned to take tough policy decisions, and this triggered something of a spiral: as Whitlock has written, 'Hamid Karzai's fraudulent reelection worsened a deluge of corruption that engulfed Afghanistan in 2009 and 2010. Dark money cascaded over the country. Money launderers lugged suitcases loaded with $1 million, or more, on flights leaving Kabul so crooked businessmen and politicians could stash their ill-gotten fortunes offshore'.[52] More seriously, the election imbroglio poisoned the relations between Karzai and the United States, at the very moment when it was vital that the two countries work together for the sake of the Republican system.

113

Almost seven years elapsed between Karzai's retirement at the end of his second term as president and the fall of Republican Afghanistan. Nonetheless, it is important to reflect on the implications of his presidency for what came later. In significant ways, the Karzai presidency initiated the decline of the Republic, although not its fall. His fluctuating attitudes towards the Taliban were particularly destructive. Increasingly during his second term, as his relations with the Americans soured, he referred to the Taliban as 'angry brothers' (rather than terrorists or Pakistani proxies).[53] In the context of the Taliban's rapid rise and increasing violence, this had major ramifications for the Republic. To the ANDSF, who were dying in the fight, it sent dangerous and dispiriting signals. To at least some elements of the population, it came to be read, whether fairly or not, as a Pushtun president sending ethnic 'dog whistles' to the Taliban.[54] It certainly muddled the Taliban's status as the unmitigated, uncontroversial enemy of the state and the nation. And it can be argued that Karzai's whitewashing of the Taliban provided a blueprint for the US's subsequent disastrous diplomacy. This was also the beginning of a loss of 'narrative' by the Republic, a weakness from which the Republic never recovered. No president, defence minister, spy chief, or other national political figure—save, perhaps, for First Vice President Amrullah Saleh from 2019—was able to provide any consistent wartime narrative. Even as the Republic neared its end, Karzai proved a difficult person with whom to deal. US *chargé d'affaires* Ross Wilson found this when he tried to induce Karzai to attend a high-level Republican delegation meeting with the Taliban ahead of a mooted international meeting in Istanbul:

> On the Afghan side, appropriate representatives of the Palace, Abdullah, Karzai and other senior political powerbrokers were to attend. It went around and around on the Islamic republic side, with Karzai being extremely reluctant to engage in that or do anything significant that would show support for President Ghani or associate him with President Ghani, so it was very difficult as I encouraged him.[55]

Wilson elsewhere remarked that he 'leaned about as hard as we could' on Karzai, even to the point of appearing 'rude', adding that

Khalilzad also 'did his best' and Dr Abdullah, too, 'worked hard'. His cooperation was not forthcoming.[56]

Throughout his tenure, Karzai enjoyed the support of a loyal team, whom he was able to inspire and mobilise. Beyond these circles, however, and especially after 2009, his ability to inspire and mobilise the wider public was compromised, and there was little love lost for him amongst those who had voted for his principal opponents. His transactional approach allowed him to balance competing interests, but at the cost of the empowerment of networks in a neopatrimonial system. It was not surprising that when different candidates were on offer in 2014, some younger technocrats, interested in something more than transactional politics, saw Ashraf Ghani as a figure to support. Unfortunately, like Karzai, he proved to have some of the skills required for effective leadership, but not others.

Ghani as a leader

An experienced American observer, well acquainted with both Karzai and Ghani, once remarked to one of the authors that 'Karzai is all politics and no policy; Ashraf is all policy and no politics'. This was of course an oversimplification, but it contained a solid core of truth. And that solid core was to have damaging consequences for the Republican system.

Mohammad Ashraf Ghani was born in 1949, into an Ahmadzai Ghilzai Pushtun family. He spent much of his adult life in the United States where he used 'Ghani' as his surname, but he made use of the name 'Ahmadzai' in the run-up to the 2014 presidential election, although thereafter he reverted to 'Mohammad Ashraf Ghani' in official circles. He studied at the American University of Beirut, where he completed BA and MA degrees and was a counterpart of Zalmay Khalilzad, and completed a PhD at Columbia University in New York in 1982, writing a thesis on 'Production and Domination: Afghanistan, 1747–1901'. This was an extremely sophisticated study, influenced by Marx, Weber, and a number of other social theorists, and while it was never published, it reflected one of Ghani's most notable characteristics, namely that he was extraordinarily widely read. He taught anthropology for some years at Johns Hopkins

University before taking up an appointment as a senior social scientist at the World Bank in Washington DC. During his academic career, he published relatively little,[57] but was a mesmerising speaker in English, much in demand for panels dealing with Afghanistan. He had suffered, however, from indifferent health, and underwent surgery for stomach cancer before his return to Afghanistan following the September 2001 terrorist attacks. He proved to be a dynamic and effective finance minister between 2002 and 2004, not least because he was obliged, at least to some degree, to find ways of cooperating with other officeholders in order to achieve his objectives.

He seemed no longer to feel any such constraints once he became president. With no superordinate figure above him and little inclination to share power with Dr Abdullah, 'Chief Executive Officer' in the 'National Unity Government' that US Secretary of State John Kerry had brokered, Ghani developed a reputation for a 'take no prisoners' approach to confrontations with other people, with little appreciation of the dangers to which this could expose him in the long run. There is a story, probably apocryphal, that when Voltaire was dying, a priest approached him and said 'Now is the time to renounce the Devil', to which Voltaire replied 'Now is not the time to be making new enemies'. Making new enemies never seemed to worry Ghani, who on occasion wore his reputation for doing so almost as a badge of pride. Sometimes he made enemies in a good cause: cracking down on malpractice will almost always leave some people feeling alienated. But given that Ghani, having once reportedly described Uzbek strongman Abdul Rashid Dostum as a 'known killer',[58] then invited Dostum to be his vice-presidential running-mate in 2014, observers were left wondering just how firm his standards actually were. One close observer poignantly remarked 'I think being the minister of finance was his comfort zone. He never grew into being a president'.[59]

What most distinguished Ghani from Karzai was Ghani's intense policy focus. His knowledge of public policy complexity was wide-ranging, and reflected the benefits not only of scholarly research but of practical experience with the World Bank. The result was a deluge of ideas, only some of which ended up being implemented. Many were concerned with putting in place a sound legal and institutional framework for future development within the country, which was no bad thing; but a consequence was that there were few immediate dividends on display from such innovation. Furthermore, some of Ghani's pet projects proved extremely difficult to implement. The classic example was the idea of an electronic identity card (*e-tazkera*) system, something that had preoccupied him since his time as finance minister when he sought to promote it as a basis for voter identification prior to the 2004 election.[60] When he became president, he had an opportunity to carry the project forward. This was when the trouble started. The foundation for the system had been laid in the 2013 Population Registration Act under Karzai, although it was only signed into law by Ghani on 9 November 2014. But in the rolling out of the *e-tazkera*, all sorts of political problems surfaced,[61] especially relating to the use of the word 'Afghan', which some groups saw as a civic identifier, while others regarded it as an attempt to impose a particular ethnic identity over the entire population. It was not until 15 February 2018 that the roll-out of the *e-tazkera* finally commenced. And while the bulk of the population remained unregistered, with the fall of the Republic, the possession of an *e-tazkera*—or at least the Taliban's potential access to Afghans' personal data—became a source of danger.[62]

Ghani also had an indifferent record in personnel management. While a number of young technocrats remained intensely loyal to him, others quietly left government service—not with much fuss, since they often remained firmly committed to the Republican ideal—because they found working with him extremely difficult. As one observer saw it, 'The president's issue was his attitude; he humiliated people … his version of Afghanistan was based on the briefs he got, most of them fabricated'.[63] James MacGregor Burns's warning comes to mind: 'Power wielders may treat people as things. Leaders may not'.[64] Rapid personnel turnover became the order of the day, making it difficult for ministers and senior officials to obtain much 'grip' on their responsibilities. Some who joined his team from abroad, for example Dr Mohammad Homayoun Qayoumi, who had been a fellow student at the American University of Beirut and a university president in the US, and who served as Acting Finance Minister from 2018 to 2020, found it difficult to adjust to the challenges of twenty-first-century Afghanistan.[65] And many, although not all, ministers were cowed by the president's temper. Few stood up to him, reminding one of the words of Cassius to Brutus in Shakespeare's *Julius Caesar*: 'Men at some time are masters of their fates: The fault, dear Brutus, is not in our stars, But in ourselves, that we are underlings'.[66]

From its outset, Ghani's presidency was deeply troubled. He, rather than Karzai, bore the burden of coping with a greatly diminished international presence and commitment, but he also carried the weight of the fraud in 2014 that had smoothed his way to the palace. Winning an election through fraud is akin to winning a time-bomb in a lottery. Electoral fraud may deliver power but it does not supply authority, and from the outset of Ghani's tenure, there were significant powerholders and groups in Afghanistan that regarded him as the beneficiary of a particular kind of theft. The low turnout at the 2019 election may have been due in part to direct Taliban threats to voters,[67] but even in the relative safety of Kabul, the turnout, as witnessed by the authors, was low—suggesting not just apprehension but disillusionment. His disposition to dominate those around him paradoxically weakened his position, since it cut him off from useful correctives when others were trying to manipulate him to their own advantage. And as Afghans increasingly lost confidence in Ghani, so did the US, which from 2018 had been going down the path of seeking direct engagement with the Taliban in the absence of the Afghan government. Ghani, not being by nature a power sharer, understood with absolute clarity that the Taliban were not power sharers either, but warnings to this broad effect from Ghani and from his National Security Advisor, Hamdullah Mohib,[68] fell on deaf ears in Washington. In this way, the scene was set for disaster.

Conclusion: Leadership failings and their implications

To reflect on whether different leaders, for example Dr Abdullah, could have protected Republican Afghanistan from decline and fall is ultimately a counterfactual exercise, much more difficult than an analysis of institutional frameworks and their implications. It seems clear, however, that the centralised, presidential system embodied in the 2004 Constitution did not serve Afghanistan well. Rather than providing opportunities for ordinary people to rule effectively, it depended upon the emergence of a leader with a suite of skills that few potential candidates were likely to have given the decades of disruption that Afghanistan had experienced. The president of Afghanistan was expected to be symbolic head of state, executive head of government, and to a significant degree *the* interagency process resolving tensions between different parts of the system. Each could have been a full-time occupation. The result was that both Karzai and Ghani found themselves severely overloaded, and while Ghani set himself a punishing work schedule, especially for someone over 70 when his second term began, its value was offset by his reluctance to delegate and his disposition to micromanage. Some of this reflected his preferred approach to the policy process: in his first term, he created 'high councils' for areas such as justice, the economy, and internally displaced persons and refugees. These were essentially working groups of sectoral ministries chaired by the president but facilitated by a staffer ('advisor'). This was where policymaking happened. This was also where ministers felt impotent, their policy proposals channelled through a Ghani staffer, their work throttled through the high councils. In Afghanistan's neopatrimonial political culture, ministries were distributed as equity to stakeholders to secure their buy-in for the administration.

The centralisation of the policy process and restricting of ministers' authority rendered their portfolios devoid of the dividends that were supposed to flow to the networks that the ministers represented. It alienated the networks that had grown under Karzai's big-tent approach and had come to depend on the resulting patronage. As successive presidential elections became contentious and failed to produce an undisputed winner, the administration's authority and the state's perceived legitimacy depended on the support of these networks, and the networks in turn depended on the state for patronage and relevance. Ghani saw his approach as freeing governance and policy from the burden of adverse influences, while those excluded saw it as the president greedily amassing power for himself. This sentiment came to be expressed by the label that the political opposition used for Ghani's administration—*jumhuriyat-e seh nafara*, the three-person Republic, helmed by Ghani and his closest aides, Mohib and Fazli. But what Ghani was up against was not just networks; it was also individuals such as his vice president, Marshal Dostum, who commanded considerable support among Afghanistan's Turkic populations. In marginalising Dostum and driving him from Afghanistan into exile in Turkey, Ghani also alienated significant segments of Uzbek and other Turkic ethnic groups. Other individuals who had lost out were able to paint Ghani's exclusionary approach as an attempt to drive out their ethnic communities from power. Ghani's leadership style, therefore, struck at the heart of the political balance that had sustained the Republic by giving equity to networks, ethnic communities, and powerbrokers. This approach, which grew under Karzai, prioritised political stability over policy efficiency. When Ghani sought to give primacy to policy, his overzealous and hurried efforts disrupted the political equilibrium.

But the final years of Ghani's presidency were also a time when his unique skill-set of policymaking became less relevant; it was a time when diplomacy and politics, his areas of relative weakness, were most needed but least exercised. Beginning with the Doha talks in 2018, the US was moving fast, and things changed so quickly that there were few policy positions that lasted for any length of time. This made the job of anyone 'not Ghani' difficult, because nobody could be sure what the latest position was on issues such as the release of Taliban convicts, the authority of the peace negotiation team, or the appropriate posture of the ANDSF.[69] With events driven at such a pace by external actors, the usual policy processes could not keep up. Uncertainty was so high and processes so deficient that subordinates were forced to send a large number of memos each day to the president seeking his instructions. These memos were often on matters so small that director-level staff would ordinarily have made the decisions, but given the circumstances, even the National Security Advisor could not pronounce on them, necessitating their escalation to the top. And the top was overwhelmed. No human is equipped to process significant volumes of information and produce good decisions consistently. What Ghani needed was to focus on the diplomacy that was driving events in Afghanistan and work to rebuild the domestic political consensus around the Republic as the US distanced itself, the Taliban waged war, and his administration found itself politically isolated internally. His efforts were too little, too late. In the pivotal year of 2021, he only made two foreign visits: in March to Tajikistan, where he got into a verbal joust with Pakistani Prime Minister Imran Khan, and in June to the US, where he encountered a strident Biden position to extricate the US with no contingency plan for supporting the ANDSF. He convened a meeting of influential politicians—the ethnic leaders and network nodes that he had marginalised—in July 2021 to build political support for the Republic. While the leaders issued a joint statement and pledged their support, the Taliban were already at a tipping point. We discuss this in greater detail in Chapter Eight. When politics and diplomacy mattered most for Afghanistan, Ghani was unable to engage.

Both Karzai and Ghani had significant abilities, but each had significant weaknesses as well, and the constitutional and political *systems* functioned in such a way as to accentuate the impact of those weaknesses. Furthermore, both Karzai and Ghani faced major problems in securing 'performance legitimacy'. To some degree this was outside their direct control. As we have noted, Karzai's approach to leadership was predominantly transactional, whereas Ghani's was more of a redefining kind. Neither was particularly qualified as a war leader. Karzai's involvement with the *Mujahideen* was not of a kind that required him to acquire strategic vision or tactical skill; and Ghani's academic background was not in the sphere of strategic studies. This mattered less for Karzai than it did for Ghani, since military operations during the bulk of Karzai's presidency were conducted by the US and its NATO and other allies in tandem with the ANDSF. It mattered more for Ghani. The problems of insurgency that Ghani faced were deeply intractable, given the sanctuaries that the Taliban enjoyed in Pakistan, but Ghani's micromanagement did not help. Some civilian leaders have had strong military backgrounds—Churchill, Eisenhower and De Gaulle come to mind. Some do not, but understand the importance of relying on strong professional military advisors. Those who meddle can run into strife. A classic case came in March 2021, when government troops in Maidan Wardak launched a major assault on an anti-Taliban Hazara strongman,

Abdul Ghani Alipour ('Commander Shamshir'),[70] whose militia had allegedly shot down a helicopter containing ANA Special Forces.[71] No matter the rights and wrongs of the situation—which were highly contested—it was no time to waste scarce military resources in what was a sideshow to the main game, namely the advance of the Taliban. For a wartime leader, sometimes the vision Ghani articulated for Afghanistan appeared to be for a country not facing imminent existential threat. As the Taliban made rapid advances and the nation needed a voice to rally it in January 2021, Ghani was articulating his three-pronged vision for Afghanistan that revolved around peace building, state building, and market building.[72] Later in the year, on 3 August, as Afghans across the country erupted in spontaneous chants of 'Allahu Akbar'[73]—God is Greatest, an allusion to similar calls in the late 1970s that started the groundswell against the Soviets— Ghani failed to channel the mood of the nation against the Taliban. 'There was a lot of resistance in many cities, which had given the Taliban the impression that the Taliban couldn't take cities as easily as they wanted', National Security Advisor Mohib said of the time in early August. 'The expectation was that this could stick ... that the provinces will defend and they will be able to hold the Taliban at bay and we will have time to negotiate an agreement with the Taliban'.[74] But Ghani did not so much as acknowledge the popular sentiment, let alone affirm and galvanise it to bolster the popular resistance in cities across the country. His silence begs the question of whether he even read the nation's mood. It was no surprise, then, that four days later the first provincial capital fell; eight days after that, Ghani fled the country.

As Chapters Seven and Eight show in more detail, after the US-Taliban deal of 29 February 2020, the political environment within Afghanistan shifted abruptly, and various players became more and more focused on short-term survival: the French expression *sauve qui peut* ('save what you can') comes to mind. Even before the Doha agreement, this danger had been highlighted by Dipali Mukhopadhyay. In a most insightful essay, she drew on Rousseau's metaphor of the Stag Hunt—where hunters impatiently awaiting the chance to capture the big prize of a deer, something only possible if they cooperate, may be tempted instead to break away to catch a passing hare—to highlight the danger of fragmentation.[75] The shift in incentive structures created by the February 2020 agreement massively complicated the task of national leadership in Afghanistan. The task was also complicated by the intensity of divisions within the national political elite. The rickety 'National Unity Government' was not revived after the 2019 election, and the bitterness that resulted from no fewer than three consecutive presidential elections contaminated by fraud—all of them with the same principal victim, Dr Abdullah—led to a situation in which too many people lost sight of the severity of the threat posed to the Republican system by the Taliban. Yet if we pose the question of what role leadership weakness played in the decline and fall of Republican Afghanistan, the answer again is not a simple one. Indifferent or erratic leadership undoubtedly contributed significantly to the decline of the Republic, and in a very specific sense to its fall when Ghani fled. But by the time Ghani boarded his helicopter, the Taliban were at the gates of Kabul, and the game was effectively over. To understand how Republican Afghanistan reached this point, it is necessary now to discuss the lethal effects of US diplomacy and of the internal realignments in Afghanistan that it triggered. That is the focus of the next two chapters.

6

DIPLOMATIC DISASTER

The beginning of the end for Republican Afghanistan came on 29 February 2020 when the United States signed its agreement with the Taliban in Doha. The US signatory, Dr Khalilzad, described it as 'A Day to Remember', which had unfortunate overtones of Walter Lord's famous book *A Night to Remember*,[1] which dealt with the sinking of the *Titanic*. The US's partner was what the agreement somewhat clumsily called 'the Islamic Emirate of Afghanistan which is not recognized by the United States as a state and is known as the Taliban'. The Taliban had every reason to be delighted that a reference to 'the Islamic Emirate of Afghanistan', the title by which they had long sought to be known, found its way into the text. The US also issued a 'Joint Declaration between the Islamic Republic of Afghanistan and the United States of America for Bringing Peace to Afghanistan',[2] but nothing in this was binding on the Taliban in any respect.

The US-Taliban agreement was completely silent on the issue of Taliban sanctuaries in Pakistan. The agreement contained no provision for a permanent and comprehensive ceasefire in the country, merely listing such a ceasefire as an agenda item for future discussion in what it vaguely called 'intra-Afghan negotiations with Afghan sides' (paragraph 4). The text provided for a reduction of

US troop numbers within 135 days to 8,600, to be followed by 'withdrawal of all remaining forces from Afghanistan within the remaining nine and a half (9.5) months' (Part One, A(1), B(1)). It also purported to bind not just the US but its allies, even though they were not parties to the agreement;[3] and it included 'all non-diplomatic civilian personnel, private security contractors, trainers, advisors, and supporting services personnel'. This withdrawal provision was not conditioned on any progress being made in intra-Afghan negotiations, or on any Taliban commitment to protect human rights or democratic processes. The agreement further provided that 'up to five thousand' Taliban 'combat and political prisoners'—euphemisms for convicted fighters, masterminds of suicide attacks, drug smugglers and would-be suicide bombers—held by the Afghan government 'would be released by March 10, 2020, the first day of intra-Afghan negotiations', with 'the goal of releasing all the remaining prisoners over the course of the subsequent three months' (Part One, C). The wording of the agreement went beyond what was contained in the 'Joint Declaration', which merely stated (Part Two, 4) that the 'Islamic Republic of Afghanistan will participate in a U.S.-facilitated discussion with Taliban representatives on confidence building measures, to include determining the feasibility of releasing significant numbers of prisoners on both sides'. All in all, what the Doha deal offered was not an agreement for bringing peace to Afghanistan, but an exit agreement for the United States.

To understand how this came to pass, it is necessary to set the Doha agreement in the wider context of US efforts to engage with the Taliban after 2001. The risks associated with talking to the Taliban were well known, but as it turned out, readily brushed aside.[4] Broadly speaking, the history of US 'peace diplomacy' in Afghanistan was marked by three fundamental paradigm shifts in America's disposition toward Afghanistan and the policies that flowed from them. The major shift under President Obama was the decision to negotiate with the Taliban after years of fighting the group. Under President Trump, the quantum leap was to conduct negotiations in the absence of the Republic and to the potential detriment of its 2004 Constitution and achievements in human rights. President Biden's contribution was to pull the plug on the American presence in Afghanistan entirely.

These fundamental changes altered the incentives and actions of the stakeholders inside Afghanistan, of the actors in its neighbourhood, and of the allies that had spent two decades supporting it. In this chapter, we look at these paradigm shifts and how they contributed to the decline and fall of the Republic.

Shifts in US diplomatic strategy

As early as 2010, the United States under President Obama seemingly concluded that there was no military solution in Afghanistan and that there should be negotiations with the Taliban. This was the first major change in the mindset of US policymakers toward Afghanistan.[5] Under Richard Holbrooke, appointed on 22 January 2009 as the US's first Special Representative for Afghanistan and Pakistan, the US position was that peace talks with the Taliban should happen with the participation of the Afghan government. Holbrooke was clear that the talks should be 'Afghan-led',[6] and his idea was that the Taliban and the Afghan government should 'reconcile', with the US assisting to 'integrate' the Taliban into the Afghan polity and society.[7] But there were also conditions that the Taliban would have to meet, as laid out by Secretary of State Hillary Clinton before the US House of Representatives Foreign Affairs Committee in October 2011: 'We have been clear about the necessary outcomes of any negotiation: Insurgents must renounce violence, abandon al Qaeda, and abide by the constitution of Afghanistan, including its protections for women and minorities. If insurgents cannot meet those red-lines, they will face continued and unrelenting assault'.[8]

Many direct and indirect efforts, as well as several false starts to peace talks, were to follow. In November 2010, it surfaced that NATO and Afghan officials, including President Karzai, had met with a man who claimed to be a senior Taliban figure, Mullah Akhtar Muhammad Mansour, and a Western diplomat reportedly said that 'the Afghan man was initially given a sizable sum of money to take part in the talks'.[9] The fortunate man who received the money, it turned out, was *not* Mullah Mansour, but a shopkeeper from the Pakistan city of Quetta.[10] This should have served as a reminder of just how little Western officials actually knew about the internal functioning of the

Taliban. But the most striking false start, rightly described by Coll as 'an episode of remarkable diplomatic incompetence',[11] came in 2013 when the Taliban opened what became known as their political office in Doha, giving the Taliban 'an address' from which they could engage with the world. Then-President Karzai objected to the flying of the Taliban flag and to a sign proclaiming that the office represented the 'Islamic Emirate of Afghanistan'. Karzai announced that his government would not participate in any peace talks as long as the Taliban had these symbols of statehood.[12] He also suspended the negotiation of a strategic partnership agreement with the United States, which was eventually signed by President Ghani in 2014. The flag and sign were later removed, but Karzai's strident protest left an indelible mark in the minds of future American policymakers.

In 2018, when Dr Zalmay Khalilzad, at the time a private citizen, was appointed Special Representative for Afghanistan Reconciliation, Secretary of State Pompeo said that his 'singular mission' was to develop 'opportunities to get the Afghans and the Taliban to come to a reconciliation'.[13] An account by one of Khalilzad's team stated that 'Pompeo empowered Khalilzad to act as he saw fit'.[14] The emphasis on reconciliation was a relic from the Holbrooke days and was soon abandoned, as were several other policy positions from that era. The most significant innovation was the decision to negotiate directly with the Taliban, without the presence of the Afghan government.[15] This constituted the second paradigm shift, and it had tectonic implications for the Taliban, America's international allies and, most importantly, the Republic. It elevated the Taliban to the status of a principal US interlocutor and sidelined the Afghan government from matters that directly affected the interests of the Afghan state. The move in effect relegated Afghanistan to a status ancillary to the US effort, a 'partner' whose unquestioning cooperation was expected, and one that could be chastised and embarrassed if and when it stood up for its interests and the rights of its people. It was hardly surprising that the agreement that resulted from these negotiations contained no protections for the Afghan constitution or the rights of the Afghan people. The US rationalised exclusive engagement with the Taliban by maintaining that it consulted with the Afghan government throughout the negotiation and implementation of the Doha deal, and that direct US talks with the Taliban constituted a bitter pill that had to be swallowed to give peace a chance: 'The longstanding US policy that the Republic must be represented effectively [would have] ensured that there wasn't going to be any negotiation and we weren't going to get anywhere', said Ross Wilson, who was US *chargé d'affaires* in Kabul from January 2020 until the collapse of the Republic. 'We had to get off that dime', he added.[16]

A lesson that the US should have learned from Karzai's insistence on denying the Taliban the outward trappings of statehood was that taking the relevant stakeholders forward together would mean that peace efforts could not safely be fast-tracked: in 2014, Münch and Ruttig wrote that 'The international community needs to understand that such a process—with its multi-faceted internal and regional dimensions—will be so multi-layered that it probably needs much more time than just three years'.[17] But the US was not interested in conducting years of patient diplomacy, and for it to move at its preferred breakneck speed, something had to give. The US could not control the Taliban's actions, but it could certainly pressure the Republic, and that was what happened. Part of the argument for this approach was that the US public had grown weary of the war in Afghanistan and the bipartisan consensus in Washington to withdraw was stronger than ever under a mercurial US president whose whims could not be predicted. 'If there's something you are absolutely forced to do, [you may as well] get something for it', Wilson said of the rationale for conducting diplomacy in this way.[18]

Two other notable shifts occurred on Khalilzad's watch. One related to sequencing. Initially, he committed very publicly to a standard diplomatic formula: 'nothing is agreed until everything is agreed'. This is an entirely defensible approach to negotiation, since it can ensure that offers are not set in stone unless and until they have been matched by appropriate commitments from the other side. Unfortunately, in 2019 he abandoned this in favour of a two-stage process under which the US would first reach its own agreement with the Taliban, with 'intra-Afghan negotiations' to follow.[19] This had an extremely damaging impact on incentives for the Taliban to negotiate seriously with the Afghan government. The Doha agreement ultimately granted the Taliban everything they really wanted—the status of a place at the table with the US, a strict timeline for the withdrawal of troops and contractors, and a promise of releases of thousands of convicted Taliban fighters— and left them with no incentive to engage seriously with their Afghan counterparts. Giving away too much, too soon, is one of the most elementary mistakes one can make in negotiating.[20] If anything, the two-stage process, and the prohibition on attacking the Americans, actually incentivised Taliban attacks on *Afghan* targets, since the more destruction they could cause, the stronger their negotiating position would be if a later phase of discussions finally materialised.

The other shift pertained to releases of convicted Taliban fighters. While this was described in the Doha agreement as a 'confidence building measure', the effect of the convict release provisions was the exact opposite, since they deprived the Afghan government of one of its main sources of potential leverage during any negotiations with the Taliban. As we noted earlier, the wording of the provisions in the US-Taliban agreement also went beyond what was contained in the Joint Declaration. The discrepancy in wording was either too clever by half, or evidence of an extremely amateurish approach to negotiation on the part of the US: again, it is an elementary mistake in diplomacy to confuse constructive ambiguity (which in certain circumstances may serve the interests of all parties) with loose wording, which can trigger immediate disputes over interpretation. This was exactly what happened over the convict release issue. There is some evidence that the convict release text found its way into the Doha agreement at the last minute. According to a US congressman, on 15 February 2020,

> during a meeting attended by more than a dozen members of Congress at the Munich Security Conference in Germany, I asked Secretary of State Mike Pompeo about a rumor that the deal might also commit the Afghan government to releasing Taliban prisoners—a huge upfront concession that Afghan President Ashraf Ghani understandably did not want to make. Pompeo told us categorically that the deal would say nothing about releasing prisoners.[21]

Three questions about the Trump administration's approach arise immediately: what was the US seeking to obtain? Was this the optimal way to obtain it? And did the Afghan government know that the US was 'forced' to withdraw? Although US policymakers insisted that the deal with the Taliban was not a withdrawal agreement, that was undeniably its net effect, to say nothing of the concessions made to the Taliban at the expense of the Afghan people and their republican aspirations. The Afghan government long complained that if the US were to withdraw, it might as well have negotiated the arrangements with the Republic instead of the Taliban.[22] There was no reason to privilege the Taliban to the exclusion of a major non-NATO ally with which the US had a bilateral security agreement and a strategic partnership agreement. There was certainly no indication that the Afghan government would not have cooperated in such bilateral negotiations, not least because it was in no position to refuse to cooperate. If anything, the Republic under Ghani went out of its way to reassure the US that it 'respected' any decision to withdraw and was prepared to work with the US to implement it.[23] That the US chose to negotiate with the Taliban in the absence of the Afghan government ignored the significant convergence of interests between the US and Afghanistan, which was a willing partner that could have provided force protection during a US withdrawal and offered counter-terrorism cooperation after it.

The question as to whether the Afghan government knew—or should have known—that the US was going to withdraw is more complicated. After the signing of the US-Taliban agreement, US officials privately hinted to Afghan officials that the US would not withdraw completely. Other major US allies were striking the same chord. For example, NATO Senior Civilian Representative Stefano Pontecorvo told the Afghans in July 2020 that if NATO withdrew completely, it would leave 'a security vacuum for the international community' in its wake. 'If we run away, 90% of the international community will blame us', he said, adding that NATO would remain 'in the numbers needed and for the duration required' even after a possible peace agreement between the government and the Taliban.[24] The following month, outgoing US Deputy Chief of Mission Karen Decker told Afghan National Security Advisor Hamdullah Mohib that the US was 'not abandoning' Afghanistan but looking for a way to stay 'without a large foreign military footprint'. To drive the point home, she said 'nobody' in Washington expected perfect adherence to the terms of the Doha agreement.[25] Similar hints continued into the waning days of the Trump administration. In January 2021, Khalilzad reminded senior Afghan leaders that the US-Taliban deal had the explicit provision that a 'political roadmap' between the Taliban and the Afghan government should be negotiated before the US 'withdrawal is complete'. The implication was that since that roadmap was not on the horizon, complete withdrawal was not likely.[26]

Immediately after being sworn in as US President, Biden announced a review of the US-Taliban deal. In his first phone call to his Afghan counterpart two days after Biden's inauguration, US National Security Advisor Jake Sullivan was categorical: the US was going to study the Doha deal not just for US commitments to the Taliban but also the Taliban's commitments to the US. If the Taliban did not live up to their commitments—including 'meaningful and sincere negotiations' with the government—they would 'bear the consequences of their choices', Sullivan told Mohib.[27] As the review continued, the numbers of US soldiers kept dropping, but the US offered no hint to the Afghan government about its intentions. In late March 2021, Mohib spoke with newly appointed CIA director William Burns, who had been sworn in two days earlier, to seek 'certainty' in 'strategic relations' with the United States.[28] Some certainty came days later. On 5 April 2021, US Deputy National Security Advisor Jonathan Finer told Afghan officials that the US was considering an extension in its troop presence, but it 'would be limited and not conditions-based', essentially abandoning the contingent link between a political roadmap and a US troop withdrawal.[29] Biden's announcement of a full and unconditional withdrawal came on 14 April.[30]

This was the third paradigm shift and a moment of shocking clarity for the Afghan government. The US had opted to abandon the Afghan Republic and effectively release the Taliban from their obligation to negotiate anything with the government—not peace, not a permanent ceasefire, not a reduction in violence. It was finally leaving the Republic to manage the consequences of Washington's agreement with the Taliban, a deal that it had depicted as offering a pathway to peace but which had resulted in historic levels of bloodshed.[31] This left the Taliban with no incentive to negotiate seriously with the Afghan government. The Afghan government had no option but to accept Biden's announcement, but its leadership felt the sting of betrayal. In February 2022, former National Security Advisor Mohib told one of the authors that he only learned after the collapse of the Republic that Khalilzad's 'mission' had been to secure a withdrawal for the US:[32]

> They never admitted to it being a withdrawal agreement. They kept saying, 'We want peace.' Only after the whole thing finished did we see transparency from Zalmay Khalilzad on the media that he had the mission to withdraw. Why didn't you tell us that this was your mission? In meetings with us, you said different things. We missed the writing on the wall. We should have known that he was going to lie to us.

Clear-eyed realists might argue that the pathology of Afghan dependency on the US and other partners was the Republic's Achilles' heel and that the writing had been on the wall long before Biden's announcement. This position merits debate, although it can be hard to disentangle Afghanistan's taking the US for granted from the US's deliberate cultivation of that attitude. As early as September 2019, the Afghan National Security Advisor asked the Office of the National Security Council to prepare a plan for the contingency that there would be zero US troops by January 2020. One of the authors was involved in developing the 'Scenario Zero' plan and seeking Ghani's approval for it. The Political-Security Plan, as it came to be known formally, rapidly became beleaguered because of bureaucratic turf wars, incompetence and the quickly changing dynamics with respect to peace, security, and diplomacy. Similar planning had been undertaken in the past, with half-baked documents—outlining how Afghanistan might conduct 'independent defence'—collecting dust on the shelves of government offices.[33] What this indicated was that the Afghan government contemplated the prospect of a full US withdrawal, initiated policy planning to prepare for it, but failed to follow through. It did not help that the US kept assuring the government that a full withdrawal was unlikely even as Afghanistan was preparing for that scenario. Afghanistan's near-total reliance on the US for weapons, ammunitions and materiel made unilateral weaning hard, and Afghan requests toward gradual independence were ignored.

After Biden's withdrawal announcement

After the announcement of a complete withdrawal, the US continued to reassure Afghanistan that it would support the Republic against the Taliban. In late May 2021, National Security Advisor Sullivan told his Afghan counterpart that the US intended to continue security and civilian assistance and was preparing a budget request for Congress reflecting funding levels 'very close' to the existing support. He promised that the US would purchase and ship 'key supplies' to the ANDSF and continue to support the Afghan Air Force. He said that the US would support the ANDSF 'at tempo and at scale' to ensure that the Taliban knew that 'a military victory is not in the offing'.[34] He promised to find a regional base for US air assets to come to the ANDSF's aid when needed and to provide continued support to the Afghan Air Force. Sullivan also said the US planned to conduct high-level diplomatic work with regional countries to seek a negotiated settlement.[35]

Months of uncertainty about the future of the US military presence were about to give way to months of uncertainty about how American support would be delivered to the Republic after the withdrawal. The longer the uncertainty dragged on, the harder it became for Afghanistan to plan for a post-US scenario, the strategic ambiguity affecting Afghanistan's politics and economy, and public confidence. The promise to purchase and ship supplies to the ANDSF ran counter to the Republic's written requests to purchase its own supplies with US financial assistance; it also fostered continued Afghan dependence on the US after withdrawal. Between April and August 2021, the US provided no clarity to Afghanistan on what bases it would use for air support to the ANDSF and how critical operational and maintenance support to the Afghan Air Force would be provided, even as US generals warned the Afghan government that its air force would grind to a halt by September unless servicing and maintenance arrangements were made.[36] The Afghan government's concept—which we discuss in more detail in Chapter Eight—for creating an Afghan National Army Special Operations Corps to spearhead the fight after the US withdrawal and function as the point of interface with the US for counter-terror purposes languished without a response. Khalilzad, who, according to Deputy National Security Advisor Finer was tasked with formulating the US response to the Afghan pitch, went incommunicado in April. As National Security Advisor Mohib explained:

> I was not at all in touch with Zal. After Biden's announcement in April, he was nowhere to be seen. He was not in touch with anyone senior—not with me, not with the President, not even with the First Vice President [Amrullah Saleh] who liked to be involved in these things.[37]

At a critical time for the Republic, one of its most important US interlocutors was unavailable to senior Afghan leadership. He was also absent from Washington DC when President Ghani and a delegation visited for talks in June 2021.

The promise of high-level diplomatic work became bogged down in the post-agreement dynamics. One idea, percolating since late 2020, crystallised around organising a major conference in Istanbul, where senior Republican and Taliban leadership would converge along with representatives of regional stakeholders to hash out a political roadmap to end the violence in Afghanistan. This idea ended up being 'stillborn', according to Wilson, who pointed out that the Taliban resisted US, Pakistani, and Russian pressure to participate,[38] partly because they had little reason to do so once the US had committed to a full withdrawal. There were also questions about the level of Taliban participation—if there were simply going to be the negotiators from Doha, as the Taliban insisted, there was little reason to believe that a change in venue from Qatar would help, and even less reason for Ghani to strike a deal with Mullah Baradar when his negotiating team could do so. Turkey was also initially reluctant to ruffle Qatari feathers by taking the action away from Doha.[39] For these and related reasons, the Istanbul meeting did not happen and America's last major diplomatic initiative to bring about a grand bargain petered out. With that, Sullivan's promise of high-level US diplomacy died, not unlike his promises of military aid and over-the-horizon assistance. Only one of Sullivan's promises—a funding request to Congress reflecting previous levels of assistance to Afghanistan—ever materialised.

Contrasts with the Trump administration

If the Biden administration's approach was to make lofty promises to limit the damage from pulling the plug, the Trump administration's policy was deliberate infliction of damage. Both Khalilzad and Pompeo elevated the Taliban to the status of a mainstream international diplomatic actor and praised Pakistan for its role, even as the former escalated violence and the latter helped it do so. They also sidelined the Afghan government, cast doubt on fundamental democratic exercises such as presidential elections, and used US military and diplomatic assistance to force the Republic into major concessions. Taken cumulatively, these actions altered the incentives of all stakeholders. The Taliban, who had achieved the US commitment to withdraw, had little incentive to negotiate peace with a government that the US was abandoning. The region, which had sensed the Taliban's ascendance, established direct and indirect relations with the group. Afghanistan's international allies, uncertain about the longevity of the Republic, reduced their assistance. Afghanistan's domestic politics also changed in response. Instead of rallying around the flag at a moment of existential peril for the Republic, major political actors such as former President Karzai distanced themselves from the government, endorsed calls for an interim government in a way that undermined the Constitution, and established or strengthened contacts with the Taliban. Taken together, the changing dynamics of domestic politics, regional diplomacy, and international support damaged the Republic in ways that significantly contributed to the disaster that occurred on 15 August 2021. We evaluate each of these factors in turn.

The Taliban enjoyed the trappings of a *de facto* state in Doha, and then some. Not only did their flag fly, they also were able to call themselves the political office of the 'Islamic Emirate of Afghanistan'. In their publicity material after every engagement with the US, they issued statements under the name of the Emirate and purported to speak for the Afghan people. Khalilzad went out of his way to treat the Taliban as on a par with the Afghan government in his public diplomatic activities and policy work. In most of his statements about violence and peace, he urged 'all sides' or 'both sides' to 'do more', disregarding that the Taliban were escalating violence, seeking to undermine a sovereign state, and killing Afghan civilians through targeted and mass-casualty terrorist attacks. In parallel with practically all his visits to Kabul, he also made a stop in Doha to meet with the Taliban political office; on more than one occasion, he met the Taliban first before coming to Kabul. Khalilzad took his efforts to maintain this equivalence to bizarre and dangerous extremes. In a January 2021 meeting with Afghan Foreign Minister Atmar and National Security Advisor Mohib, he presented a suggestion for a 90-day 'reduction in violence' period. Mohib explained that 'reduction in violence' periods in the past had been bloody for the ANDSF because the Taliban, who had a military deconfliction mechanism with the US but not with Afghanistan, could choose to hit Afghan forces at will and decide which attacks counted toward the elusive 'reduced' state of violence. Mohib suggested that there should be a ceasefire so that the ANDSF could work to regain the military initiative. Without hesitation, Khalilzad retorted: 'Balance of initiatives'.[40] As Afghanistan struggled to respond to a Taliban emboldened by the Doha deal, US diplomacy actively sought to contain Afghan troops' ability to address Taliban aggression.

Furthermore, once the Taliban's role as diplomatic actor was mainstreamed thanks to US diplomacy, the floodgates of international engagement with the group opened. The UN and human rights organisations met the group in Doha with the purported aim of sensitising them to international humanitarian law and human rights, or negotiating humanitarian access. Regional countries invited them to their capitals, where the Taliban were able to discuss matters that a sovereign state would normally handle, such as the condition of

Afghan refugees and migrants, cross-border trade and protection of multinational economic and energy projects.[41] Some countries—such as Uzbekistan, China, and Pakistan—went out of their way to give the group a red-carpet reception. Members of the Taliban's political office visiting Pakistan in December 2020 and January 2021 not only met with the country's foreign minister, they were also able to inspect their human assets. Mullah Baradar visited wounded Taliban fighters receiving treatment at a Karachi hospital, and Mullah Fazal met a squad of suicide bombers.[42]

Afghanistan and China's bilateral security commission, which was supposed to meet every six months alternately in Beijing and Kabul at the level of national security advisor, held its meetings over videoconference in 2020 and 2021 because of the COVID-19 pandemic. But the pandemic was apparently no barrier to a Taliban visit to meet the Chinese foreign minister.[43] During one Taliban visit after the US commenced its engagement with the group, China promised the Taliban delegation medical and humanitarian assistance; the Chinese embassy only told the Afghan government about the pledge when it came time to ship the goods through the Afghan Red Crescent Society.[44] During a Taliban visit to Uzbekistan in August 2019, the Uzbek foreign minister received the Taliban delegation at the airport before formal talks at the foreign ministry. The governor of Samarkand gave the delegation a tour of the ancient city, and the Taliban celebrated the Muslim festival of Eid in Tashkent.[45] Such hospitality would hardly have been justified even if the Taliban had demonstrated peaceful intent with behaviour to match. But the more their violence grew, the more countries in Afghanistan's neighbourhood appeared to flout diplomatic sensitivities and give the group VIP treatment. Khalilzad even urged countries such as India, which had studiously avoided engagement with the Taliban, to talk to the group.[46] With every major country in the region establishing ties with the Taliban, the strategic rationale of not being left out won over and Indian officials established a backchannel with them.[47] India did not have the courtesy to inform the Republic of its intention before the meeting.[48] For India, which had ostensibly favoured 'Afghan-led, Afghan-owned and Afghan-controlled' peace efforts, this was quite a reversal. It is difficult to imagine another example in contemporary diplomacy where a sovereign state was undermined by other states through such conspicuous elevation of the group seeking to overthrow it by violent means.

Wider implications of the US-Taliban agreement

But diplomacy was not the only sphere in which the behaviour of stakeholders operated to the detriment of the Republic. A November 2020 conference in Geneva, designed to renew international assistance to Afghanistan and demonstrate support for the Republic, provided a glaring example. International assistance announced at Geneva fell to less than a third of what had been pledged at a similar conference four years earlier in Brussels.[49] America's own commitment fell from $4.2 billion to $600 million.[50] Part of the reason for the precipitous drop was the uncertainty about the looming withdrawal deadline for US troops in May 2021 and questions about whether the talks between Afghanistan and the Taliban would preserve the constitutional, republican order to which the donors were pledging their assistance. Khalilzad's diplomacy had the net effect of altering the behaviour of Afghanistan's international allies to the detriment of the Republic. And that was not all. The US itself conditioned half of its $600 million pledge on progress in the talks, where of course the Republic could only control its own conduct and not the Taliban's. For Afghanistan to receive the $300 million in critical development assistance, it had to make unpleasant concessions at the negotiation table. The US was in effect using aid conditionality to set the Republic up for capitulation to the Taliban in a bid to advance negotiations because of timelines imposed by its Doha agreement with the group.

American disregard for the Republic had a longer history. Just as the Khalilzad-led talks with the Taliban were starting in late 2018, doubts began to appear about whether the presidential elections, slated for the spring of 2019, should move ahead. The debate that emerged set the prospect of 'peace' against the constitutional requirement of holding elections. The apparent 'logic' was that if the Taliban were going to make peace and Afghanistan's political system was going to adapt to accommodate them, it would be counterproductive to hold any elections at all. In a context where Afghanistan and its allies were seeking to preserve the gains of the previous two decades, raising questions about the most fundamental of these gains—the principle of constitutional order and popular sovereignty—was a stunning turn of events, an outcome that hugely favoured the Taliban. The group had done its best to disrupt all of Afghanistan's elections by mounting violent nationwide attacks on candidates, campaigners, electoral officials and voters. By positing his initiative as a possible alternative to the elections, Khalilzad had altered the calculations of broad segments of the Afghan political class. And bizarrely, some of Republican Afghanistan's political class aligned themselves with the Taliban's vision. One of the major presidential candidates, Hanif Atmar, called for Ghani to step down at the end of his first term so a caretaker government could take over and pave the way for a peace deal.[51] Former President Karzai went so far as to call elections a threat to peace.[52] Dr Abdullah, another major presidential candidate, said he was prepared to 'quit the elections for the sake of peace'.[53] There is little doubt that some of Ghani's political rivals were using the debate to score political points, but US negotiations with the Taliban were having grave consequences for the Republic. The 'peace-versus-elections' debate put the democratic exercise into serious doubt, undermining the funding, logistical preparation, political buy-in, popular participation and security measures for the nationwide undertaking. It was not until August 2019 that Khalilzad gave his blessing for elections, removing the cloud of uncertainty that had resulted in delays twice already.[54]

As we noted in Chapter Two, the blemished elections finally took place in September 2019 with low turnout, and the results were contested.[55] Both Ghani and Abdullah announced victories and held parallel inaugurations within about 500 metres of each other on the same day.[56] Khalilzad along with other US officials attended the Ghani inauguration even as they pressured Ghani and Abdullah to reconcile their differences to present a unified Republican front in the talks that were expected to begin with the Taliban in Doha. Pompeo made an unsuccessful visit to Kabul in late March 2020 to resolve their differences but left the capital announcing a cut of $1 billion in assistance and a threat of a further cut of the same amount.[57] Ross Wilson explained Pompeo's rationale:

> On March 23 Pompeo came to Kabul for a day. The purpose was to try to secure a resolution of the domestic political crisis having to do with duelling presidential inaugurations, which weakened and divided the republic's negotiating position vis-à-vis the Taliban. That made it nearly impossible to see the way forward for negotiations. A not insignificant part of the way forward was the commitment in the Doha agreement to reduce US forces from 12,000 to 8,600 by June-July 2020. The leverage was declining. On the Afghan side there was not a coming together—there was a bickering and pulling apart—that undermined the Islamic Republic side in the negotiations. It made it almost impossible to negotiate—who would they [the Taliban] negotiate with? They didn't have a side that commanded broad enough support to negotiate credibly. Pompeo's announcement was to help the Republic by spurring action on their end.[58]

Although correct in assessing that declining US leverage and continued bickering in Kabul hurt prospects for peace, opting to cut security assistance to the ANDSF—who had just successfully secured the presidential elections and were contending with escalating Taliban violence—was a destructive, lazy, and uncreative way to exercise US leverage on Afghanistan. In an effort to pressure Ghani and Abdullah, the US did its own damage to the Republic's image and sent a message to the ANDSF that the US, which was making peace with the Taliban, had no qualms about undermining them (nor was it the first time that the US had diverted millions of dollars in assistance from the ANDSF—that honour went to Trump's efforts less than a year earlier to build his border wall with Mexico).[59] If the Ghani-Abdullah bickering weakened the position of the Republic's negotiators, US efforts effectively communicated to the Taliban that US assurances to support the Republic were open to revision. Few signals could have been more favourable to the Taliban's negotiating position.

Ultimately, the problem that blighted 'intra-Afghan negotiations' was not bickering in Kabul, but the lack of incentive for the Taliban to negotiate in good faith. As Semple, Raphel and Rasikh concluded, the Taliban 'appeared to be ready to accept little short of capitulation by the Kabul government, which guaranteed there would be no progress in intra-Afghan negotiations'.[60] The much-touted 'intra-Afghan' engagement—supposedly a great achievement of the Doha process[61]—offered no more than an *illusion* of meaningful diplomacy. When this happens, delegations may appear to be fully engaged, seeking instructions from their principals, giving media interviews, and offering off-the-record briefings. But it may all be for show, and it is easy for those inexperienced in diplomacy to be deceived into assuming that this amounts to progress. Many observers, unfortunately, were taken in, leading to what Kate Clark of the Afghanistan Analysts Network called 'fantasy castles of research, advocacy and new institutions'.[62]

As the US elevated the position of the Taliban and changed the incentives of Afghan politicians and international allies, it also lauded Pakistan for its role. Publicly, Khalilzad lavished praise on Pakistan,[63] and privately, US officials assured the Afghan Government that Pakistan was playing a positive role. Newly appointed CIA Director William Burns told the Afghans that the US was 'pleased' with Pakistan's role,[64] his comments coming weeks after those of National Security Advisor Sullivan, who had assured his Afghan counterpart that Pakistan was 'certainly in a different frame of mind now' and showed greater 'motivation' to 'manage' the Taliban.[65] The US maintained that Pakistan was helpful in getting the Taliban to the negotiating table with the US and Afghanistan and was supportive of the Doha agreement. The US also maintained that Pakistan supported the government's negotiations in Doha and did not want them to fail.[66] There is little reason to doubt that Pakistan wanted the US-Taliban deal to succeed because it had everything to gain from a full US withdrawal, leaving an ascendant Taliban pitted against a beleaguered Republic, and a possible half-baked deal between them at best. Pakistan was enjoying US approval for its efforts without having to do anything to affect the Taliban's ability to escalate its violence. By only asking Pakistan to use its influence to urge the Taliban to negotiate, the US was absolving Pakistan from other responsibilities—such as cutting the supplies of ammonium nitrate from Pakistan that the Taliban used in improvised explosive devices, dismantling Taliban training camps and recruiting grounds, and disrupting Taliban fundraising on its soil. By 2021, Pakistan even allowed Taliban members to regulate Afghan schools in Pakistan, despite Afghanistan's protests.[67] Freed from US pressure, the head of the ISI told Ghani in May 2021, as Pakistan Chief of Army Staff Bajwa and a senior British diplomat looked on, that he was in no mood to 'start a war on my soil' against the Taliban because of Afghanistan— an episode we discuss in more detail in Chapter Eight. In its haste to extricate itself from Afghanistan, the US was getting just the minimum level of cooperation it required from Pakistan and nothing more—certainly not enough to advance peace in Afghanistan. An example of such Pakistani cooperation came in July 2021 when the ISI and Army chiefs purported to visit the Taliban in Doha to pressure them on peace. One of the authors heard Qatar's envoy, Mutlaq Al-Qahtani, respond to the Pakistani effort by saying that he felt that the two chiefs should focus their activities in Pakistan 'because Hibatullah is not in Doha'.[68] To Afghan officials, the US praise of Pakistan simply provided further evidence of Washington's naïveté, but there was little or nothing they could do about it.

Conclusion: America's shifting goalposts in Afghanistan

During the negotiation and implementation of its agreement with the Taliban, the US shifted its objectives, policy positions, and conditions vis-à-vis the Taliban in ways that advantaged the group. US backsliding on these issues compounded the flaws of a deal that created misaligned incentives for the Taliban, whose interests lay in stalling, and for the government, which was increasingly pressured to strike an agreement on the Taliban's terms.

A cardinal act of backsliding was America's abandonment of the ideal of a 'permanent and comprehensive ceasefire' in Afghanistan, in favour of a vague and amorphous 'reduction in violence'. This left important questions such as demobilisation of the Taliban, reintegration of their fighters, the relations of the Taliban's Haqqani Network with the ISI, the imperative of a ceasefire during peace talks, and other critical questions out of the deal. The effect was that it allowed the Taliban to retain not just the freedom to escalate violence during any 'intra-Afghan' talks but also the capacity to return to violence even if there were a 'permanent and comprehensive ceasefire'. The second major act of backsliding was Khalilzad's abandonment of his earlier precept that the four major components of the Doha deal were interrelated and that complete US withdrawal was linked with the Taliban agreeing to a political roadmap with the government. Benchmarks are of real use only if they are enforced. Abandoning this interconnectedness left intact only the US withdrawal commitment and the Taliban commitment not to harass US forces during withdrawal. The third major act of backsliding was to abandon holding the Taliban even to their vague commitment of reducing violence and resorting merely to feeble admonitions that the Taliban should not pursue a strategy of military takeover because there was no military solution to the war in Afghanistan.[69] The fact that the American position went from demands (that the Taliban should at least agree to a permanent ceasefire) to mere handwringing (to the effect that there was no military solution) indicated the increasing modesty of American ambitions in Afghanistan. Of course, it could hardly have been otherwise, as the architecture of the Doha deal and subsequent political decisions by the Trump and Biden administrations decreased US leverage and strengthened the Taliban's hand.

In all of this, US diplomacy failed to bring the region together around the common objective of avoiding the return to power of Islamist fundamentalists intimately linked to the international narcotics trade. As early as March 2020, just days after the signing of the Doha agreement, the UN Security Council passed a resolution with the unequivocal proclamation that 'the Islamic Emirate of Afghanistan is not recognized at the United Nations, and furthermore that the UN Security Council does not support the restoration of the Islamic Emirate of Afghanistan'.[70] China, Russia and the US can rarely have agreed so categorically on a matter of importance and yet have failed so spectacularly to work effectively toward their stated objective.

Despite the increasing modesty of American ambitions in Afghanistan, the United States treated the acquiescence of the

Republic on all actions in the implementation of its Doha deal as a natural and expected mode of behaviour. The US was prepared to use blunt trauma to effect the desired outcome when compliance was not readily forthcoming. By cutting military aid, reducing civilian assistance, sending terse letters to Ghani that were then leaked to the media,[71] and circulating proposals for an interim government at a time when the Republic was negotiating with the Taliban,[72] the US consistently undermined the Republic without any apparent regard to the likely effects of this treatment on Afghan mass psychology, the morale of the ANDSF, the behaviour of the Taliban, and the incentives for the region.

It pushed increasingly ambitious timelines on the Republic to negotiate 'peace' with the Taliban at a time when the Taliban had no incentive to reciprocate. The desperation of the Republic at the US-imposed timeframe of fourteen months was only met with delays by the Taliban, who correctly calculated that they could simply wait out the US. The US had no contingency plan for what to do if the Taliban did not live up to their commitment to negotiate peace and reduce violence. Kate Clark captured the problem precisely:

> Khalilzad had gambled all on the Taleban genuinely wanting to negotiate. He never had a Plan B of what to do if the insurgents were playing for time and actually intent on military conquest. Bizarrely, he and other US officials clung to their fantasy peace process into August, even as huge swathes of Afghanistan fell to the Taleban.[73]

This approach left the Republic to languish over long periods of policy uncertainty when it was bleeding, and it left undelivered the diplomatic and military support that US officials promised to the Republic.

It is true that in the eyes of some US observers, Khalilzad shone, although others called him a tragic figure, or worse.[74] A sometime member of his team, in a study published just weeks before the final collapse, wrote that Khalilzad was 'all energy' and 'was too good to be thrown off course by the vagaries of diplomacy, bureaucratic resistance in Washington, or complaints in Kabul'.[75] But given the disastrous results of Khalilzad's diplomacy, this was akin to arguing that the captain of the *Titanic* was 'too good' to be thrown off course by warnings of icebergs, fire in a coal bunker, and a shortage of lifeboats, and it overlooked Konrad Adenauer's prescient warning 'never to confuse energy with strength'.[76] Sometimes entanglement in the day-to-day work of negotiation can bring with it a critical loss of perspective, where hyperactivity is mistaken for progress and one can no longer see the forest for the trees.

All of this does not absolve Afghanistan of its own faults, weaknesses, and miscalculations. This book chronicles critical leadership failures, a lack of resolve to fight the Taliban, stratospheric levels of corruption, a heavily centralised state structure that at moments of crisis became even more exclusive, and ethnic frictions stemming from real and perceived grievances that the Republic's leadership did nothing to resolve. But corrupt, weak, politically divided states can drift through years, often decades, of bloody war with entrenched domestic insurgents. In Afghanistan, it took the US-Taliban deal to trigger the collapse of the Republic.

7

CASCADE EFFECTS AND THE UNRAVELLING OF MILITARY POWER

The US-Taliban agreement had lethal consequences for Republican Afghanistan, in two respects. One was its psychological impact. It does not pay to be on the losing side in Afghanistan, and once people felt that they were being abandoned, they quite naturally undertook a prudential assessment of how to position themselves for the future. The other impact was strictly military: the withdrawal of US contractors—as promised to the Taliban—had a crippling effect on the operational capabilities of the Afghan armed forces. Even the finest vehicle is of little value as a source of transportation if its tyres have been deflated, and this, metaphorically speaking, was what the Doha agreement did to the ANDSF. Of course, this then fed back into the popular sense of abandonment, and ultimately created a downward spiral that any Afghan government would have been hard-pressed to reverse. This should have surprised no one: as we noted in Chapter Two, 84% of respondents in the 2019 Asia Foundation survey strongly or somewhat agreed that the Afghan National Army needed foreign support to do its job properly. Putting aside larger strategic and organisational issues, basic military capability has two key dimensions: the morale of personnel and the effectiveness of their tools. It was the unique achievement of US diplomacy to strike fatal blows to both. In doing so, the United States triggered what social scientists call a cascade.

'Public opinion' is a complex phenomenon. If one is quizzed as to what 'public opinion' on a particular issue might be, the most accurate answer is typically that public opinion is divided. What one then needs to do is explore how it is divided, what positions different members of the public hold, and with what intensity they are attached to particular positions. Well-crafted survey research is one of the best devices for mapping public opinion. There is also much to be said for interviews and even conversations as a way of picking up what issues might concern particular individuals, but it is much harder to generalise about wider public opinion from such sources. This has been known for millennia: in ancient Rome, Cicero recorded that

> Diagoras, named the Atheist, once came to Samothrace, and a certain friend said to him, 'You who think that the gods disregard men's affairs, do you not remark all the votive pictures that prove how many persons have escaped the violence of the storm, and come safe to port, by dint of vows to the gods?' 'That is so,' replied Diagoras; 'it is because there are nowhere any pictures of those who have been shipwrecked and drowned at sea'.[1]

But in some circumstances, developing sophisticated maps of public opinion may be very difficult. Nowhere is this likely to be more challenging than in addressing the issue of whether particular actors or systems enjoy 'support'. As we have noted earlier in the book, Asia Foundation survey data from 2019 suggested that 85.1% of respondents had no sympathy at all for the Taliban. Yet this lack of support did not provide a bulwark against the Taliban takeover in 2021.

To understand why, it is necessary to recognise that there are several reasons why making sense of 'support' can be difficult. First, the support—or lack of support—of some sections of the public may be more important than that of others. Not everyone opposed to a Taliban takeover was necessarily in a position to do much to stop it. Second, there are different forms of 'support'. Support can be normative, based on genuine sympathy, or it can be prudential, based on calculations of interest. In practice, 'support' may involve a mixture of the two, but circumstances may conspire to make one dominate the other. These different kinds of support need to be carefully distinguished. Normative commitments may not be enough to protect a regime if overwhelming prudential considerations make it appear rational to abandon it. Third, the decision whether to accord prudential support to an actor or system is not one made in a vacuum; rather, it may critically depend upon actors' perceptions of how other actors are positioning themselves or are likely to position themselves. It is this interdependence that gives rise to the possibility of cascades.

What are cascades?

A common refrain among policymakers after 15 August 2001 was that no one expected a collapse to come so quickly. This may have been true of intelligence agencies, but there were plenty of warnings in the public domain. Even before the Doha agreement was signed, a published study argued that

> a negotiation process can have the paradoxical effect of incentivising violence, by prompting actors to seize as much territory as they can before negotiations reach a critical phase. Such a process also runs the risk of triggering fragmentation if political actors conclude that they will serve their interests better by acting unilaterally rather than collectively.[2]

On 11 September 2020, Dr Nishank Motwani of the Afghanistan Research and Evaluation Unit wrote that:

> Afghanistan desperately needs a Plan B, a strategy to protect the fragile democracy the country has built over the last two decades. Otherwise, a regression to the dark days of the past is practically inevitable … In the end, the intra-Afghan talks will become less relevant as events on the ground overtake the negotiating positions of either party. By that time, it will be too late to rescue an overwhelmed partner.[3]

On 8 July 2021, one of the authors published an article that warned that:

> Afghanistan is teetering on the brink of an almost unimaginable disaster. The withdrawal of US and allied forces, scheduled by President Joe Biden to be completed by September 11, threatens to precipitate the unravelling of the most pro-Western government in Southwest Asia ... With dozens of districts falling to the Taliban in late June and early July, this could happen quickly. US intelligence estimates that it could take two or three years for the country to fall under Taliban control appear dangerously sanguine.[4]

And in a judgement in the Federal Court of Australia on 19 July 2021, the judge quoted from an opinion supplied by one of the authors that stated, *inter alia*, that the:

> security situation in Afghanistan is deteriorating rapidly, and is exceptionally fluid ... there is a grave risk that Afghanistan will fall victim to what social scientists call a 'cascade', where even people who despise the Taliban decide to shift support to them because they think they are going to come out on top anyway ... This can lead to unexpected and very dramatic power shifts. It is pertinent to note that in 1992, when the beleaguered communist regime collapsed, only 29 days elapsed between the onset of the regime's final crisis on 18 March, and the regime's disintegration on 16 April.[5]

Those who took a more relaxed view of the prospects in Afghanistan in 2020 and 2021 had not only forgotten the speed with which the Communist regime collapsed in 1992 and the Taliban regime in 2001, but they had overlooked the role of cascades in bringing about regime change.

What is a cascade? The logic underlying cascades has long been recognised: as Machiavelli wrote in *The Prince*, 'men almost always follow in the footsteps of others, imitation being a leading principle of human behaviour'.[6] 'As cascades occur', Cass Sunstein has noted, 'beliefs and perspectives spread from some people to others, to the point where many people are relying, not on what they actually know, but on what (they think) other people think'.[7] This can embrace a range of distinct phenomena, and in the spheres of marketing and regulation, cascades have understandably attracted a considerable amount of attention in recent years. Asset price bubbles, such as Tulipmania in the Dutch Republic in 1637 or the South Sea Bubble of 1720, are examples of cascades, and as Sunstein puts it, 'When there are speculative bubbles, people are typically relying not on fundamentals but on their judgments about what other people are likely to think and do'.[8] In the following paragraphs, we detail some of the specific kinds of cascade that have proved to be salient, most importantly 'informational' cascades, 'reputational' cascades, and 'availability' cascades. We then show how the phenomenon of cascading can play out politically in a 'bandwagoning' cascade, of a kind which had a positive effect in 1989 in bringing about the collapse of the Soviet sphere of influence in Eastern Europe but can also be negatively mirrored in the collapse of resistance to tyrannical or oppressive forces.

The distinction between informational and reputational cascades is a fine one, but it is also significant. An informational cascade 'occurs when people with little personal information about a particular matter base their own beliefs on the apparent beliefs of others'.[9] By contrast,

> in the case of a reputational cascade, people do not subject themselves to social influences because they think that others are more knowledgeable. Their motivation is simply to earn social approval and avoid disapproval. Even the most confident people sometimes adjust their expressions in the interest of building or preserving their reputations; they go so far as to silence themselves.[10]

This kind of calculation was famously reflected in Hans Christian Andersen's nineteenth-century story *The Emperor's New Clothes*.[11] Reputational cascades can be very dangerous; for example, Timur Kuran has highlighted how cascading can fuel ethnic conflict, drawing on ethnification in the former Yugoslavia in the 1990s as an example.[12] Perhaps the most potent cascades of all are 'availability cascades' that bring together informational and reputational dimensions: an availability cascade, according to Kuran and Sunstein, 'is a self-reinforcing process of collective belief formation by which an expressed perception triggers a chain reaction that gives the perception increasing plausibility through its rising availability in public discourse'.[13]

In the sphere of politics, and particularly for the purposes of our analysis, a critically important form of cascade is what we call a 'bandwagoning cascade'. This kind of cascade has been manifested in a number of different forms, but perhaps the most spectacular has been the occasional overthrow of a dictatorial regime or set of regimes. The underlying logic flows from the interplay of normative convictions and prudential calculations: in a dictatorship, people's normative convictions may be overridden by considerations of prudence, simply for the sake of safety or day-to-day survival. While some truly heroic individuals may on occasion take uncompromising stands of principle even in circumstances of immense danger—the 1935 Nobel Peace Prize laureate in Nazi Germany, Carl von Ossietzky, comes to mind[14]—many individuals do not. Kuran's analysis explains why: 'A person who chooses to follow the call of his conscience will merely compound his misery—unless, of course, he derives immense satisfaction from expressing his antigovernment feelings'.[15] But if some triggering shock occurs to shift people's calculations, surprising events may ensue. As James C. Scott has put it,

> social scientists, not to mention ruling elites, are often taken by surprise by the rapidity with which an apparently deferential, quiescent, and loyal subordinate group is catapulted into mass defiance. That ruling elites should be taken unaware by social eruptions of this kind is due, in part, to the fact that they have been lulled into a false sense of security by the normal posing of the powerless. Neither social scientists nor ruling elites, moreover, are likely to fully appreciate the incitement a successful act of defiance may represent for a subordinate group, precisely because they are unlikely to be much aware of the hidden transcript from which it derives much of its energy.[16]

The Romanian revolution of December 1989 provided the canonical example from the late twentieth century. Once the Ceauşescu regime's image of invincibility was punctured, it went into immediate and rapid free fall.[17] A similar point could be made about the 1989 fall of communist regimes in Eastern Europe, which directly preceded the events in Romania. Once Soviet President Gorbachev confirmed that the USSR would not intervene militarily in Eastern Europe, the writing was on the wall for the Soviet Bloc regimes.[18]

A bandwagoning cascade, however, can cut two ways. Repressive regimes can be overthrown if the perceived costs of opposing them go down, shifting the balance between the normative and prudential calculations of individuals. But equally, repressive insurgent movements may succeed if their success increasingly appears so likely that resisting them comes to be widely seen as pointless. In this kind of situation, it is indeed the case that nothing succeeds like success. And it may only require a minority initially to reposition themselves for disaster then to ensue.

Historical cascades in Afghanistan

Afghanistan has an unhappy recent history of involuntary regime change: in 1973, 1978, 1979, 1992, 1996, 2001 and 2021. The first two of these were classic examples of the *coup d'état*, namely the palace coup of 1973 against Zahir Shah and the coup of April 1978 that brought the People's Democratic Party of Afghanistan to power, but strikingly, three of the next five examples of regime change—in 1992, 2001 and 2021—involved cascades. Given the events of 1992 and 2001, it remains something of a mystery why policymakers in Western countries in 2020 and 2021 did not have the possibility of yet another cascade firmly in mind: recent historical experience alone should have alerted them to the possibility. Exactly why it did not will probably not become clear anytime soon, but some possible explanations come to mind: inexperience and lack of historical knowledge on the part of analysts catapulted into agency desks dealing with Afghanistan; a disposition on the part of some analysts with more anthropological than social-scientific backgrounds to think in broad 'culturalist' terms rather than focus on individual motivations and incentives; and an inclination amongst area specialists to see earlier cascades as singular events rather than examples of a wider phenomenon.

An understanding of cascades can help make sense of why particular things happen at particular times. Culturalist explanations can be much less effective in doing so. For example, an American historian recently wrote that:

> The Taliban exemplified an idea—an idea that runs deep in Afghan culture, that inspired their fighters, that made them powerful in battle, and that, in the eyes of many Afghans, defines an individual's worth. In simple terms, that idea is resistance to occupation. The very presence of Americans in Afghanistan was an assault on what it meant to be Afghan. It inspired Afghans to defend their honor, their religion, and their homeland.[19]

This rather sweeping claim is not nearly as persuasive as one might initially be inclined to think. In the 2019 Asia Foundation survey, only 6.6% of those who considered that the country was moving in the wrong direction pointed to foreign intervention as the reason, and amongst the small number of respondents who showed sympathy for the Taliban, only 2% voiced sympathy because 'they fight against foreign forces'.[20] More seriously, a culturalist approach is of little use in explaining why the final collapse of Republican Afghanistan did not come until years after the bulk of foreign forces had left the country, or in explaining why it came in 2021 in particular. That ceases to be a problem if one analyses the collapse through the prism of cascades. One of the notable features of cascades is that they have a trigger—that there is a particular development or event that sets the cascade in motion. The fall of the Berlin Wall in November 1989 became the trigger for the cascade that saw the Soviet sphere of influence in Eastern Europe unravel. In addition, cascades can come in stages, with a first triggering event lighting the fuse and a subsequent trigger acting as an accelerant. In the case of Afghanistan, the Doha agreement discussed in the previous chapter lit the fuse, with President Biden's 14 April 2021 endorsement of a time-based rather than conditions-based withdrawal adding vast amounts of fuel to the flames.

Of course, not every striking event will necessarily be a trigger for a cascade. In 1989, immediately after the completion of the Soviet withdrawal from Afghanistan, there was an attack on the eastern city of Jalalabad orchestrated by the ISI and the *Hezb-e Islami* of Gulbuddin Hekmatyar, with the US Ambassador to Pakistan reportedly in the loop.[21] The objective, capitalising on the uncertainties that the Soviet withdrawal had produced, was clearly to trigger a cascade. But it did not have that effect. Poorly coordinated, it proved to be a shambles.[22] Hekmatyar tried to pin the blame on Ahmad Shah Massoud,[23] but no one took his claim seriously. What is critical for an event to function as a trigger is that the event be one that appears to expose a seemingly dominant force as significantly weaker than it would like people to think. As Thomas Hobbes remarked in the seventeenth century, 'Reputation of power, is Power'.[24] The 2014 end of the US combat mission in Afghanistan created tremendous anxiety and triggered a large exodus from Afghanistan, but—carefully managed in cooperation with the Afghan government—it did not trigger a cascade. When Kunduz was occupied by the Taliban in September 2015, and Ghazni in August 2018, the Republic managed to preserve its reputation of power by demonstrating that it could re-take them, and no cascades ensued. In 2021, it was a different story.

The collapse of the regime of Dr Najibullah in 1992 was a classic example of a cascade. What lit the fuse was the discontinuation of all aid to the regime from the Soviet Union at the end of 1991. What precipitated the final collapse was a public statement by Najibullah on 18 March 1992 that 'once an understanding is reached through the United Nations process for the establishment of an interim government in Kabul, all powers and executive authority will be transferred to the interim government as of the first day of the transition period'.[25] The regime collapsed on 16 April 1992, a sobering reminder of how quickly things can move in Afghanistan once a cascade begins. Najibullah's statement prompted all sorts of erstwhile regime supporters to reposition themselves, including senior military figures. On 15 April, Najibullah reportedly confronted these figures directly, accusing them of treason,[26] but by then it was far too late for him to do anything but attempt to leave the country. This he failed to manage, ending up instead as a somewhat unwelcome guest at the United Nations premises in Kabul, from which he was dragged and killed when the Taliban seized Kabul in 1996.

The 2001 cascade took the form not of defections from the Taliban leadership, but of the loss of Taliban control over key parts of the country once it became clear that the arrival of a massively superior force—a United States enraged by the 11 September 2001 attacks—meant that the Taliban regime's days were numbered. The launch by the United States of 'Operation Enduring Freedom' on 7 October 2001 inaugurated a period of conflict that symbolically reached its height on 13 November 2001 when anti-Taliban forces took Kabul. This phase of the conflict lasted just 37 days. The US aerial assault on Taliban positions was ferocious,[27] but what was striking, and emblematic of a cascade, was the speed with which multiple towns and cities were lost by the Taliban, not through street-to-street fighting but as resistance collapsed once it was clear from which direction the wind was blowing. One is reminded of Churchill's characterisation of the near-simultaneous October 1918 collapse of Ottoman and Austrian operations as the First World War came to an end: 'A drizzle of empires, falling through the air'.[28] On 9 November, Mazar-e Sharif was taken by forces under Abdul Rashid Dostum, the Hazara Shiite leader Mohammad Mohaqeq, and *Jamiat-e Islami* commander Atta Muhammad Noor. On 10 November, Khwajaghar, Eshkamesh, Hairatan, Shiberghan, Baghlan, Pul-e Khumri, Nahrin, Aibak, and Bamiyan all fell, as did Maimana on 11 November, and Herat the following day. As we noted in Chapter One, Kunduz, where Arab and Pakistani extremists were holed up, took a little longer to fall, as did Kandahar. But by 13 November, the operation to displace the Taliban regime was largely over.

Ways of averting cascades

Cascades have been relatively common in recent Afghan history, but they have been quite rare in other contexts, and it is therefore worth reflecting on what factors might militate against a cascade starting in troubled times of war. Once one identifies such factors, one can explore the extent to which they were, or were not, put into play in Afghanistan to try to protect the Republic.

The first factor to note is resolute and determined national leadership. From dramatically different perspectives, this was something that was understood during the Second World War by both Churchill and Hitler. When Churchill became the British Prime Minister in May 1940, he set out an uncompromising position:

> We shall go on to the end, we shall fight in France, we shall fight on the seas and oceans, we shall fight with growing confidence and growing strength in the air, we shall defend our Island, whatever the cost may be, we shall fight on the beaches, we shall fight on the landing grounds, we shall fight in the fields and in the streets, we shall fight in the hills; we shall never surrender.[29]

One reason why he was able to speak with such confidence was that he had put in place a truly national government, with leaders of the erstwhile opposition holding senior ministerial positions, as they were to do until 1945. This stood in stark contrast to the feeble 'National Unity Government' brokered in Afghanistan in 2014, which was never a manifestation of national unity and simply papered over severe elite divisions that resurfaced more strongly in the 2019 elections and persisted until the fall of the Republic. These divisions worked against halting a cascade. Hitler also proved resolute, but long prevented a cascade not by having an inclusive government, but through credibly threatening terrible consequences against any persons at mass or elite level who might step out of line. As Ian Kershaw recorded, 'Anyone showing the least sign of opposing the regime's own death wish of senseless "holding out" against impossible odds faced great peril'.[30] This way of preventing a cascade required a willingness to use extreme terror, and it was to the credit of the Afghan Republic that—in contrast to the Taliban—it did not take that step.

A second factor is the support of loyal players beyond the realm of the commanding heights of the state. On his 80th birthday in 1954, Churchill credited 'the whole nation' for the outcome of the war: 'Their will was resolute and remorseless and, as it proved, unconquerable'.[31] Britain, of course, was an industrialised power during the Second World War, and the war effort indeed owed much to ordinary people who not only served in the military, but worked in factories to produce essential armaments, enduring both the burden of wartime rationing and the risk of bombardment. In a country such as Afghanistan where agriculture, horticulture, and pastoral activities provided livelihoods for much of the population, the scope for direct involvement in war other than as a victim was much more limited. The loyal players whose support really mattered were legitimate regional and local actors who could potentially mobilise some sort of following, but these were precisely the individuals who had either been marginalised as a result of the centralised character of the state or challenged by the central state on the grounds that they were 'warlords'. A significant overarching difference between the political approaches of Presidents Karzai and Ghani was that while Karzai nurtured favoured powerbrokers and sought to cultivate them, albeit at the expense of local institutional development, Ghani treated them as detrimental to his power and sought to weaken them. But as Ghani was to discover, one could only safely weaken such figures if the state had strong claims to procedural legitimacy (notably through free and fair elections) that entrenched the state's standing with the public. Otherwise, by isolating such powerbrokers from the neopatrimonial system, one separated them from their base. This was partly why figures such as Ismail Khan, Abdul Rashid Dostum, and Atta Mohammad Noor proved too weak to put up much resistance once the cascade really gathered pace in 2021 and failed to mobilise in Balkh, Herat, Jawzjan, and elsewhere.

A third factor is a powerful strategic narrative. Narratives are 'compelling story lines which can explain events convincingly and from which inferences can be drawn', and are strategic 'because they do not arise spontaneously but are deliberately constructed or reinforced out of the ideas and thoughts that are already current'.[32] As we noted in Chapter Four, the Taliban after 2001 invested heavily in improving their propaganda reach and the narratives that they disseminated using their propaganda tools. The Republic proved much less effective in doing so, partly because the free media environment created a more cluttered space into which state narratives were projected, partly because competitive and often extremely bitter politics drowned out a powerful narrative, and partly because the narrative that was most likely to resonate, namely one that tagged Pakistan as the enemy, was also one that allies of Republican Afghanistan (other than India) did not want to hear it deploy.

A fourth factor is an understanding of how words and deeds can potentially affect mass psychology. This was something of which the United States appeared blithely unaware as it negotiated with the Taliban. Ghani understood it better, but with lamentable consequences. George Packer recorded that in June 2021, Ghani:

> came to the White House and asked Biden to hold off on evacuating Afghans, to avoid initiating mass panic. Afterward, Ghani met with a few members of Congress. Jason Crow used his time to make the case for evacuations. 'I know what you're trying to do, Mr. Crow,' Ghani replied with some heat. 'It's undermining what we're trying to do in creating some stability and security.'[33]

Given Ghani's decision to evacuate himself on 15 August, hardly a step calculated 'to avoid initiating mass panic', it is no surprise that many Afghans felt a cold fury on learning of how he had earlier sought to block the safe evacuation of others.

A final factor in averting a cascade is a high level of political legitimacy for the system or structures one is seeking to defend. This is not a simple factor to build into one's calculations, because what is relevant is the trade-off between normative and prudential calculations. Thus, a regime with relatively low levels of generalised normative support may survive if the prudential incentive to abandon it is not especially strong, while conversely, a regime with much higher levels of generalised normative support may crumble if the prudential incentive to abandon it is stronger too. What one can say, however, is that it is better to face a threat when one has higher levels of legitimacy than lower; the weaker the legitimacy of a system or structure, the greater the danger that enough people will either abandon it, or simply sit on the fence, to put its survival in peril. This was clearly something that happened in Afghanistan.

Ways of precipitating cascades

What kinds of event might trigger a cascade? All cascades occur in a specific context, and for that reason, it is difficult to compile a comprehensive list of potential triggers. Nonetheless, there are some obvious ones to note, bearing in mind that whether they actually will trigger a cascade will always be a situational question. Actions that trigger a cascade are not necessarily designed to do so; it is the effect of the action, rather than the underlying intention of the actor, that is relevant. That said, however, there are certain kinds of action that so plainly run the risk of triggering a cascade that if they are undertaken without attention to their possible consequences, those responsible can certainly be deemed negligent in the extreme.

One kind of action that runs the risk of triggering a cascade occurs if the ostensible allies of a leader or system depict that leader or system as dispensable. This was plainly a problem even before the Doha agreement was signed, something captured in the words of an Afghan army captain in 2019:

> I wonder what kind of peace talks are these. The Taliban are killing us on the battlefield, but they talk with Americans in Doha. The ongoing peace talks have a very bad effect on the morale of our soldiers, because we think that our fight in the last 17 years was wrong and not worth it. The Taliban are fighting, and we are begging them for peace.[34]

Things then got worse with the decision of the United States to sign a bilateral agreement with the Taliban, from which the Afghan president had been excluded from negotiations, and to include in that agreement a provision—namely that relating to prisoner releases— that would require the absent president to free prisoners whom he plainly would have no desire to let loose at that stage. The signal that this sent was that in the eyes of the US, the Afghan president was substantially irrelevant to the future trajectory of the country.

In theory, one could undermine an individual leader without undermining the entire constitutional system of a country. But US actions contrived to do the latter as well. On 28 February 2021, with its 'peace process' manifestly floundering, the Biden Administration produced a draft 'Afghanistan Peace Agreement' and proposed a major conference in Istanbul to finalise it.[35] The initiative was plainly a face-saving device for the Biden administration. The text, which Steve Coll and Adam Entous laconically described as 'breathtakingly ambitious',[36] proposed a vaguely defined 'Peace Government' and stated that 'All elections to be held pursuant to the current Constitution are cancelled during the tenure of the Peace Government'. In their intrusiveness into the minutiae of Afghan constitutional affairs, the US proposals were hauntingly reminiscent of the notorious 23 July 1914 demands sent to Serbia by the Austro-Hungarian Empire, on the eve of the First World War.[37] No president of the Republic could realistically have been expected to accept the proposals, especially given that the US proposals were put forward before President Biden on 14 April 2021 committed to an unconditional withdrawal but after the bipartisan Afghanistan Study Group, established by Congress in December 2019, had recommended that the US should not 'simply hand a victory to the Taliban', and should 'ensure that a complete withdrawal of U.S. troops is based not on an inflexible timeline but on all parties fulfilling their commitments, including the Taliban making good on its promises to contain terrorist groups and reduce violence against the Afghan people, and making compromises to achieve a political settlement'.[38] As we noted in the previous chapter, the Taliban showed no interest in taking up the proposals, and the Istanbul meeting never materialised: all that the US initiative did was weaken the position of Afghanistan's constitutional system by suggesting that it was something to be brushed aside as an inconvenience.

One can also precipitate a cascade by withdrawing moral, political, or military support for an ally *in practice*, even while purporting verbally to remain committed to that ally's wellbeing. A state that opts to sell out an ally is highly unlikely to admit that that is what it is doing, partly because others might consider its behaviour disgraceful, but also because it may wish to protect its reputation, as a broader asset in its international relations, even though the strength of a link between reputation and past behaviour remains the subject of ongoing debate.[39] But words can work for only so long to hide the import of deeds, and as any discrepancy between words and deeds becomes more and more obvious, this in itself can have an inflammatory effect.

One further thought about the triggering of cascades comes to mind. Sometimes it may be unclear exactly what set things alight.

Reflecting on the 1989 revolutions in Eastern Europe, Timur Kuran, in responding to the question 'What specific events set the bandwagon in motion?', answered that 'Attempting to answer this question is akin to identifying the spark that ignited a prairie fire or the cough responsible for a flu epidemic'.[40] Even rumours can trigger collective action responses.[41] A cascade is a complex phenomenon that can occur only because a population is heterogeneous: otherwise, side-switching would occur *en masse* rather than sequentially.[42] Its complexity lends it to 'pattern prediction'[43] rather than prediction of all the twists and turns that a particular cascade may take. But that said, since cascades come in stages, what is most important is to identify the *critical* upheavals that triggered *significant* shifts in the orientation of elements of a population. In some cases, it may be quite difficult to pin these down, but that was hardly the case where the fall of Republican Afghanistan was concerned.

Conclusion: The fatal cascade of 2021

The decline of the Afghan Republic was a slow process over more than a decade, dating back at least to the fraud that contaminated the 2009 presidential election. The fall of the Afghan Republic, however, began with the signing of the Doha agreement discussed in the previous chapter. As a British commentator put it, 'the key element that undermined Afghan army morale was the US beginning negotiations with the Taliban behind the back of the elected Afghan government. This clear act of bad faith was not lost on the soldiery, who realised the likelihood of a future Taliban takeover'.[44] We have already outlined the negative signals that it sent about US commitment to the Republic, but it had other consequences as well. One, which we discuss in the next chapter, was that Ghani ordered the ANDSF to adopt an 'active defence' posture—essentially to avoid US charges that the government was seeking to function as a 'peace spoiler'—which ensured that momentum remained on the side of the Taliban. This did not last forever, but it lasted long enough to cause damage to the standing of the state. The Doha agreement came on top of an already tense internal political situation that followed the 2019 presidential election. In an effort to bring the contending candidates together, US Secretary of State Pompeo threatened a massive aid cut if they did not bury their differences. A former US military official was scathing in his appraisal of this intervention: 'Asked what $1 billion U.S. aid cuts this year and next would do to Afghan security forces' ability to fight the Taliban, he replied: "They will be toast"'.[45] President Ghani and Dr Abdullah did bury their differences, but only on paper; the damage had already been done.

A further factor contributing to a cascade was the sheer speed with which the Doha agreement unravelled in the implementation phase. The failure of intra-Afghan negotiations to begin on 10 March 2020 as the agreement had provided, and the unwillingness of the US to act swiftly to require that the Taliban honour their commitment to commence such negotiations at that time, indicated very plainly that the Trump Administration saw the agreement as an exit agreement for its own benefit and was not about to pressure the Taliban to implement its provisions in good faith. In a television interview in October 2021, Khalilzad claimed that 'we could have pressed President Ghani harder' and that 'we didn't press him hard enough'.[46] It would be difficult to find a clearer indication of what the US approach to implementation actually was: to minimise pressure on the Taliban and look to the Republic to make concessions. Needless to say, it is a mark of weak diplomacy to pressure the party that seems easiest to pressure, rather than the party that needs to be pressured.

An even stronger contributor to a cascade was the dramatic impact of the withdrawal of US forces and contractors on the operational capabilities of the ANDSF. Even before the completion of the US withdrawal, this was highlighted in a powerful and candid article in *The New York Times* by Afghan General Sami Sadat:

> It's true that the Afghan Army lost its will to fight. But that's because of the growing sense of abandonment by our American partners and the disrespect and disloyalty reflected in Mr. Biden's tone and words over the past few months ... Losing combat logistical support that the United States had provided for years crippled us, as did a lack of clear guidance from U.S. and Afghan leadership.

Expanding on this last point, Sadat noted that:

> The Afghan forces were trained by the Americans using the U.S. military model based on highly technical special reconnaissance units, helicopters and airstrikes. We lost our superiority to the Taliban when our air support dried up and our ammunition ran out. Contractors maintained our bombers and our attack and transport aircraft throughout the war. By July, most of the 17,000 support contractors had left. A technical issue now meant that aircraft—a Black Hawk helicopter, a C-130 transport, a surveillance drone—would be grounded. The contractors also took proprietary software and weapons systems with them. They physically removed our helicopter missile-defense system. Access to the software that we relied on to track our vehicles, weapons and personnel also disappeared. Real-time intelligence on targets went out the window, too.

Sadat's arguments have all the more force because he made no attempt to gild the lily, writing that 'Disruptions to food rations and fuel supplies—a result of skimming and corrupt contract allocations – destroyed the morale of my troops'.[47] Critically, the points he raised about airpower were known to the US months before the collapse. In a classified report in January 2021, the Special Inspector General for Afghanistan Reconstruction warned that 'the sustainability of Afghanistan's Air Force was contingent on continued U.S. support', particularly 'the critical role played by contractors in maintaining aircraft'.[48] From this, one can begin to appreciate the enormity of the US promise to the Taliban 'to withdraw from Afghanistan all military forces of the United States, its allies, and Coalition partners, including all non-diplomatic civilian personnel, *private security contractors, trainers, advisors, and supporting services personnel*'.[49] Once this happened, the effects were felt on the ground; Afghans increasingly could see exactly what was happening, and Afghans increasingly moved to reposition themselves in the light of how they saw events playing out. One reflection of this was desertion from the ranks. Desertion can result from a range of different factors—the collapse of logistics, a sense that the cause is lost, and the erosion of bonds of trust, just to mention a few.[50] When one links these factors to the phenomenon of cascades, it becomes increasingly clear that large-scale desertion is better seen mainly as a consequence rather than a cause, albeit with feedback potential.

The next chapter examines the final phase of the Republic in more detail. The US abandonment at the beginning of July 2021 of the Bagram airbase north of Kabul[51] was the trigger for the final phase of disintegration, with the Taliban moving quickly to seize customs posts at Afghan borders in order to deprive the state of revenue before attacking or bargaining their way into provincial capitals. Just as in 1992 and 2001, it was the rapid fall of these capitals that signalled that the end was imminent. In US circles, a belief—by this time little more than a fantasy—that diplomacy could rescue something from the wreckage was still in the air. In a television interview on 31 October 2021, US Secretary of State Anthony Blinken stated that

> I was on the phone with President Ghani on a Saturday night pressing him to make sure he was ready to agree with the plan we were trying to put into effect to do a transfer of power to a new government that would've been led by the Taliban but been inclusive and included all aspects of Afghan society.[52]

The Saturday in question was 14 August, the day before the Taliban entered Kabul, and the notion that at that point the Taliban—and especially the Haqqani network—would have been prepared to share power with anyone simply beggars belief. Ghani's flight the next day symbolically marked the end of the Republic, but as a matter of practical reality, its life was by then already over.

8

THE FINAL DAYS OF KABUL

From its formal inauguration at a ceremony in Kabul on 22 December 2001 until its fall on 15 August 2021, the Afghan Republic lasted for 7,176 days. This chapter is concerned with the last phase of the Republican era. In it, we explore some of the most notable events after the signing of the US-Taliban deal on 29 February 2020. We reconstruct a semi-chronological timeline of major developments in the realms of military and security affairs, diplomacy, and politics to account for the increasing atmosphere of impotence in Kabul, the occasional surges of defiance, and the ultimate inability of the government to take decisive action as the Republic crumbled around Kabul. These events show that the collapse of the Republic happened over a period through different individual actors across Afghanistan deciding, in an atmosphere of uncertainty, to take action appropriate to their circumstances—out of a desire for self-preservation, out of greed, or on the basis of other considerations. Collapse, once triggered, was not a single chain of events logically following each other, but an unravelling along multiple axes that brought about a death by a thousand cuts.[1]

How the unravelling commenced

The proposed US-Taliban agreement was premised on the Taliban's engaging in a one-week period of 'reduction in violence' in late February 2020. While some observers saw this as tokenistic to the point of being virtually meaningless, supporters of the Doha process attached great importance to it. The Taliban movement, wrote one supporter, 'has made an impressive offer of significant and lasting reductions in violence nationwide that cover both Afghan and U.S.-coalition forces'.[2] Things played out rather differently. The Taliban's attacks—largely unencumbered by US and Coalition airstrikes—increased drastically once the agreement was signed. But as we noted in the previous chapter, Ghani responded by ordering the ANDSF to assume a posture of 'active defence', an under-defined term which meant they could only hit the Taliban if the Taliban were massing to attack the Republic. Ghani seemingly hoped that his conciliatory posture would elicit a similar response from the Taliban, and give US officials room to pressure the group to reduce violence. Although it was not part of the deal, US officials insisted in public that the Taliban were expected to reduce violence and move toward a 'permanent ceasefire'.[3] But the US failed to convince the Taliban of this, and after a series of destructive attacks in Nangarhar and Kabul, Ghani finally ordered his troops in mid-May 2020 to 'abandon the defensive posture and assume an offensive posture'.[4] But the ANDSF were unprepared to ramp up attacks, not least because US airstrikes, and NATO support in planning and executing operations, had diminished significantly. The result was that the gap between the number of Taliban attacks and ANDSF operations widened after the US-Taliban deal. Over the next five months, the Taliban conducted over four times as many attacks as operations by the ANDSF and the US's 'Operation Resolute Support' combined.[5] This had a devastating effect on the ANDSF: between March and October that year, 21,911 soldiers deserted or were killed, injured, or taken prisoner.[6]

Violence continued unabated even when negotiations between Afghanistan and the Taliban finally started in September 2020. Any hopes that the Taliban would match their battlefield behaviour with their stated policy of wanting peace disappeared at this point. Under

Figure 1

Taliban attacks versus Afghan and Resolute Support operations after the US-Taliban deal in February 2020

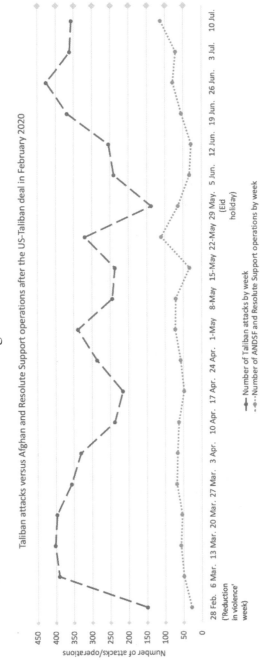

Source: Afghan Office of the National Security Council.

the Doha deal, the Taliban reduced their mass-casualty attacks in major cities but switched to targeted assassinations of journalists, activists, politicians, religious scholars, and civil servants.[7] A UN report found that attacks against activists and journalists became 'premeditated and targeted' in 2020, a contrast from the previous trend of activists mainly being killed in large attacks targeting other entities. Although the UN stopped short of pointing a finger at the Taliban, it urged the group to 'hold to account Taliban members that order or implement the killing' of activists and journalists.[8] The US, which had expected its deal would bring relative calm to major cities, was caught flat-footed by the Taliban's shrewd adaptability. On 19 October 2020, Khalilzad tweeted that 'Continued high levels of violence can threaten the peace process and the agreement and the core understanding that there is no military solution'. By then, of course, it was clear that there was no such 'core understanding'.[9] Khalilzad and his acolytes had been gulled.[10] He visited Islamabad to meet the ISI Director-General, Lieutenant-General Faiz Hameed, in December 2020 to pressure the Haqqani network, a proxy of the ISI, to stop the attacks,[11] but his behind-the-scenes efforts were ineffective, prompting the US to marshal 35 nations in a joint statement in March 2021 condemning the Taliban and the Haqqani network.[12] More diplomatic statements followed more Taliban violence until the collapse of the Republic. They did nothing to slow the Taliban's advance.

Violence also increased outside major cities, with the Taliban proving able to maintain operational tempo during the traditionally calmer winter months. This strategy ensured that the ANDSF continued to experience casualties year-round and was unable to use the winter to regroup and plan for spring campaigns. The ANA sustained more casualties in the first two quarters of 2021 than in the same period in 2020.[13] Without previous levels of US air support and with mounting casualties, Afghanistan's security leadership became increasingly alarmed. The response was to introduce leadership changes, rally the troops, and seek new military hardware. The end of a US military presence across Afghanistan meant that intelligence cover over large swathes of Afghanistan was also ending. The government concluded that the qualitative difference between Afghan forces and Taliban fighters, who were increasingly using conventional warfare techniques, was negligible at best, and the increasingly stretched Afghan Air Force was unable to offer an edge. Armed and surveillance drones were going to be critical. National Security Advisor Hamdullah Mohib visited Azerbaijan in December 2020 to seek so-called Kamikaze drones, which Baku had used against Armenia to devastating effect that year.[14] The government also made technical-level outreach to Turkey, and an initial draft Memorandum of Understanding was exchanged with Ukraine's National Security and Defense Council in April 2021. More significantly, the government sought MQ-9 Reapers and MQ-1 Predator drones to be deployed as part of an Air Weapons Team under the newly established Afghan National Army Special Operations Corps (ANASOC), which brought together the special forces components of the National Directorate of Security, Afghan National Army, and Ministry of Interior.

Planning ahead

The proposed ANASOC was designed to be the 'tip of the spear' for the ANDSF and to conduct counter-terrorism, counterinsurgency, and counter-narcotics operations. The combined strength of the various Afghan special forces was 22,091 highly trained troops, their ranks free of 'ghost soldiers'. Most of their commanders had trained with, or in, the US or other NATO nations. Most also had experience fighting alongside international forces. The government planned to increase the force to 90,000 and make ANASOC the main conduit of US military assistance and counter-terrorism cooperation. The objective was that ANASOC's effectiveness and integration with US counter-terrorism agencies would minimise the need for a US troop presence in Afghanistan. This was consistent with the broader trajectory of American policy to pull forces out from Afghanistan and cut costs. ANASOC would help the US achieve both of those objectives, and only cost US$4 billion a year. In late 2020, Ghani authorised the formation of ANASOC, and the funding concept was pitched to the US in 2021. It was presented again to Biden in late June 2021 when Ghani visited Washington

DC. On both occasions, however, the US approach was only to listen politely.

Ghani also presented to Biden a wide-ranging list of requirements for the ANDSF. Among the things he requested was expediting the overhaul of 44 aircraft of the Afghan Air Force, delivering nearly 100 aircraft that the US had committed to provide in years past but failed to supply, providing additional advanced aircraft, supporting expedited training of pilots, and extending aircraft service contracts until three major aircraft maintenance hubs could be built across Afghanistan in 2024. The document handed to the Pentagon and National Security Advisor Jake Sullivan outlining these requests included an offer to conduct joint counter-terrorism operations after US soldiers had pulled out; it also requested intelligence exchange and operations support. The document, which was drafted by one of the authors, also asked the US to clarify how it intended to provide 'over-the-horizon' support to the ANDSF after the US withdrawal: such 'over-the-horizon' support entailed air strikes in Afghanistan from regional US bases, and training, procurement, and equipment support for Afghan forces from abroad. These requests were less ambitious than they appeared. US generals had warned Afghanistan in June 2021 that most Afghan Air Force aircraft would grind to a halt by September because of wear and tear and the expiration of service contracts. Some US defence contractors who provided critical services had already left by April 2021; all would depart by 31 August. Despite promises—some made by Sullivan to his Afghan counterpart Mohib—the US failed to present Afghanistan any plans for 'over-the-horizon' support, keeping the Republic in the dark as to how its forces could sustain themselves or receive critical enabling services after the US left. There was also no response to the ANASOC pitch or the weapons wish-list.

A major component of the US response was to send seven aircraft—a combination of light attack, transport, and passenger planes—from Kabul to the United Arab Emirates for maintenance in June. Weeks of back-and-forth between Afghanistan and the US over which flight path and refuelling stop to use delayed the project. The US opposed the use of Iran, whereas Afghanistan opposed the only other option, Pakistan. Afghanistan eventually relented and, after some foot-dragging, the Pakistani Air Headquarters issued permits to Afghan aircraft. A C-130 and an A-29 were to leave Kabul on 12 and 15 August, respectively, and return in early September.[15] They never returned.

There were other instances where military planners were caught off-guard by the swift pace of events. The US was working with Afghanistan to deliver a pay raise to the ANDSF to boost motivation. Plans in June 2021 included Afghanistan purging the rolls of 'ghost' soldiers to prevent US assistance from going to unintended recipients. Parallel to this, NATO planned to train Afghan forces abroad. The first batch of 20 Afghan special forces was sent to Turkey in July 2021, with a second batch scheduled for August. NATO planned to expand these courses to cover the entire ANDSF by January 2022. NATO's future role in Afghanistan was subject to conversations at various levels in the Republic's last year. The Office of the NATO Senior Civilian Representative proposed three possible scenarios for a post-US-withdrawal NATO presence. They ranged from a military mission headquartered at the Ministry of Defence and Ministry of Interior to a political liaison office with a defence assistance mandate. Afghanistan preferred the most robust engagement possible and suggested a refreshed Enduring Partnership Agreement to include work on deepening inter-operability, intelligence sharing, participation in military exercises, institutional capacity building and counter-corruption to embed the ANDSF within the NATO universe. The Senior Civilian Representative's office welcomed the proposal, and President Ghani shared it with NATO Secretary-General Jens Stoltenberg in July 2021. All these initiatives—a refreshed Enduring Partnership Agreement, a pay raise for the ANDSF, and training of the ANDSF abroad—were overtaken by events.

Military diplomacy

Parallel to these efforts, the British Chief of the Defence Staff, General Sir Nicholas Carter, was attempting a high-stakes diplomacy effort with his Pakistani counterpart and the Afghan National Security Advisor.[16] The initiative, in which one of the authors was involved, entailed several secret rendezvous between Pakistan Army

Chief General Qamar Javed Bajwa, ISI Chief Lieutenant-General Faiz Hameed, Afghan National Security Advisor Mohib, and Afghan National Directorate of Security chief Ahmad Zia Saraj. In an effort to find a neutral third-party venue for a meeting, the British suggested that the sides meet inside General Carter's plane on the tarmac of an airport in Bahrain. While this Bond-like scenario never panned out, the initiative included a secret and ultimately fruitless visit by Saraj to Rawalpindi to meet his counterpart in February 2021 to attempt to forestall a Taliban 'spring offensive'. The last major step of the initiative included a secret visit to Kabul by Bajwa and Hameed on 9 May 2021. The United Kingdom Foreign, Commonwealth and Development Office had worked up an elaborate arrangement with Mohib: General Bajwa would meet with President Ghani, and Hameed would simultaneously meet his counterpart in a separate room at the Arg presidential palace. The British deemed Bajwa more reasonable and inclined to cooperate, so the plan was for Ghani to reach an understanding with him on steps that Pakistan could take to pressure the Taliban and weaken its military momentum. A senior British diplomat would witness the conversation. Hameed and Saraj would finish their meeting and join Ghani and Bajwa, where Hameed would be socialised into the agreements as *fait accompli*. The hope was that he would be unable to contradict his superior in front of Afghan and British officials. But Hameed baulked immediately, protesting that he was not prepared to 'start a war on my soil' because of Afghanistan.[17]

Between May and July, Afghanistan was actively working with Norway, Turkey, and the United Kingdom to keep their troops in Afghanistan after the NATO withdrawal. Turkish personnel would secure the airport, and Norwegian troops would run a trauma centre there to replace the one at Bagram and enable diplomatic missions to remain in Afghanistan. On 21 July, Afghanistan also finalised a text that would enable British troops to remain in Afghanistan. Against the advice of its legal counsel, the Office of the National Security Council decided to enable the military presence of these countries through an exchange of diplomatic notes instead of taking the legal path of concluding a treaty and ratifying it in parliament. The rationale was that a formal treaty would take time, and there was no guarantee that parliament would approve it. These nations' soldiers were to be present only in modest numbers and for purposes other than direct military assistance. But—like allied personnel in West Berlin during the Cold War—they had the potential to provide strong signalling value to the Afghan population, the Taliban and international community. And Afghanistan needed those signals. The position of the Republic had weakened very considerably after it was excluded from the negotiation and conclusion of the US-Taliban deal. This change in political currents prompted Afghan politicians to reposition themselves to what they saw as the new reality. Many of them established private contacts with the Taliban,[18] and some softened their public rhetoric against the group. Former President Karzai consistently spoke of 'the Afghan sides involved in the war'— ignoring the Taliban's skyrocketing violence, targeting of civilians, and all-out effort to uproot the Republic over which he had once presided.[19] Former finance minister and Ambassador to Pakistan, Hazrat Omar Zakhilwal, founded a political party in March 2021 with former education and interior minister Farooq Wardak. A senior leader of his party called for a transitional government,[20] not just rejecting the continuation of Ghani as president but also casting doubt on the continuity of the Republic as the political system of Afghanistan.

Final weeks

In the waning days of July, First Vice President Amrullah Saleh had pitched what one high-level defence official had called the 'Cuff Strategy', meaning that the government would use all it had in its *cuff*, Dari for the palm of the hand, to resist the Taliban. The idea included arming the loyal Kuchi tribes around Kabul, exhorting the city's residents to pitch in, and mustering ANDSF personnel and materiel from elsewhere to join the Kabul-based 111 Division of the 201st ANA Corps. This would make the defence of Kabul solely a Republican endeavour, the kind of 'independent defence' that Afghanistan's security planners had considered but never seriously planned to do because the prospect of the complete withdrawal of international forces was never deemed imminent. The idea withered on the vine for lack of Ministry of Defence support.[21]

Also around this time, the United States and United Kingdom were pushing the Republic to retreat from 21 provinces and focus on major population centres, arterial highways, and the border posts to protect customs revenues and maintain state viability. General Sir Nicholas Carter had pressed Mohib on this point during the latter's visit to London in late July 2021, advising him also to plan for a few targeted special forces operations to wrest certain locations from the Taliban to signal that the plan was not simply a wholesale retreat. He told Mohib that the Republic had to maintain such a 'stalemate' long enough—nine months—for it to sink in for the Taliban that they could not win militarily.[22] Ghani initially resisted the idea, but on 31 July 2021, he convened a meeting in the palace of major political leaders—mostly ones who risked losing political equity if their strongholds were ceded—and secured their support.[23]

But events were moving fast. Districts were falling unstoppably, and the ANDSF was in retreat. By 5 August, government figures showed that 218 of the 304 districts across Afghanistan had fallen, and the administrative centres of 18 others had been relocated to avoid Taliban threats. Most of the remaining provinces were deemed 'under threat'.[24] The ANDSF was in crisis, and executing an organised repositioning was going to be difficult—with the ever-present danger that even a well-organised repositioning would be a new cascade trigger. Furthermore, the chain of command at the tactical level was breaking down. A week before the fall of Herat, the corps commander of Herat's 207 Zafar Corps complained to the Ministry of Defence leadership that 'nobody wants to follow my orders'.[25] In other instances, ANDSF commanders cut deals with the Taliban out of a desire for self-preservation, or out of opportunism, or both. For example, the battalion commander in Ghaziabad district in the eastern province of Kunar struck a deal with the Taliban, handed the base to the militants, and split the weapons and ammunition with them before slipping across the border into Pakistan in early August 2021.[26] The brigade commander in the province of Laghman, next door to Kabul, was found to have had nightly rendezvous with the Taliban for several months in 2021.[27] In another adjoining province, the commander of the combat outpost in Saidabad district, which the ANA had taken over from US forces, sold it to the Taliban in late June 2021. The deal included mine-resistant ambush protected (MRAP) vehicles, Humvees and other armoured vehicles; the commander also abandoned hundreds of soldiers to the Taliban.[28]

Apart from possible Taliban infiltration, what prompted these commanders to take such measures? Human motivation can be complex, but it is possible to identify a few key indicators that help explain why some soldiers and commanders in certain circumstances decided to stop fighting. They all made sense in the context of the developing cascade as US forces were withdrawn. First, the sense of abandonment that pervaded Afghanistan after the signing of the US-Taliban deal gave way to a sense that it was futile to fight after the US announced in April 2021 its intention to withdraw without a plan to support the ANDSF. The Taliban read the mood and exploited it. As early as May 2021, they sent local elders in several provinces— Maidan Wardak, Logar, and Ghazni—to ANDSF units with a simple message: 'The US has handed Afghanistan to the Taliban. You are fighting for nothing. The Taliban are offering you safe passage if you drop your weapons'. This message of 'amnesty' resonated with soldiers in dozens of checkpoints, which fell to the Taliban overnight. The surrendering soldiers received a small amount of cash from the Taliban to make their way home. The government arrested the tribal elders involved in the incidents,[29] but the damage was done.

The combination of a sense of abandonment and Taliban outreach might have had more limited success if it had been effectively countered early by the Republic. But Ghani, whose mode of expression tended to sail over people's heads, failed to give soldiers a wartime narrative for which to fight, and the country's political elite, deeply fractured in the aftermath of not one but three suspect presidential elections, was far from rallying behind the Republic or the constitution. The security leadership was aware that many soldiers were asking themselves why they should die in a war in which the Taliban's victory appeared all but inevitable.[30] The Taliban were also able to convert their biggest weakness—their well-earned reputation for brutality against ANDSF prisoners—into a relative strength by offering amnesty to surrendering soldiers. Amnesty was applied inconsistently and surrendering ANDSF troops were still massacred,[31] but it was practised just often enough for some desperate soldiers to take the chance. The resulting desertions and surrender had a direct impact on ANDSF strength and casualties. For the first time in years, in the last six weeks of the Republic, ANDSF casualties actually declined.[32]

That was partly in the context of a drastically reduced fighting force. Although the Ministry of Defence paid salaries to 163,000 personnel in the month prior to collapse, the real numbers were drastically smaller. One week before the collapse, the Ministry of Defence's database showed a force of under 129,000. The database had a natural lag because paperwork associated with casualties and desertions had to be processed to reflect the changes, and the depleted army units likely did not have the administrative staff to carry out this work consistently. And so, this number was almost certainly a significant overestimation of the Ministry of Defence's strength, as revealed by a commission comprising the Ministry of Defence's Human Resources, Administration and Operations (*Pezhantoon, Tashkilat wa Operasiyoon*) departments that had been tasked in June and July with purging the rolls of so-called 'ghost soldiers'. This commission was able to verify only a fighting force of 30,000–35,000 soldiers, excluding the Defence Ministry's administrative and civilian staff.[33]

Not all of the ANDSF surrendered, deserted, or cut deals. As districts fell and regular infantry became less effective, the Afghan special forces became the workhorse. Comprising about 10% of the Afghan National Army, the ANA special forces conducted nearly 60% of the operations in 2019–20.[34] That percentage only went up in 2020–21. Although the increasing reliance on these soldiers was wearing them down and the forces were worried about the safety of their families as the Taliban advanced,[35] they remained the most reliable and effective component of the ANDSF until the end. But that said, for the reasons we mentioned in Chapter Four relating to the selection-destruction cycle, this was not a sustainable situation, and it began to show. The aforementioned Ministry of Defence commission also found a 'noticeable' decline in the strength of the ANA special forces.[36]

In early August, the Ministry of Defence considered creating two defensive lines around Kabul but soon concluded that it lacked the

3,000 troops required because of competing priorities. How the security leadership came to this conclusion was partly a function of their morale. 'I never saw the minister of defence speak of resistance in our internal meetings', a high-level defence official said, adding that the minister told him how the tide was in the Taliban's favour: 'My brother-in-law is optimistic about the Taliban; they don't mistreat people and are not corrupt'. This apparent lack of resolve among the top leadership was happening in the context of a mismatch between the Republic's aspirations and its instruments. The Chief of Army Staff and the Director-General of Military Operations felt that the palace changed plans and priorities too fast for the Ministry of Defence to keep up. 'In the final couple of months, the Chief of Army Staff and the Director-General of Military Operations would laugh at decisions that came from security meetings at the palace. They said, "Our soldiers are surrounded by Taliban and cannot even leave their bases, yet they want us to conduct clearance operations"', the high-level defence official said.

The forces had two other related difficulties: high-level political pressure on defence tactics and the increasingly hands-on involvement of the Office of the National Security Council. Vice President Saleh pressured the Chief of Army Staff to pay greater attention to the rapid gains the Taliban made in the north.[37] The Office of the National Security Council, derided for its micromanagement of security institutions, became involved to the extent that some defence officials felt no sense of ownership or agency in the conflict. One official, who had been moved from the National Security Council to a high-level Ministry of Defence post in March 2021, described what he saw in the ministry: 'I found that the Ministry of Defence did not take responsibility for effective implementation of anything. They knew that both political and security responsibility for failure would fall on the Office of the National Security Council'.[38]

There were also differences between the US and Afghanistan. Although the US had informed Afghanistan that its withdrawal would be unconditional, meaning the US would not be holding the Taliban to its commitments under the US-Taliban deal,[39] at their end the US generals felt bound by it, including parts that the Afghan government came to understand to be 'secret annexes'. According to one high-level Afghan security official, the US officer in charge of US air operations in Afghanistan, Rear Admiral Peter Vasely, explained that the US would not conduct air strikes on Taliban forces unless they were within 1,000 meters of a major city, or their vehicles had a visible 'DShK' machine gun mounted on them. This self-imposed limitation advantaged the Taliban, who exploited it to devastating effect. Undaunted by air strikes, they would concentrate dozens of forces against an ANDSF base. Groups of Taliban fighters would take turns shooting at the beleaguered outpost, which was equipped to deal with a four- or eight-hour firefight but not a twenty-four-hour siege.[40] On the increasingly rare occasion that the US sent a drone, Taliban fighters would fall back to avert a strike, only to return after the drone left.[41] This allowed the Taliban to tighten their hold around major cities. But when the group, contrary to its commitment under the Doha deal, attacked provincial capitals, the US was hesitant to conduct airstrikes in urban centres.[42] This is why, as the Taliban took over Herat city, Lashkargah, Spin Boldak or the border town of Islam Qala in August, the US did not conduct air strikes.[43]

Final days

The end came faster than many had predicted. After the wholesale collapse of districts across Afghanistan between May and July, provincial capitals followed. It started with the fall of Zaranj, capital of the western province of Nimroz.[44] Shiberghan, the capital of Jawzjan in the north, followed on 7 August; Taloqan, the capital of Takhar in the north, was next. Over the next seven days, nearly thirty of Afghanistan's thirty-four provinces fell. Capturing a provincial capital had always been a significant marker of Taliban strength, but not all provincial capitals were of equal significance. Nor did the manner of their fall matter equally. The Taliban push into the north, which had begun several years earlier in Kunduz, Baghlan, and Badakhshan, was followed up with a sudden and sharper thrust in mid-2021 that caught northern powerholders by surprise: they seemed to have anticipated that the Taliban would focus on consolidating their positions in Pushtun-dominated areas rather than attempt a *Blitzkrieg* into other parts of the country. The strategic province of Kunduz—

linking Kabul to the north and functioning as a conduit of opium smuggling for the Taliban—fell on 11 August after the collapse of the 217 Pamir Corps. Significant amounts of military hardware from the Corps fell into the hands of the Taliban. They had now cut off Kabul's main road access to the north, including to the key province of Balkh that was home to another military corps. The following morning, on 12 August, the governor of the strategic province of Ghazni—which sat on the main highway linking Kabul to the south—reached a deal to hand the province to the Taliban in exchange for safe passage out of the province. Capitulation by Governor Daud Laghmani, who had been appointed in May with the backing of the Office of the National Security Council over the objections of Ghazni's public and political elites, sent shockwaves across Afghanistan.[45] A contingent of the ANDSF was still making a last stand in Ghazni as Laghmani handed it to the Taliban and left town.[46]

On the same day, Governor Hayatullah Hayat of Maidan Wardak, which neighbours Kabul, visited the capital with an urgent request for 'PK' and 'DShK' machine guns for the resistance. After Ghazni, Maidan Wardak was the only province standing before the Taliban reached Kabul. He received the guns and ammunition on 13 August from the depot of the National Public Protection Force and returned to his province,[47] where panic had set in after officials saw a convoy of vehicles speeding toward the provincial capital. Concluding that a large Taliban force was coming to capture the province, the officials scrambled out of Maidanshahr and were less than an hour's drive to Kabul when the National Directorate of Security reassured them that the convoy was, in fact, the governor of Zabul and his retinue, coming to Kabul after cutting their own deal with the Taliban! The jittery officials returned to their province.[48]

Context was important in understanding the officials' scramble: Ghazni had capitulated the day before, and the key provincial capitals of Herat, Kandahar, and Helmand—each province home to a military corps—would also fall that day, 13 August. Panic was setting in right across the country, with no apparent plan by the government to stop the Taliban's rapid advance. A plan was shaping up in the presidential palace at noon that day: as the shellshocked Maidan Wardak officials drove back, Ghani chaired a meeting attended by both vice presidents, all the security chiefs and Dr Abdullah, Chairman of the High Council for National Reconciliation.[49] It was decided at the meeting that the Republic would concentrate its remaining resources to defend Kabul.[50] To rally the public, Ghani went to the historic Bala Hissar fortress on the Sher Darwaza mountains in the southeast of the city and taped a defiant message calling on the people of Kabul and the ANDSF to resist. His minister of defence, General Bismillah Khan Mohammadi, stood next to him in the frame.[51] But neither the video nor any other announcement about the meeting came from the Arg (the presidential palace) that day. At that point, Amrullah Saleh took to his Facebook page to announce the decision, proclaiming that 'all the required resources would be provided to the ANDSF'.[52] This set off alarm bells at the National Directorate of Security and the Office of the National Security Council, which were engaged in a delicate effort to secure the evacuation of the governor, intelligence chief, corps commander, and local powerbroker Ismail Khan from Taliban captivity after the key western province of Herat and the 207 Zafar Corps had fallen that day.[53] National Security Advisor Mohib gave another reason for Ghani's tape not airing:

> [After the security meeting] I was talking to Dr Fazli [Head of the Administrative Office of the President] and telling him that these people are saying that they could resist, but the reality is that I have been following the situation, and places are falling like dominoes. They are going to make the President issue this statement but nothing from my observation to back it up with. And he [Fazli] said … that after the [security] meeting, he had had a talk with Zia Saraj, who told him [about] similar concerns. I didn't know about this conversation. We were all trying to put up a brave face. Nobody wanted to talk of weakness, but when I heard that, I felt that it was an important juncture to have an honest conversation with these leaders.[54]

On 13 August, five of the six provincial centres in the vicinity of Kabul—in Parwan, Kapisa, Laghman, Maidan Wardak, and Nangarhar—were in the government's hands. Only the provincial centre of Logar to the southwest had fallen, but the ANDSF had regrouped and were putting up stiff resistance in Dasht-e Saqawa, along the Kabul-Logar highway.[55] Mazar-e Sharif in the north of Afghanistan with its 209 Shahin Corps was also standing. But the Head of the National Directorate of Security, Saraj, privately expressed doubts to Fazal Mahmood Fazli, Head of the Administrative Office of the President and one of Ghani's trusted confidants, that the ANDSF could defend the city. He cited low morale and lack of organisation, adding that Taliban sleeper cells inside the city were being activated.[56] When Ghani was alerted to this, he ordered Mohib to seek a unified view of the ANDSF's senior security leadership about the possibility of resistance. Mohib convened a meeting of the security chiefs in the evening of 13 August at the Ministry of Defence[57] and found that they shared the spy chief's assessment.[58] Mohib described the exchanges that took place at the meeting:

> [T]he minister [of defence] had just come back from the recording of the message by the President. I told him that what I had been observing is that in fact your troops are not fighting, you just had the President recording this message. Is that something you can back up with [your] forces? This is where they all (security chiefs) came back and said there is no military solution, we have to find a political solution. NDS had the assessment that MoD didn't have the strength it claimed it had and soldiers were not in the mood to fight. And police had significant issues. The minister of defence himself ... gave me a few examples of people who were from Panjsher that he had personally spoken to, one of whom was a *qumandan* (commander) who had asked his soldiers to fight and they threatened him and told him that if he forced them to fight, they would kill him first, then move on to go home. The other was a pilot from Panjsher who had not turned up to work and the minister called him and he told the minister that his family told him not to go to work and endanger the family. The minister told me, This is the mood of the people you would expect to be most willing to fight the Taliban.[59]

Mohib then asked the minister of defence if the Republic could resist in Panjsher province, a highly defensible valley north of Kabul that had resisted the Soviets in the 1980s and the Taliban in the 1990s:

[The minister] went on to say we couldn't even resist in Panjsher because when resistance took place there [in the 1990s], it was after it had been a base for resistance against Soviet Union for 10 years. Following that were five years of government when [Ahmad Shah] Massoud was minister of defense. Before Kabul fell [in the 1990s], they had moved a lot of forces and ammunition and weapons to Panjsher. And at that time, there was only one way into Panjsher. It had Badakhshan and Takhar at its back to protect it. Right now, it is an island. His argument was that we cannot even resist in Panjsher.[60]

That night, thousands of Taliban prisoners in Kabul's maximum-security prison at Pul-e Charkhi staged a violent riot. The Taliban were also pressing on ANDSF positions in Surobi, 70 kilometres from Kabul, which had been reinforced by troops sent from the capital.[61]

Parallel to these internal consultations, Mohib and Fazli had been having discussions with US *chargé d'affaires* Ross Wilson from 7 August to negotiate a transfer of power. Mohib described the content of his discussion thus:

The main question there was, is there a way to rescue some of the Republic? [Save] some institutions and provide for some guarantees that would allow normal life in Afghanistan for people? The point was, if we could guarantee that a peaceful transition of power took place, and a peaceful transition of power [that] has some level of representative decision-making— we couldn't have elections, obviously, but if we could have had a *Loya Jirga*, maybe that would endorse any decision-making which would allow for a respectful and dignified transfer of power.[62]

Mohib was hoping to negotiate guarantees with respect to ANDSF, employees of the Republic, human rights and women's rights protections, and have them endorsed in a *Loya Jirga*, or grand assembly of political leaders. But Wilson saw it differently, with important practical questions:

Three sessions I had with Mohib and Fazli in the last week— the week of Aug 7—telling me the President was prepared to hand over power, but there was the question of how it would work and to whom it would be handed over. ... The President's expectation as conveyed by Mohib/Fazli changed from discussion to discussion: [transfer of power would be] unconditional but then it had to be in the context of a loya jirga, which would have been hard and time-consuming, unpredictable and probably unsatisfying to the Talibs. [It would be] unconditional but there were conditions, and it went around and around. There were questions in my mind as to how much it reflected the President and how much of it was creative representation ... It was not known by any political circles outside [the palace] and didn't include Abdullah, who had a mutually agreed role in the peace process, Karzai or any of the other powerbrokers or political leaders. Among others, VP Saleh's exclusion was a bit of a problem.[63]

From Mohib's perspective, the discussions had to be tightly held because news of any such discussions would further demoralise the 'security forces and people across the country'. But partly at Wilson's suggestion and partly out of the need to create a broad enough political consensus for a handover, Mohib met with Dr Abdullah on the evening of 13 August and briefed him about his discussions with the security chiefs and asked him to convene a meeting of political leaders under the auspices of the High Council for National Reconciliation 'to create a consensus' around a handover. Abdullah offered to hold such a meeting the following afternoon, 14 August. 'From the speed of the collapse, we don't have much time', Mohib told Abdullah. 'Perhaps we should do it in the morning'. Abdullah agreed to hold the meeting as soon as logistically possible and promised to come to the palace with the leaders at 2.00 pm on 14 August to see the president for final consultations. In the meantime, Mohib and Fazli met with First Vice President Saleh 'and had a long discussion and told him why the [president's] message was not released and what our thinking was about what should be done'. After that meeting, Fazli met with Vice President Danesh, who was 'a lot easier to relay this [information] to', Mohib said. 'He agreed that we needed to pursue a political path forward'.[64] When the political leaders arrived at the palace that afternoon, they proposed sending an 'empowered delegation' to Doha. Mohib added:

By empowered, they meant a delegation that could negotiate the dissolution of the Republic and had authority that the other [peace negotiation] delegation [led by Masoom Stanekzai] didn't have. This effectively took the President's power away from him: the delegation would be the decisionmaker about what future there would be for Afghanistan. The President agreed. We continued negotiations with the Americans. That evening, President Ghani spoke with Secretary of State Blinken and told them that what I had been negotiating with Wilson is his position and he is fully behind it.[65]

The delegation would be kept small, and discussions on the composition of the delegation led to an initial understanding that Dr Abdullah would take with him former President Karzai, Gulbuddin Hekmatyar or one of his representatives, former Vice President Karim Khalili or former Deputy Chief Executive Mohammad Mohaqeq, and one representative from the *Jamiat-e Islami* party, most probably Salahuddin Rabbani. President Ghani would send National Security Advisor Mohib, his chief of staff Matin Bek, former minister for peace Salam Rahimi, and the head of the negotiation delegation in Doha Masoom Stanekzai. Secretary Blinken agreed to send Salman Ahmed, director of the State Department's Policy Planning Staff, instead of Zalmay Khalilzad. 'This was one of the things we had been negotiating with Wilson', Mohib said. 'We needed an envoy that could be trusted by President Ghani'.[66]

Parallel to these efforts, US military officials advised the Republic on 14 August to execute another consolidation: hold Kabul and maintain a 'corridor' to the north in Balkh, where the 209 Shahin Corps was still standing, and a corridor to the east, where the Nangahar provincial capital was still standing 'and then give up on the rest'.[67] Even this consolidation was going to require significant logistical work in the middle of chaos, but the Ministry of Defence started working on the plan that day. There was also a separate track of diplomacy, the one the US had with the Taliban. Although Mohib said that Zalmay Khalilzad was not in touch with him, or the president, or Vice President Saleh, Khalilzad did maintain contact with the Taliban and worked to obtain assurances from their leadership in Doha that their forces would not enter

Kabul by force. Wilson explained the assurances and the doubts that American policymakers had about it:

> Zal[may Khalilzad] appeared to have had a set of conversations with [Mullah] Baradar. At a certain point [US Central Command commander] General McKenzie intersected on this, though I'm thin on details, about the nexus of issues involving rapid advance of Taliban forces from the southeast toward Kabul (Ghazni and Paktika to Kabul) but advances elsewhere too. The question was, what would happen if they got to the outskirts of Kabul city? At a certain point, I was told that the Talib representatives told us their forces would not advance toward Kabul and would pause before reaching the city or probably the province while the terms [of a handover] could be worked out or defined. At the same period, we had reason to believe that in fact such instructions were given to Taliban fighting forces, which in fact did not stop. That led to some questions on our part about the extent to which senior Taliban leadership in general, and maybe especially Baradar, and people in Doha—and even others in Quetta and Peshawar— were in control of the Taliban units on the ground who were rapidly advancing and smelling blood.[68]

The presidential palace was growing frustrated at Washington's slow pace. 'The sense of urgency that was expected was not really, I think, understood by Washington', Mohib said. 'It was a lot of very slow negotiation'.[69] At its end, the US Embassy thought the idea of a *Loya Jirga* was time-consuming and inconsistent with the rapidly unfolding situation. Either way, there was less time than either the Republic or the US anticipated. 'None of us knew how short the timeline was', Wilson said. 'Everybody assumed there was more time to work with than there actually was'.[70]

The situation changed dramatically on 14 August. Mazar-e Sharif and the 209 Corps fell, completing the Taliban's control of the north. Atta Muhammad Noor, the northern powerbroker who had vowed to defend the province at any cost,[71] fled the city along with other high-ranking security officials, including fellow northern powerbrokers Mohaqeq and Dostum, the provincial governor, members of parliament, and a deputy director-general of the National Directorate of Security, General Ebadullah Ebad.[72] Three eastern provinces—Paktia, Paktika, and Kunar, which formed the better part of Ghani's popular base—also fell that day.[73] But 14 August had another big blow in store for Ghani. Governor Ziaulhaq Amarkhil, his loyal supporter who had been Chief Electoral Officer at the time of the suspect 2014 presidential election, cut a deal with the Taliban in the eastern province of Nangarhar, another of Ghani's strongholds.[74] This left only two of the five provincial centres surrounding Kabul in government hands: Parwan and Kapisa, where, on 14 August, US forces conducted what would be their last air strike while Republican Afghanistan still stood.[75] Shortly after noon, Ghani aired a taped message on the state-run RTA television. It was not a message of defiant resistance but one that simply stated that he was 'consulting' with the international community about peace and would update the nation about his progress 'soon'. Panic was already setting in across Kabul city: when one of the authors visited a bank that evening, throngs of residents were seeking to withdraw their savings, and the bank was instituting withdrawal limits. BBC journalist Yalda Hakim saw an exodus at the airport.[76]

Mohib described the whirlwind of meetings and the near-simultaneous set of events that constantly unfolded in the final thirty-six hours thus:

> [T]he difficulty of the story is that there were multiple realities happening at the same time. There was no sequence in which these events happened … With every passing moment, realities were changing. Every meeting made sense at that time. Decisions were for that moment. In a few hours, those realities would change … a lot of the realities that were assumed [to remain unchanged] had started to change … Balkh fell, Maidan Wardak fell … Jalalabad fell, and I received pictures of Taliban sitting with the governor in his compound … this was around 4 a.m. [on 15 August]. I knew we had a long day the following day. I decided to catch some sleep. I woke up and things had stayed the way I went to sleep, not better. Now we had a city surrounded by the Taliban.[77]

At around 8 am on 15 August, the Taliban broke through the Maidanshahr line.[78] Except for a police checkpoint in Arghandeh, just outside Kabul city, the capital had no defensive line: it was fully exposed to a Taliban assault.[79] In the panic that ensued as forces retreated from Maidanshahr, even the Arghandeh checkpoint folded and retreated into Kabul city's Company locality in the fifth Police District (PD5).[80] This was when panic and chaos reached the palace. A senior national security official at the palace described the confusion about the situation in the city: around 10 am, the head of the Presidential Protection Service, General Kochai, told National Security Advisor Mohib that PD5 had 'fallen' to the Taliban. He returned at 11.15 am to report that the Taliban had been sighted in Chaman-e Hozouri, within three kilometres of the palace. Around the same time, some Presidential Protection Service guards started clearing the palace, telling the few employees who had turned up to go home. The Presidential Protection Service also tried to evacuate the national intelligence and security coordination office (*Markaz-e Melli-e Tawheed*), which received updates from all branches of the ANDSF, sent out high-level defence and security directives, and provided briefings to the president about the military situation.[81] In the confusion of the moment, the president's guards were attempting to render inoperative the national coordination cell. They were eventually talked down.[82]

One of the authors received a call from a relative around this time that informed him that officers in Police Districts 5 and 13 had abandoned police stations and changed into civilian clothes to blend in. Taliban had also been sighted in the nearby Company area. This seemed to corroborate what Saraj had told Mohib around 10 am that day: that the Taliban were activating sleeper agents across the city, contrary to their promises to the US and their public pronouncements that they would not enter Kabul city. Earlier, at around 9.15 am, Vice President Saleh—who said he was 'angry' that Ghani had not announced the joint decision to resist—had left the city to go to Panjsher 'to coordinate resistance' from the province.[83] He had overseen the security of Kabul since October 2020, but there was confusion over whether his mandate was limited to fighting Kabul's rising crime levels, or also included defending the city against a Taliban takeover. He took the narrower interpretation of his powers, but the Office of the National Security Council believed he also oversaw the city's defences. His departure that morning only added to the confusion at a critical time and left the chain of command unclear.

The 15 August was also payday for employees of the Office of the National Security Council. In the panic, the normally staggered payment schedule was disrupted and a mob of employees gathered in the finance office. Agitation hit a boiling point when support staff learned that they were not going to get their *emtiazi* pay, concession payments on top of their civil service salary. As intimidated finance officers scrambled to manage the shouting and shoving,[84] Second Vice President Sarwar Danesh's SUVs drove past them to meet Ghani, who was distracted and going from one room to another as he spoke to close advisors.[85] Deprived of a normal meeting, Danesh called his chief of staff at 12.15 pm to decide what to do. The question was whether he should go home or go straight to the airport for his 3.00 pm Emirates flight to the United Arab Emirates, with the ultimate destination of Istanbul (the vice president's concerned family had obtained a ticket for him the night before, 14 August, as they watched provinces around Kabul fall). Danesh was initially told he could use Ghani's helicopters to fly to the airport, but he eventually drove to the airport before 2.00 pm. He was not on the manifest for Ghani's escape flight.[86] US Marines, however, had assumed control of the airport and paused all commercial flights, ostensibly because more troops were arriving and US embassy officials and documents were being evacuated on military flights. Danesh would miss his flight that day and remain trapped in Kabul as the Taliban took over the city.

Back in the Arg, General Kochai was growing increasingly concerned about the security of the president. Mohib, who was supposed to leave Kabul with the wife of the president, Rula Ghani, on a special plane arranged by the United Arab Emirates at 2.00 pm, had his own growing worries as the plane took longer and longer to materialise. At one point, Kochai turned to Mohib and said he could not keep the president safe if Mohib left Kabul.[87] Not only did Kochai lack authority over the ANDSF, but coordination among his own Presidential Protection Service personnel was also breaking down: unbeknown to him, some Presidential Protection Service personnel, whose duty required them to be dressed in suits, had changed into the traditional *peran tunban*, apparently hoping to blend in and melt away if the Taliban stormed the gates. Meanwhile, other Presidential Protection Service units appeared to be organising a possible resistance inside the walls of the palace. A palace maintenance worker, whom one of the authors met around 1 pm on 15 August, told him that the Presidential Protection Service had asked him to pick up a weapon and assume a position on the perimeter of the palace. The worker had no military training and refused the request. The Presidential Protection Service did not insist, and shortly thereafter the flight of the president—between 2.15 and 2.30 pm[88]—rendered the issue moot. Everything else was also rendered moot: one of the authors saw how some of the last security checkpoints in the city, which were protecting the airport, began melting away within hours of Ghani's flight. The idea of sending the empowered delegation to Doha, which rested on the assumption that the Republic would hold Kabul and that the Taliban would not force their way in, was now dead. The city had fallen and the Taliban were in Kabul, ostensibly 'invited' by former President Karzai.[89] One of the authors saw several of the leaders who were supposed to fly to Doha as part of that delegation trying to flee Kabul. Some of them—including Vice President Danesh—left Kabul on the same charter flight as one of the authors on 16 August.[90]

Conclusion: Dynamics of final collapse

It is unclear how long the Republic could have held on if the 13 August decision to defend Kabul had been implemented. Only swift and resolute implementation of the decision to resist could have helped, but neither Ghani nor his security chiefs had the requisite resolve. There may be merit in the claim, made to one of the authors, that resistance would have 'turned Kabul into Damascus', with urban warfare proving devastating to civilians. Any defence would have been a last-ditch effort to slow the inevitable fall of the Republic, through surrender or outright defeat. As we noted in the previous chapter, US Secretary of State Blinken had pinned his hopes on an 'inclusive' new government led by the Taliban, and some have suggested that a display of resistance could have given efforts to broker a deal between Ghani, the US and the Taliban a chance.[91] One can understand why the idea of such a deal had a certain appeal: it might have seemed to provide an opportunity to negotiate safety for ANDSF members, the continuation of thousands of civil servants in their jobs, and preservation of certain fundamental human rights such as girls' education. But even though Mohib had worked towards such negotiations, after the fall of the Republic his view was that such a deal would have amounted to the handover of the Republic and legitimising the Taliban;[92] given how blithely the Taliban had ignored the spirit of the Doha agreement, the probability that they would have honoured any such deal in good faith was vanishingly small. There could have been one possible marginal benefit of a potential deal: a managed transition to Taliban takeover could have possibly calmed the nerves of anxious Kabul residents, reduced the chances of a wholesale economic collapse, and reduced the anxiety that fuelled a run on the banks, among other things. Writers will continue to argue these and other points as the judgement of history takes shape with the benefit of more time and evidence. But one thing is certain: when the Taliban were at the gates, Kabul's defenders were in disarray, its international partners fleeing, and its political class abandoning it. Negotiating anything but total surrender in such circumstances would have been virtually impossible.

The final months of the Republic show that collapse happened after a trigger—the US-Taliban deal—prompted stakeholders to act out of fear, opportunism, greed, self-preservation, political considerations, or similar factors. The overcentralised and neopatrimonial dimensions of the system had heightened the danger that this would happen, but the trigger was necessary to set the cascade in motion. Most individual actors doubtless believed their actions would not sink the ship. In fact, most actors typically do not see themselves as part of a grand picture, or their individual actions in ideological or hugely consequential terms. The true power of most individual actions lies in their signalling value. In an environment of high uncertainty and low organised direction, these actions serve as signals to others; they help change the mass psychology and quicken the pace of events as nobody wants to be left high and dry when the curtain falls. This was the unpleasant place in which the soldiers of the combat outpost in Saidabad found themselves when their commander sold them out. The defenders of Ghazni were in a similar situation when the governor cut his deal with the Taliban. And, ultimately, the people and government in Kabul found themselves in the same place after Ghani and Saleh abandoned the city. The vast majority of Afghans—including one of the authors—were simply left to fend for themselves.

In fleeing, the Republic's leaders followed the quasi-Machiavellian logic that Robert Greene explains thus: '... martyrdom ... is a messy, inexact tactic ... For every famous martyr, there are thousands more who have inspired neither a religion nor a rebellion, so that if martyrdom does sometimes grant a certain power, it does so unpredictably. More important, you will not be around to enjoy that power, such as it is'.[93] When the chips fell, none of its leaders wanted to be a martyr for the Republic.

Collapse hardly follows the sequential logic of dominos; it is chaotic, with the various events seemingly happening simultaneously and quickly. After a tipping point, the incentive for all levels to act fast for self-interest is high; commitment to an ideal or cause, or slowness in acting, may produce martyrs but carry no reward otherwise. And they did not in the final days of the Republic. The forgotten soldiers who made a last stand in Ghazni chose martyrdom, but they remain unremarked.

9

CONCLUSION

In 1876, the German Chancellor, Count Otto von Bismarck, remarked that the Balkans were not worth the bones of even a single Pomeranian grenadier. But not for nothing were the Balkans known as the powder keg of Europe, and when the heir to the throne of the Austro-Hungarian Empire, Archduke Franz Ferdinand, was assassinated in Sarajevo on 28 June 1914, it proved to be the spark that set off a world war.[1] Analyses of dramatic historical events often focus on agency and structure, occasion and cause, or, putting it more colloquially, 'powder keg and spark'.[2] These distinctions are broadly reflected in the analysis of this book.

These distinctions usefully parallel our analysis of decline and fall as conceptually distinct phenomena. 'Fall' is typically a far more dramatic and obvious development than 'decline': in a notable history of the Roman Empire, Max Cary and Howard Scullard wrote that 'Not all elements in a culture may be declining at the same time, nor universally throughout it'.[3] In Republican Afghanistan, many things went wrong, but there were also significant achievements, and the fact that not everyone benefitted from them immediately was as much a reflection of the scale of the challenges that Republican Afghanistan faced as of the failings of the system. The distinction between decline and fall is important, because it goes to the issue of responsibility for events in Afghanistan.

Where decline is concerned, the discussion in this book shows that the picture was a complex one, with multiple factors contributing to decline, and many problems being the product of human action but not of human design.[4] When things go terribly wrong, it is both psychologically and emotionally understandable that a search may begin for a simple explanation, and a single scapegoat. But in the real world, disasters tend to have complex roots,[5] and it is important that they be properly explored. To make sense of the *decline* of Republican Afghanistan, it is necessary to go back to its origins, and identify some of the structural weaknesses in the political system that interacted with personal and policy failings on the part of Afghan leaders and their foreign backers, cumulatively contributing to diminished generalised normative support for the Afghan government. It is also necessary to recognise the fundamental role of Pakistan in undermining the Republican project in Afghanistan. Its responsibility—both causal and moral—should not be under-emphasised. Without the sanctuaries provided by Pakistan for the Taliban, the story of the two decades after 2001 might have been very different.

Explaining the *fall* of Republican Afghanistan is a different matter. Many political systems have found themselves in a state of decline, usually in the ragged way that Cary and Scullard highlighted. Not all end up collapsing: some simply stagger on. To explain the fall of the Afghan Republic, more specific and immediate factors need to be identified. This book has made an effort to highlight what those factors might have been. Once one enters this realm, individual agency rather than simply structure begins to loom more prominently as a critical causal factor. And the activities of different agents of course can come into play.

Revisiting the 2021 collapse

In Chapters Two to Five, dealing with political legitimacy, pathologies of aid, the persistence of insurgency, and problems of leadership, we highlighted some of the critical factors that contributed to the decline of Republican Afghanistan. Chapters Six to Eight, by contrast, focus on the factors that contributed to its fall: maladroit diplomatic endeavours that lit the fuse for a cascade that finally brought the Republic down once it became clear that President Biden was going to adhere unconditionally to the approach adopted by President Trump. At this point, however, there is some value in also briefly exploring what factors in the politics of the United States contributed to its abandonment of the most pro-Western regime in West Asia.

The cost of ongoing involvement in Afghanistan hardly seems an adequate explanation of what happened. As we noted in Chapter Two, the number of 'hostile deaths' of US personnel in Afghanistan fell dramatically after the completion of the withdrawal of the bulk of international forces by the end of 2014. Furthermore, total US appropriations for Afghanistan in fiscal year (FY) 2020 amounted to just $4.62 billion, down from a peak of $16.75 billion in FY2010.[6] To put this in perspective, for FY2020, total US federal outlays totalled $6.6 trillion; appropriations for Afghanistan were thus only 0.0007% of total outlays.[7] In March 2021, the US Defense Department produced a larger '"war-related" estimated costs' total for FY2020 of $39.67 billion, but this included 'related regional costs that support combat operations in the U.S. Central Command area of responsibility'; this amounted to 5.5% of FY2020 defence outlays of $714 billion and 0.006% of total US federal outlays. The cost per US taxpayer in FY2020 was less than half of what it had been in FY2013.[8]

Nor does pressure from the public seem to have been especially intense. An opinion poll conducted in April 2021 found a net approval for withdrawal of 73% of respondents, but the proportion of respondents who 'strongly' approved was only 29%.[9] Afghanistan after 2014 was not even remotely the kind of political issue in the United States that Vietnam had been for President Lyndon Johnson in the late 1960s,[10] when conscription was also a major issue; and as it continued to be for President Richard Nixon after a shooting of demonstrators at Kent State University on 4 May 1970 led to mass protests across the United States. The Vietnam situation fitted a scenario traced out by Andrew Mack: 'As the war drags on and the costs steadily escalate without the "light at the end of the tunnel" becoming more visible, the divisions generated within the metropolis become *in themselves* one of the political costs of the war'.[11] These costs for the US were large in the case of Vietnam, but vastly less so in the case of Afghanistan.

At the elite level, there were certainly voices advocating withdrawal from Afghanistan, and from diverse backgrounds. Traditional US isolationism found voice in Republican Party circles; a kind of progressive 'neo-isolationism' was articulated by groups such as the Quincy Institute for Responsible Statecraft. Various 'realists' argued that if the US withdrew from Afghanistan, it would be better placed to confront emerging challenges from China[12] and for that matter Russia—although the alacrity with which Russian President Vladimir Putin then moved to pursue brinksmanship over Ukraine, culminating in Russia's 24 February 2022 invasion, suggested that the US abandonment of Afghanistan had dispelled any fear in Moscow that the US would take active steps to protect Washington's friends in Kyiv.[13] If one of the direct or indirect consequences of the Afghanistan withdrawal was the Russian invasion of Ukraine, the cost-benefit calculus of the withdrawal begins to shift dramatically, but there is no evidence that 'realists' took this possibility into account. There was also backing for negotiations with the Taliban from commentators who had earlier been associated with the office of the Special Representative for Afghanistan and Pakistan, which had functioned from 2009 to 2017.[14] These diverse elite circles provided some of the tropes such as 'endless war' that found their way into wider discussion. But that said, within both Republican and Democrat circles, there were also voices decrying any abandonment of Afghanistan and the Afghans and warning of the dangers that might—and ultimately did—result. There was no shortage of credible arguments for staying the course that US presidents could have adopted had they been so inclined. With neither cost, nor mass public pressure, nor elite consensus providing an irresistible force driving total withdrawal, we are brought back to individual agency, above all that of Presidents Trump and Biden, and their all-too-compliant associates. There are limits as to how far one can go in accounting for the motivations, and perhaps even the whims, of individual decision-makers. However, some tentative observations are in order.

Amongst students of the presidency, there would be little doubt that Trump was one of the most impulsive, unstable, and frankly bizarre occupants ever of the Oval Office, something which a number of studies have confirmed.[15] As president, he proved incapable of methodical policy formulation, and to seek to link his approach to Afghanistan to any kind of serious appraisal of options from a policy perspective is probably to treat his approach to office too kindly. It remains a complete mystery how 'progressive' supporters of the withdrawal of US forces from Afghanistan could have felt even the slightest confidence that Trump, as final decision-maker in the US system, could be trusted to finesse a complex and delicate 'peace process' of which he was ultimately the linchpin. Compounding this problem was that of a Secretary of State who was out of his depth across a range of policy areas[16] (although he had the nous to ensure that his own signature was not attached to the Doha agreement), and an envoy whom a former senior CIA official described as 'a private citizen dabbling on his own in 2018 with a variety of dubious Afghan interlocutors against whom the intelligence community warned, trying opportunistically to get "back inside"'.[17] Seeking to negotiate a meaningful 'peace deal' with the Taliban while the likes of Trump and his team occupied the White House was truly playing with fire in a gasoline dump.

With the change of administration in January 2021, despite the turmoil that accompanied it,[18] there were hopes of a more mature approach to Afghanistan. This, unfortunately, did not eventuate. As we noted in Chapter Seven, Biden ignored even the modest recommendations of the Afghanistan Study Group, and proceeded to endorse a withdrawal without conditions or support for the ANDSF to continue fighting, setting the scene for the mayhem that then ensued. In doing so, he exposed his own severe limitations, which probably would have received a lot more attention during the presidential campaign of 2020 had he not been running against an incumbent with sociopathic tendencies. There was simply less to Biden than met the eye. He was the oldest president in the history of the United States,[19] potentially bringing with him some of the rigidities in thinking that can accompany old age.[20] His earlier run for the presidency had imploded in 1987 when he was exposed as a plagiarist.[21] His background in foreign policy was also widely misunderstood. While as a senator he had been a long-serving member of the Senate Foreign Relations Committee (which he chaired from 2001 to 2003 and 2007 to 2009), until he became president he had never held a major office with distinct executive authority and had never occupied a position where he was routinely required to make final decisions on matters of high policy with significant associated risks. Dr Robert M. Gates, who served as Defense Secretary in both the Bush and Obama Administrations, wrote in his memoirs that Biden had 'been wrong on nearly every major foreign policy and national security issue over the past four decades'.[22] Some progressive Democrats regarded him with suspicion because of his ardent support for the invasion of Iraq in 2003,[23] and it is possible that he tilted in their direction over Afghanistan in order to offset any damage that his earlier position on Iraq might have caused him in Democrat circles. But he also appeared to have had a cold indifference to the wellbeing of Afghans. He famously clashed with Karzai when he visited Kabul,[24] and his discourtesy did not go unremarked. As one writer put it, 'The Afghans present, even those with little sympathy for Karzai, found it offensive. They saw Biden as not just impolite but condescending'.[25] An even more scathing judgement was offered in February 2022 by Jennifer Brick Murtazashvili in the wake of Biden's issuing of an executive order dealing with frozen Afghan assets:[26]

> This move also is another harsh blow for America's reputation, as it reminds the world once again of American incompetence during the withdrawal. It leads us to wonder whether Biden has personal animus towards Afghanistan. His previous public postures on Afghanistan are riddled with malice, yet not anchored in a coherent strategy. At every opportunity, he has spoken with unparalleled cruelty about Afghanistan and its people. His disdain was on display in April when he announced the withdrawal of troops. It was even more evident during a series of speeches in August when he spoke without remorse about the haphazard U.S. withdrawal.

The misfortune that Afghanistan suffered from the Trump and Biden presidencies might be regarded simply as incredibly bad luck, but it does raise a wider question that goes beyond the scope of this book but which is nonetheless important to note for the future of world affairs in the twenty-first century—namely whether this situation reflects fundamental defects in the capacity of the US political system to produce capable elites and competent leaders. This problem had been recognised even before the rise of Trump,[27] but Trump-style populism has certainly brought it into sharper focus.[28]

Given how disastrously the policies of Trump and Biden played out for Afghans, it is perhaps useful to engage in a small thought experiment, although it is inevitably counterfactual with all the limitations which that involves.[29] Would Republican Afghanistan have fallen (or have fallen when it did) if, instead of the US striking a deal with the Taliban, it had confronted the issue of sanctuaries in Pakistan and worked cooperatively with the Afghan government to manage the withdrawal of remaining US troops from the country—with proper planning for maintenance of ANDSF capabilities by civilian contractors, and for the use of drones for counter-terrorism strikes? This approach would have held out no hope for ambitious players to head to Oslo to collect a Nobel Peace Prize, but would have mirrored much more closely the approach to transition that was put in place before 2014, which allowed the Afghan government to manage the challenge of mass psychology and avoid a destructive cascade. It would not necessarily have made much direct difference to the factors that had contributed to decline, but it might have created space for those factors to be addressed differently.

Some final thoughts

Before the Taliban seized Kabul, an increasingly ubiquitous narrative within or on the edge of Western policy circles maintained that a desire for international recognition and for substantial international assistance would oblige the Taliban to moderate their behaviour.[30] Such optimism had a long history: when the Taliban took Kabul in 1996, Khalilzad had written that 'once order is established, concerns such as good government, economic reconstruction and education will rise to the fore'.[31] But once the violent overthrow of the Republic had been accomplished in August 2021, it became rather clear, rather quickly, that while the Taliban were indeed keen to obtain aid and recognition, they were not so desperate for aid and recognition that they were prepared to moderate their behaviour in the ways that Western optimists had expected or hoped.[32] In the wash-up from the takeover, the ISI-backed Haqqani network came out on top, something plainly demonstrated by the appointment of Sirajuddin Haqqani, a sanctioned terrorist whose presence in a Taliban government would predictably be anathema to Western actors, as interior minister, and by the appointment of a cabinet made up entirely of men and almost entirely of members of a single ethnic group. The Taliban figures who had featured prominently in the Doha negotiations were no longer calling the shots, if indeed they ever had.

There were plenty of warnings, in the public domain, as to the perils of misreading the Taliban's intentions.[33] In a particular insightful commentary in June 2019, Sayed Madadi wrote the following:[34]

> U.S. policymakers have erroneously developed an assumption that the Taliban have grown equally frustrated with the longevity and cost of war. The reality, however, has been almost the opposite. American impatience and desperation have only further invigorated the Taliban, who see it as a sign of victory from God. Unlike the United States, the Taliban have proven that they understand their adversaries and have been extremely adaptive to changing circumstances—all while strictly adhering to their own set of medieval beliefs. Unless the United States corrects course to see the Taliban as they are rather than as what the United States prefers them to be, the peace process will either miserably fail or come at a staggering cost in an intensified and renewed conflict.

With the surfacing of arguments for recognising the Taliban diplomatically, it is pertinent also to note the same writer's sobering recent comments on the desirability of empowering the Taliban:[35]

> The international community's first priority has been to avert an unprecedented humanitarian and economic crisis, which has

been severely exacerbated by the Taliban's takeover of Afghanistan ... These efforts ignore the fact that the main drivers of the crisis are political, not economic. The Taliban's incompetence, discrimination, and intimidation have caused massive human and physical capital flight, disrupted the public sector and the economy, and undermined any sense of trust or stability ... Inclusive and representative governance is only meaningful in a pluralistic and democratic system, where the voice and approval of the people drive state legitimacy and public policies ... During the negotiations in Doha, I observed how compromises made as confidence-building measures only solidified the Taliban's intransigence and their refusal to abandon their maximalist positions ... Helping Afghanistan must begin by acknowledging that the Taliban are at the heart of the problem, not the solution.

Those who so gravely misread the Taliban before August 2021 would be wise not to repeat their earlier mistakes. Nevertheless, they may well do so. One Western writer who had strongly supported the Doha process—despite warnings as to its dangers from informed Afghans—recently voiced the opinion 'that this round of Taliban rule "probably ranks as the most peaceful six-month period that Afghanistan has enjoyed in four decades"'.[36] While this may end up being the last-refuge argument for the defenders of the 'peace process', many Afghans would not share this sunny assessment.[37] Nor should the wider world, for two reasons, both related to the meaning of 'peace'.

First, the idea of peace is more complex than such a simplistic usage would suggest. Richard Caplan has warned that peace viewed simply as the absence of armed conflict 'is of very limited value for the purpose of understanding the nature or the quality of a given peace and thus for devising appropriate peacebuilding strategies and for assessing how consolidated a peace may be'.[38] This builds on an older insight from Hobbes:

> For WARRE, consisteth not in Battel onely, or the act of fighting, but in a tract of time, wherein the Will to contend by Battel is sufficiently known: and therefore the notion of *Time*, is to be considered in the nature of Warre; as it is in the nature of Weather.

For as the nature of Foule weather, lyeth not in a showre or two of rain, but in an inclination thereto of many dayes together: So the nature of War, consisteth not in actuall fighting; but in the known disposition thereto, during all the time there is no assurance to the contrary. All other time is PEACE.[39]

The Taliban may not be confronted by armed groups similar to the *Mujahideen*, but they remain highly vulnerable to the risk of violent protests flowing from an upsurge in contentious politics,[40] given that the totalitarian mindset of the Taliban militates against the kind of institutionalised politics that can function as a safety-valve.

Second, there is something distinctly unsettling about the notion that the path to peace is to hand power to the actor that has proved most willing to breach the peace in order to achieve its objectives. The Taliban were consistently responsible for the bulk of civilian casualties in Afghanistan, and to see them as bringing 'peace' is to downplay the Carthaginian character of their approach, focused on stamping out all resistance. What the Taliban offered was a 'peace' without welfare, a 'peace' without liberty, and a 'peace' without a semblance of due process or justice.[41] But the decimation of Afghanistan's once-lauded independent media,[42] the flight of international journalists, and the effective winding-back by the UN Assistance Mission in Afghanistan of its role to investigate and report on harm to civilians[43] has meant that much of the violence that the Taliban have directed against Afghans has not been reported. The reports that do make it out of Afghanistan paint a picture of the Taliban engaging in widespread campaigns of forced displacement of Hazaras and Turkic populations in the north and conducting reprisals against Tajik populations.[44] The Taliban have also executed hundreds of former ANDSF personnel,[45] including ethnic Hazara members[46] and detained dozens of others. But the change in tactic by the Taliban from all-out insurgency to targeted attacks has brought numbers of reported violent incidents down, eliciting the label 'peace'. One is irresistibly reminded of the verdict of the Roman historian Tacitus on the behaviour of the Romans: *solitudinem faciunt, pacem appellant*— 'they make a desolation and they call it peace'. This is where the decline and fall of Republican Afghanistan ultimately led.[47]

AFTERWORD
ON BETRAYAL

On 15 September 2021, President Biden issued a statement to mark the 'International Day of Democracy'. His tone was forthright and uncompromising:[1]

> This International Day of Democracy, we reaffirm a basic truth: that democracy—government of the people, by the people, and for the people—is humanity's most enduring means to advance peace, prosperity, and security. It is how we best safeguard the universal human rights, fundamental freedoms, and dignity that belong to every person. And in a moment when democracy is increasingly challenged by those who seek to govern through force and repression, it is incumbent on democracies to prove that we are able to deliver for the needs of our people as we strive toward a more equitable, inclusive, and sustainable world ... Together with our partners, the United States will continue the vital work of strengthening democratic institutions, defending civil society and independent media, promoting free and fair elections, protecting human rights, and insisting on accountability for those who commit abuses and foster corruption.

Bracing as these words might have appeared, they had a hollow ring coming just a month after decisions of the Biden Administration had abandoned the people of Afghanistan to the mercies of a theocratic tyranny. Many ordinary Afghans, hearing these words, would have had every reason to feel that they had been betrayed. But this gives rise to some issues with which it is useful to wind up our discussion: what exactly might we mean by 'betrayal', what forms might betrayal take, and what patterns of betrayal did Afghanistan experience in recent times?

The phenomenon of betrayal is ubiquitous in political, social, and human relations, but the meaning of the word 'betrayal' has often seemed elusive—much more than that of the legal concept of treason—to the point that a recent major study has suggested that it may be an essentially contested concept.[2] One way of circumventing this challenge, however, is to focus on how one might stipulate a useful definition of betrayal. Here, there are several candidates. One is that offered by the political theorist Judith Shklar:[3] 'For a simple act of betrayal, one person should have both intentionally convinced another person of his future loyalty, and then deliberately rejected him. The latter then, not surprisingly, feels betrayed. There is nothing ambiguous about this, the hard core of treachery'.

Another approach is offered by the philosopher Avishai Margalit, for whom betrayal is 'ungluing the glue of thick human relations', where 'belonging' is 'the most important general feature of thick relations'.[4] Of course, one can always demand ever-greater levels of clarity over the exact meaning of terms such as 'loyalty' and 'belonging'. But it may not be especially useful to do so, since many examples of alleged betrayal plainly fall within any meaningful definition. Betrayal, it seems, is a little like poetry—hard to define, but relatively easy to recognise.[5]

One other point to note is that not all forms of betrayal are equally serious, and not every form of betrayal is automatically evil, just as not every example of duplicity is necessarily wrong. During the Second World War, heroic figures in occupied countries who hid Jews from the Gestapo had to lie about their activities,[6] and it would be absurd to judge them harshly for doing so. Indeed, to have told the truth to the Gestapo would itself have been an act of betrayal. Furthermore, to betray friends, family or associates who are planning to do something evil is hardly an evil itself. But the fact that not all acts of betrayal have evil consequences, and that there may be difficult cases at the margin, is not an argument for regarding betrayal in general as a trivial issue. On the contrary, it deserves to be taken very seriously, as some forms of betrayal have consequences that are catastrophic, and, as T.S. Eliot remarked about the betrayal of Czechoslovakia at Munich in 1938, raise doubt about 'the validity of civilization'.[7]

Forms of betrayal

Betrayal can come in many shapes and sizes, and the following discussion can hardly claim to be comprehensive. Nonetheless, some forms of betrayal stand out. One very obvious example is betrayal through breach of a promise. Promises are classic examples of 'speech acts': when one says 'I promise', one is not simply saying something; one is also doing something.[8] This is one reason why words that seem promissory in character actually matter. One of the oldest of all ethical propositions is captured in the Latin expression *pacta sunt servanda*—promises are to be kept. The legal theorist Joseph Raz has expanded on this point, arguing that there is a general interest to have 'voluntary special bonds with other people' and that it is this 'general interest that explains why every promise, and not only those performance of which is to the specific advantage of the promisee, creates a right in the promisee'.[9] To make a promise does not require the specific use of the word 'promise', which in any case is an English word that may not have a direct equivalent in all languages; what is important is the conveying of a commitment in a particular way.[10] Commitments may be conveyed in speeches by leaders, assurances by diplomats, or in the signing of formal treaties where nations promise to come to each other's aid, such as in Article Five of the North Atlantic Treaty of 1949 that established NATO.

Somewhat less specific than betrayal through breach of promise is betrayal through breach of *trust*. 'All standard accounts of trust', Russell Hardin has written, 'assume that it involves reliance on someone or some agency when there is at least some risk that the agent will fail the trust'.[11] This can be formulated in terms of betrayal: Nicholas Wheeler defines trust as 'the expectation of no harm in contexts where betrayal is always a possibility'.[12] In assessing betrayal, however, it is useful to draw a further distinction:

between strategic trust and moralistic trust. 'Strategic trust', writes Eric Uslaner,[13]

> reflects our expectations about how people *will* behave … Moralistic trust is a statement about how people *should* behave. *People ought to trust each other.* The Golden Rule does *not* demand that you do unto others as they do unto you. Instead, you do unto others *as you would have them* do unto you.

It is not hard to see how a bitter sense of betrayal can emerge if one party to a relationship views it in terms of moralistic trust while the other does not. 'Generalised trust', based on 'a broad belief that others are largely trustworthy', has played an important role in fostering international amity, as it 'begins a *reciprocity circle* of trust, cooperation and enhanced trust'.[14] Spectacular acts of betrayal can come at a heavy cost for the betrayer, fracturing such a reciprocity circle.

Beyond looking at modes of betrayal, it is also useful to distinguish between different categories of person who might be betrayed. Again, the potential range of categories is very large, but there are two on whom it is useful to focus. The first is allies. At one level, one might argue that allies come into existence *as* allies when interlocking promises and trustful expectations are combined. Typically, however, what marks their distinctive relationship is some kind of formalised alliance document that specifies the obligations that alliance partners assume towards each other, and the specific responsibilities that they are to discharge in particular circumstances. Thus, a *modus vivendi* such as the 1904 *Entente Cordiale* between the United Kingdom and France would not qualify as an alliance, although it could lay the foundation for alliance-like behaviours. Alliances differ from mere association, common organisational membership, or friendship. They also differ from 'coalitions of the willing'[15] (or the obedient). Alliances are constituted through some recognisable process or set of steps. They reflect some shared purpose. They involve a joint commitment of resources, either immediate or prospective. Finally, alliances involve some degree of joint decision-making. And to work, they must ultimately be sustained by a sense of trust. From this it flows that allies can betray one other in various ways: by abandoning a shared purpose, by withdrawing crucial resources, or by acting unilaterally behind the back of an alliance partner on a matter in which it has a vital concern. Betrayal may be triggered by a sense that previously shared interests, ideology or values are no longer important; but it can also be a product of domestic pressures, erratic leadership, or sheer bloody mindedness.

The second category of persons who might be betrayed are the vulnerable. Betraying the vulnerable is often a particularly despised form of activity, since it exploits an asymmetry in power between different actors, manifested in what Andrew Linklater has called 'the power hierarchies that explain unequal vulnerabilities to harm and the uneven distribution of security, and which invariably lead to perceptions of injustice'.[16] This asymmetry has been recognised for millennia as a basis on which the vulnerable might be betrayed. As the Athenians famously put it in the *Melian Dialogue*,[17]

> you know as well as we do that, when these matters are discussed by practical people, the standard of justice depends on the equality of power to compel and that in fact the strong do what they have the power to do and the weak accept what they have to accept.

Yet while the exploitation of such asymmetries of power may be ubiquitous, it nonetheless has a poor reputation and can rebound to the disadvantage of the treacherous actor if power hierarchies prove to be unstable in the long run.

One other form of betrayal cries out for attention: betrayal of one's *own proclaimed values*. 'Hypocrisy', Shklar writes, 'has always been odious'.[18] It has long been reviled in different times and cultures. As Polonius observed to Laertes in Shakespeare's *Hamlet*, 'This above all,—to thine own self be true; And it must follow, as the night the day, Thou canst not then be false to any man'.[19] This later dawned on the murderous King Claudius: 'My words fly up, my thoughts remain below; Words without thoughts never to heaven go'.[20] Hypocrisy is equally the subject of scorn in Islam: an entire chapter of the Koran is devoted to 'The Hypocrites' (*al-Munafiqun*). Of course, it is quite common in political life. On the eve of the Soviet invasion of Czechoslovakia in 1968, Soviet General Secretary L.I. Brezhnev reportedly stated to the Czechoslovak leaders 'Don't talk to me about "socialism". What we have we hold'.[21] This did not prevent the Soviet leadership from promulgating—following the invasion—the 'Brezhnev Doctrine' that asserted a collective responsibility to protect the gains of socialism.[22] Hypocrisy is particularly distasteful when manifested by states or actors seeking to portray themselves as moral leaders of unique stature and standing. To promote values with one breath and betray them with the next will inevitably leave a bad taste in many people's mouths.

Patterns of betrayal

On what bases might one see the phenomenon of betrayal as pertinent or central to Afghanistan's recent experiences? The answer is not simple, but a little reflection suggests that there has been quite a lot of betrayal in the air. That is not to say that Afghanistan's sad fate can be exclusively blamed on betrayal: as this book has shown, the aetiology of the decline and fall of Republican Afghanistan was multifaceted, with the unintended consequences of well-intentioned actions, as well as the self-interest of a multiplicity of actors, on occasion playing tragically destructive roles. But this should not give a 'leave pass' to those leaders in the wider world who chose to wash their hands of Afghanistan and its people. There are good reasons why the Roman Prefect of Judea, Pontius Pilate, has rarely been seen as a respected role model.

A first form of betrayal to note is the betrayal of Afghanistan as an ally. A key theme in the propaganda of extremist groups such as ISIS is that the US can never be trusted, and will betray its 'allies' in the Muslim world.[23] In July 2012, following the signing of a 'Strategic Partnership Agreement' in May 2012, Afghanistan was designated a 'Major Non-NATO Ally' under US law. US Secretary of State Hillary Clinton, in Kabul for the announcement, was effusive in her language: 'We are not even imagining abandoning Afghanistan. Quite the opposite. We are building a partnership with Afghanistan that will endure far into the future'.[24] This was reinforced by a 'Bilateral Security Agreement' between the United States and Afghanistan, signed on 30 September 2014. To mark the signing, the Office of the

Press Secretary at The White House issued a statement by President Obama that the Agreement:[25]

> reflects our continued commitment to support the new Afghan Unity Government, and we look forward to working with this new government to cement an enduring partnership that strengthens Afghan sovereignty, stability, unity, and prosperity, and that contributes to our shared goal of defeating Al Qaeda and its extremist affiliates.

A cynic, reading these words, might suggest that it was naïve on the part of Afghan leaders to attach any weight to them in the first place—although as Rochefoucauld remarked, 'It is more shameful to distrust one's friends than to be deceived by them'.[26] But even if Afghan leaders treated such commitments with a grain of salt, they could be excused for not having foreseen that the US would later go behind their backs to sign its own agreement with the Taliban enemy, and—in the absence of any ceasefire—commit the Afghan government to release thousands of Taliban combat and political prisoners. It is hard to imagine how anyone could not see this as betrayal of an ally.

But a second form of betrayal is even more disturbing: the betrayal of ordinary Afghan people. Here we are not talking about those who inhabited the corridors of power, but simply people who saw the international interest in Afghanistan after 2001 as offering a once-in-a-lifetime opportunity to escape from the misery that had marked so much of the period following the communist coup of April 1978. These included, most notably, Afghan women, whose grim experiences under the Taliban had been extensively documented, and members of the historically marginalised Hazara ethnic group. For these people, promises of ongoing commitment by Western leaders were not like complex contracts, to be carefully parsed by lawyers tasked with checking whether the fine print matched the beautiful rhetoric. They were invitations to trust the West, and on the strength of them, many people had committed themselves to high-profile activities in defence of democracy, freedom, and human rights. These were activities that had made them targets for terrorist groups such as the Taliban and left them acutely vulnerable in the event that the door was opened for a Taliban return, as many were to discover as attacks on civil society activists mounted in 2020–21. In May 2010, Secretary of State Clinton met with women leaders in Afghanistan and stated 'We will not abandon you. We will stand with you always'.[27] In January 2011, Vice-President Biden publicly stated in a joint news conference in Kabul with President Karzai that the US would not abandon Afghanistan after the bulk of US forces withdrew in 2014, and added 'We are not going if you do not want us to leave'.[28] Even earlier, in 2007, then Senator Biden had published a book, somewhat ironically entitled *Promises to Keep*, in which he described meeting a young Afghan girl during a visit to Afghanistan.

> I looked up and saw a thirteen-year-old girl standing ramrod straight in the middle of the classroom, so brave and so determined. 'America can't go,' she said. 'I must learn to read. I will be a doctor like my mother.' I wanted to walk over and hug her 'No. No. No, honey,' I said, 'America is going to stay'.[29]

It is even possible that he genuinely meant what he said.[30] But with the passage of time, he seemed to have forgotten the words of Yeats's poem:[31]

> But I, being poor, have only my dreams;
> I have spread my dreams under your feet;
> Tread softly because you tread on my dreams.

To be fair, as detailed earlier in this book and as many Biden supporters have claimed, the fatal agreement with the Taliban was signed not by Biden but by Zalmay Khalilzad under President Trump. But Biden then adopted it as his own and even retained Khalilzad as his envoy. It is thus not surprising that similarities between aspects of the foreign policies of both Trump and Biden have caught the attention of some acute observers. Professor Anne-Marie Slaughter, an eminent scholar[32] who served as Director of Policy Planning at the US State Department during the Obama Administration, remarked on social media on 19 September 2021 that 'Alliances require side-payments, sacrifice, and fair dealing. What the world sees is that the US is willing to abandon Afghans and betray allies. Another version of America First'.[33] It is hard to disagree.

One other reality of which it is easy to lose sight is that it was not only Afghans who felt betrayed at the way that the international involvement in Afghanistan ended. Almost from the outset in 2001, the United States was aided in multiple ways by forces from NATO countries, as well as other allies such as Australia. For years on end, the situation in Afghanistan was one of the greatest strategic and foreign policy preoccupations for NATO civilian and military leaders, topping the agenda at NATO summits and raising a diverse range of challenges for the alliance as a whole.[34] Many soldiers from NATO and other allied countries died in Afghanistan, and substantial resources were committed to Provincial Reconstruction Teams when the US invasion of Iraq diverted US attention from the Afghan theatre.[35] Yet in 2020 and 2021, under both President Trump and President Biden, Washington's allies increasingly found themselves kept in the dark about US activities and objectives, and when they cautioned Biden as to the risks associated with his approach, he ploughed ahead anyway.[36] Under Trump, this might have seemed a way of signalling to Washington's NATO partners that the US expected them to share more of the burden of the alliance; under Biden, it seemed more like a lamentable lack of judgement. Trump committed to the Taliban that America, its NATO allies, and its non-NATO partners such as Australia would withdraw. Biden, on his part, decided to maintain Trump's commitment to the Taliban. These consequential US decisions made it harder for these nations—many of whom had signed bilateral security agreements and strategic partnership agreements with Afghanistan—to keep their promises to Kabul.

Perhaps the most serious betrayal of all in Afghanistan was the betrayal of core values. From the motto *E pluribus unum*—'one out of many'—to the complex early American conceptions of democracy and liberty,[37] US values had an individualist character. There is simply no disguising the fact that while Afghanistan's 'Republican' system, for all its flaws, was modernist and pluralist in character, the anti-modernist Taliban were monist and totalitarian in their vision, actively hostile to individualism, democracy, and freedom. They represented the antithesis of every single key value that the modern United States purported to defend. Yet once US leaders grew bored

213

with Afghanistan and soaked up their own recycled rhetoric about 'endless wars', they had no qualms about opting to partner with the Taliban in order to ease their own exit.

Given the triggering role of the US exit from Afghanistan in bringing the Taliban back to power, it is not surprising that the US received the bulk of the criticism for acts of betrayal. It is important, however, to ensure that the blame falls where it should, and is not crudely spread to those who deserve no criticism. It is one thing to say that President Biden's credibility was shredded in Afghanistan.[38] It is entirely different to pin the blame on Americans in general. Edmund Burke in 1775 wrote 'I do not know the method of drawing up an indictment against a whole people'.[39] Many Americans made huge sacrifices for the Afghan people, from diplomats and commanders who warned of the dangers of rushed withdrawal, to brave aid workers who stood by their Afghan staff, to the scholars who warned of the risks associated with a spurious 'peace process', and to the young American soldiers who died at the hands of a suicide bomber at the perimeter fence of Kabul airport on 26 August 2021.[40] Indeed, a September–October 2021 survey found that 73% of US veterans who had served in Afghanistan themselves felt 'betrayed' by the US withdrawal from Afghanistan.[41] The charge of American betrayal is properly levelled not against 'the Americans', but against the state, those in command of it, and their willing and eager agents.

'The state', remarked Friedrich Nietzsche, 'is the coldest of all cold monsters'.[42] This can easily be manifested in the phenomenon of betrayal, and the experiences of the people of Afghanistan at the hands of their ostensible allies provide yet another sad example. For advocates of cruder varieties of *Realpolitik*, this may simply be part of the package.[43] It is all too easy to walk in the steps of British Prime Minister Neville Chamberlain, who referred to the 1938 Czechoslovak crisis as 'a quarrel in a faraway country between people of whom we know nothing'.[44] But those who trivialise such betrayal would do well to reflect on the implications not just for the betrayed, but also for the betrayer, whom those betrayed—as well as others witnessing the betrayal—may regard with utter contempt.[45] And as Nietzsche put it, 'When you gaze long into an abyss the abyss also gazes into you',[46] a sobering reminder that the act of betrayal does not only harm the victim but also corrupts the perpetrator. In *The Prince*, Machiavelli warned that 'it cannot be called virtue to kill one's fellow citizens, to betray one's friends, to be treacherous, merciless and irreligious; power may be gained by acting in such ways, but not glory'.[47] Shakespeare understood this too. In *The Tragedie of Macbeth*, Lady Macbeth, the instigator of the slaying of King Duncan of Scotland, initially took a sanguine view of her role: 'A little water clears us of this deed'.[48] But this mood did not last: 'Here's the smell of the blood still: all the perfumes of Arabia will not sweeten this little hand'.[49]

NOTES

PREFACE

1. For background, see David Stevenson, *1914-1918: The History of the First World War* (London: Penguin, 2004) pp.503–29; Michael S. Neiberg, *The Treaty of Versailles: A Concise History* (Oxford: Oxford University Press, 2017) pp.35–50; Leonard V. Smith, *Sovereignty at the Paris Peace Conference of 1919* (Oxford: Oxford University Press, 2018) pp.15–59.

2. See Donald Markwell, *John Maynard Keynes and International Relations: Economic Paths to War and Peace* (Oxford: Oxford University Press, 2006) pp.90–139.

3. Quoted in Alan Sharp, *Versailles 1919: A Centennial Perspective* (London: Haus Publishing, 2018) p.2.

4. Julian Jackson, *The Fall of France: The Nazi Invasion of 1940* (Oxford: Oxford University Press, 2003) p.9.

5. Winston S. Churchill, *The Second World War: Volume II: Their Finest Hour* (London: Educational Book Company, 1954) pp.38–9.

6. Julian Thompson, *Dunkirk: Retreat to Victory* (New York: Arcade Publishing, 2015) p.306.

7. Quoted in Roy Jenkins, *Churchill* (London: Macmillan, 2001) p.597.

8. Ronald C. Rosbottom, *When Paris Went Dark: The City of Light under German Occupation, 1940–44* (Boston: Little, Brown & Co., 2014).

9. René Dollot, *L'Afghanistan: Histoire, Description, Moeurs et Coutumes, Folklore, Fouilles* (Paris: Éditions Payot, 1937) p.15.

10. William Maley, 'Looking Back at the Bonn Process', in Geoffrey Hayes and Mark Sedra (eds), *Afghanistan: Transition Under Threat* (Waterloo: Wilfrid Laurier University Press, 2008) pp.3–24.

11. *Agreement for Bringing Peace to Afghanistan between the Islamic Emirate of Afghanistan which is not recognized by the United States as a state and is known as the Taliban and the United States of America* (Washington DC: Department of State, 29 February 2020).

12. Claims that he took millions of dollars with him have not, however, stood up to close scrutiny. See *Theft of Funds from Afghanistan: An Assessment of Allegations*

Concerning President Ghani and Former Senior Afghan Officials (Arlington: SIGAR 22-35-IP Final Report, Special Inspector General for Afghanistan Reconstruction, 9 August 2022).

13. See, for example, David Kilcullen and Greg Mills, *The Ledger: Accounting for Failure in Afghanistan* (London: Hurst & Co., 2021); Brian Brivati (ed.), *Losing Afghanistan: The Fall of Kabul and the End of Western Intervention* (London: Biteback Publishing, 2022); Andrew Quilty, *August in Kabul: America's Last Days in Afghanistan* (Melbourne: Melbourne University Press, 2022); Elliot Ackerman, *The Fifth Act: America's End in Afghanistan* (New York: Penguin, 2022); Jean-Pierre Perrin, *Kaboul: L'humiliante Défaite* (Paris: Éditions des Équateurs, 2022); David Martinon, *Les Quinze Jours Qui Ont Fait Basculer Kaboul* (Paris: Éditions de l'Observatoire, 2022); Serge Michailof, *Afghanistan: Autopsie d'un Désastre 2001–2021: Quelles Leçons pour le Sahel?* (Paris: Gallimard, 2022); Marco Seliger, *Das Afghanistan Desaster: Warum wir am Hindukusch gescheitert sind* (Hamburg: Mittler in Maximilian Verlag, 2022); *Why the Afghan Government Collapsed* (Arlington: SIGAR 23-05-IP, Special Inspector General for Afghanistan Reconstruction, 15 November 2022).

1. INTRODUCTION

1. Richard Pipes, *Russia under the Old Regime* (Harmondsworth: Penguin, 1977) p. 83.

2. See Seymour Becker, *Russia's Protectorates in Central Asia: Bukhara and Khiva, 1865–1924* (Cambridge: Harvard University Press, 1968).

3. Hope Verity Fitzhardinge, 'The Establishment of the North-West Frontier of Afghanistan, 1884–1888', unpublished PhD thesis, The Australian National University, 1968.

4. Percy Sykes, *Sir Mortimer Durand: A Biography* (London: Cassell & Co., 1926) pp. 205–23.

5. See B.D. Hopkins, *The Making of Modern Afghanistan* (Basingstoke: Palgrave Macmillan, 2008); Martin J. Bayly, *Taming the Imperial Imagination: Colonial Knowledge, International Relations, and the Anglo-Afghan Encounter, 1808–1878* (Cambridge: Cambridge University Press, 2016).

6. https://worldpopulationreview.com/countries (accessed 17 October 2021).

7. https://worldpopulationreview.com/world-cities/kabul-population (accessed 17 October 2021).

8. *Estimated Population of Afghanistan 2020-2021* (Kabul: National Statistics and Information Authority, June 2020) p. 3.

9. See Erwin Orywal, *Die ethnischen Gruppen Afghanistans: Fallstudien zu Gruppenidentität und Intergruppenbeziehungen* (Wiesbaden: Dr. Ludwig Reichert Verlag, 1986); Conrad Schetter, *Ethnizität und ethnische Konflikte in Afghanistan* (Berlin: Dietrich Reimer Verlag, 2003).

10. For an excellent overview, see Nile Green (ed.), *Afghanistan's Islam: From Conversion to the Taliban* (Oakland: University of California Press, 2017).

11. See Torunn Wimpelmann, *The Pitfalls of Protection: Gender, Violence, and Power in Afghanistan* (Oakland: University of California Press, 2017); Sonia Ahsan-Tirmizi,

Pious Peripheries: Runaway Women in Post-Taliban Afghanistan (Stanford: Stanford University Press, 2021); Andrea Chiovenda, *Crafting Masculine Selves: Culture, War, and Psychodynamics in Afghanistan* (New York: Oxford University Press, 2020).

12. For an informed discussion, see Omar Sadr, *Negotiating Cultural Diversity in Afghanistan* (London: Routledge, 2020).

13. Charles Tilly, *Coercion, Capital and European States, AD 990–1992* (Oxford: Blackwell, 1992) pp.67–95.

14. Mancur Olson, *Power and Prosperity: Outgrowing Communist and Capitalist Dictatorships* (New York: Basic Books, 2000) p.11

15. See Jonathan L. Lee, *Afghanistan: A History from 1260 to the Present* (London: Reaktion Books, 2022) pp.51–115; Christine Noelle, *State and Tribe in Nineteenth-Century Afghanistan: The Reign of Amir Dost Muhammad Khan (1826–1863)* (London: Curzon Press, 1998). For an overview of state formation in Afghanistan, see Niamatullah Ibrahimi and William Maley, *Afghanistan: Politics and Economics in a Globalising State* (London: Routledge, 2020) pp.8–46.

16. Joel S. Migdal, *Strong Societies and Weak States: State-Society Relations and State Capabilities in the Third World* (Princeton: Princeton University Press, 1988) p.4.

17. Joel S. Migdal, 'The State in Society: An Approach to Struggles for Domination', in Joel S. Migdal, Atul Kohli, and Vivienne Shue (eds), *State Power and Social Forces: Domination and Transformation in the Third World* (Cambridge: Cambridge University Press, 1994) pp.7–34 at p.16.

18. See Thomas J. Barfield, 'Weak Links on a Rusty Chain: Structural Weaknesses in Afghanistan's Provincial Government Administration', in M. Nazif Shahrani and Robert L. Canfield (eds), *Revolutions and Rebellions in Afghanistan: Anthropological Perspectives* (Berkeley: Institute of International Studies, University of California, 1984) pp.170–84.

19. See Nivi Manchanda, *Imagining Afghanistan: The History and Politics of Imperial Knowledge* (Cambridge: Cambridge University Press, 2020) pp.105–42.

20. For a critical discussion of this idea, see Susan L. Woodward, *The Ideology of Failed States: Why Intervention Fails* (Cambridge: Cambridge University Press, 2017) pp.11–25.

21. Elisabeth Leake, *The Defiant Border: The Afghan-Pakistan Borderlands in the Era of Decolonization, 1936–1965* (Cambridge: Cambridge University Press, 2017) p.9.

22. See Robert D. Crews, *Afghan Modern: The History of a Global Nation* (Cambridge: Harvard University Press, 2015).

23. On the 1978 coup, see William Maley, *The Afghanistan Wars* (London: Macmillan/Red Globe Press, 2021) pp.23–4.

24. See Barnett R. Rubin, *The Fragmentation of Afghanistan: State Formation and Collapse in the International System* (New Haven: Yale University Press, 2002) pp.81–105; Ibrahimi and Maley, *Afghanistan: Politics and Economics in a Globalising State*, pp.17–21.

25. See Anthony Arnold, *Afghanistan's Two-Party Communism: Parcham and Khalq* (Stanford: Hoover Institution Press, 1983).

26. Frud Bezhan and Petr Kubalek, 'The Afghan President (To Be) Who Lived A Secret Life In A Czechoslovak Forest', *Radio Free Europe/Radio Liberty*, 3 November 2019.

27. See William Maley, 'Social Dynamics and the Disutility of Terror: Afghanistan, 1978–1989', in P. Timothy Bushnell, Vladimir Shlapentokh, Christopher K. Vanderpool, and Jeyaratnam Sundram (eds), *State Organized Terror: The Case of Violent Internal Repression* (Boulder: Westview Press, 1991) pp.113–31.

28. See Anthony Arnold, *Afghanistan: The Soviet Invasion in Perspective* (Stanford: Hoover Institution Press, 1985) pp.85–95; G.M. Kornienko, 'Kak prinimalis' resheniia o vvode sovetskikh voisk v Afganistan i ikh vyvode', *Novaia i noveishaia istoriia*, no.3, 1993, pp.107–18; Henry S. Bradsher, *Afghan Communism and Soviet Intervention* (Karachi: Oxford University Press, 1999) pp.75–117; Rodric Braithwaite, *Afgantsy: The Russians in Afghanistan 1979–89* (London: Profile Books, 2011) pp.58–81; Elisabeth Leake, *Afghan Crucible: The Soviet Invasion and the Making of Modern Afghanistan* (New York: Oxford University Press, 2022).

29. See Susanne Schmeidl and William Maley, 'The Case of the Afghan Refugee Population: Finding Durable Solutions in Contested Transitions', in Howard Adelman (ed.), *Protracted Displacement in Asia: No Place to Call Home* (Aldershot: Ashgate, 2008) pp.131–79.

30. See Olivier Roy, *Islam and Resistance in Afghanistan* (Cambridge: Cambridge University Press, 1990) pp.110–48; Abdulkader Sinno, *Organizations at War in Afghanistan and Beyond* (Ithaca: Cornell University Press, 2008) pp.119–72.

31. On the history of the *Hezb-e Islami*, see Chris Sands with Fazelminallah Qazizai, *Night Letters: Gulbuddin Hekmatyar and the Afghan Islamists Who Changed the World* (London: Hurst & Co., 2019).

32. On Pakistan and the Afghan resistance, see Mariam Abou Zahab and Olivier Roy, *Islamist Networks: The Afghan-Pakistan Connection* (London: Hurst & Co., 2004); Rizwan Hussain, *Pakistan and the Emergence of Islamic Militancy in Afghanistan* (Aldershot: Ashgate, 2005).

33. Olivier Roy, *The Failure of Political Islam* (Cambridge: Harvard University Press, 1994) p.113.

34. William Maley, *The Afghanistan Wars* (London: Macmillan/Red Globe Press, 2021) pp.49–52, 54–5.

35. On Gorbachev and Afghanistan, see William Taubman, *Gorbachev: His Life and Times* (New York: W.W. Norton, 2017) pp.271–4.

36. On the Soviet withdrawal, see Amin Saikal and William Maley (eds), *The Soviet Withdrawal from Afghanistan* (Cambridge: Cambridge University Press, 1989); Artemy M. Kalinovsky, *A Long Goodbye: The Soviet Withdrawal from Afghanistan* (Cambridge: Harvard University Press, 2011); Katya Drozdova and Joseph H. Felter, 'Leaving Afghanistan: Enduring Lessons from the Soviet Politburo', *Journal of Cold War Studies*, vol.21, no.4, Fall 2019, pp.31–70.

37. William Maley, *The Afghanistan Wars* (London: Macmillan/Red Globe Press, 2021) pp.149–55.

38. See William Maley, 'The Future of Islamic Afghanistan', *Security Dialogue*, vol.24, no.4, December 1993, pp.383–96.

39. See *Casting Shadows: War Crimes and Crimes Against Humanity: 1978-2001* (Kabul: The Afghanistan Justice Project, 2005) pp.82–8; *Blood-Stained Hands: Past Atrocities in Kabul and Afghanistan's Legacy of Impunity* (New York: Human Rights Watch, 2005) pp.70–100; Niamatullah Ibrahimi, *The Hazaras and the Afghan State:*

Rebellion, Exclusion and the Struggle for Recognition (London: Hurst & Co., 2017) p.191.

40. For background on the emergence of the Taliban, see William Maley (ed.), *Fundamentalism Reborn? Afghanistan and the Taliban* (London: Hurst & Co., 1998); Neamatollah Nojumi, *The Rise of the Taliban: Mass Mobilization, Civil War, and the Future of the Region* (New York: Palgrave, 2002) pp.117–24; Steve Coll, *Ghost Wars: The Secret History of the CIA, Afghanistan and Bin Laden, from the Soviet Invasion to September 10, 2001* (London: Penguin, 2005) pp.280–300; Alex Strick van Linschoten and Felix Kuehn, *An Enemy We Created: The Myth of the Taliban/Al Qaeda Merger in Afghanistan, 1970–2010* (London: Hurst & Co., 2012); Roy Gutman, *How We Missed the Story: Osama Bin Laden, the Taliban, and the Hijacking of Afghanistan* (Washington DC: United States Institute of Peace Press, 2013) pp.63–82.

41. See Anthony Davis, 'How the Taliban Became a Military Force', in William Maley (ed.), *Fundamentalism Reborn? Afghanistan and the Taliban* (London: Hurst & Co., 1998) pp.43–71.

42. See S. Iftikhar Murshed, *Afghanistan: The Taliban Years* (London: Bennett & Bloom, 2006) p.45; Jane Perlez, 'Onetime Taliban handler dies in their hands', *The New York Times*, 24 January 2011.

43. *The Taliban's War on Women: A Health and Human Rights Crisis in Afghanistan* (Boston: Physicians for Human Rights, 1998).

44. Ahmed Rashid, *Taliban: Militant Islam, Oil and Fundamentalism in Central Asia* (New Haven: Yale University Press, 2000) p.73.

45. On Al-Qaeda, see Jason Burke, *Al-Qaeda: Casting a Shadow of Terror* (London: I.B. Tauris, 2003); Jonathan Randal, *Osama: The Making of a Terrorist* (New York: Alfred A. Knopf, 2004); 9/11 Commission, *The 9/11 Commission Report: Final Report of the National Commission on Terrorist Attacks Upon the United States* (New York: W.W. Norton, 2004); Anne Stenersen, *Al-Qaida in Afghanistan* (Cambridge: Cambridge University Press, 2017).

46. William Maley, *The Afghanistan Wars* (London: Macmillan/Red Globe Press, 2021) pp.199–201.

47. For details of the operation, see William C. Martel, *Victory in War: Foundations of Modern Military Policy* (Cambridge: Cambridge University Press, 2007) pp.223–42.

48. See Barack Obama, *A Promised Land* (New York: Viking, 2020) pp.676–701.

49. For a detailed account, see Ahmed Rashid, *Descent into Chaos: The United States and the Failure of Nation Building in Pakistan, Afghanistan, and Central Asia* (New York: Viking Press, 2008) pp.90–3.

50. Ayesha Jalal, *The Struggle for Pakistan: A Muslim Homeland and Global Politics* (Cambridge: Harvard University Press, 2014) p.327.

51. For detailed discussion of the agreement, see William Maley, *The Afghanistan Wars* (London: Macmillan/Red Globe Press, 2021) pp.215–19.

52. See Alex Strick van Linschoten and Felix Kuehn, *An Enemy We Created: The Myth of the Taliban/Al Qaeda Merger in Afghanistan, 1970–2010* (London: Hurst & Co., 2012) pp.219–60.

53. See Hamid Enayat, *Modern Islamic Political Thought: The Response of the Shīʿī and Sunnī Muslims to the Twentieth Century* (London: Macmillan, 1982) p.132.

54. See John Locke, *Two Treatises of Government* (Cambridge: Cambridge University Press, 1988) pp. 330–49; Jean-Jacques Rousseau, *The Social Contract and Discourses* (London: J.M. Dent, 1973) pp. 173–5.

55. Quoted in William Maley, *The Foreign Policy of the Taliban* (New York: Council on Foreign Relations, 2000) p. 22.

56. There are also distinct echoes, from the nineteenth century, of Dostoevskii's 'Legend of the Grand Inquisitor', where a returning Christ is arrested as a heretic for threatening the Inquisitor's totalitarian order: see F.M. Dostoevskii, *Brat'ia Karamazovy* (Moscow: Izdatel'stvo "Khudozhestvennaia literatura", 1985) pp. 161–73.

57. See Omar Sadr, *The Republic and Its Enemies: The Status of the Republic in Afghanistan* (Kabul: Afghan Institute for Strategic Studies, January 2021).

58. J.G.A. Pocock, *The Machiavellian Moment: Florentine Political Thought and the Atlantic Republican Tradition* (Princeton: Princeton University Press, 1975).

59. Philip Pettit, *Republicanism: A Theory of Freedom and Government* (Oxford: Oxford University Press, 1997) pp. 51–79.

60. Philip Pettit, *On the People's Terms: A Republican Theory and Model of Democracy* (Cambridge: Cambridge University Press, 2012) p. 13.

61. Philip Pettit, *On the People's Terms: A Republican Theory and Model of Democracy* (Cambridge: Cambridge University Press, 2012) p. 22. See also Quentin Skinner, *Liberty before Liberalism* (Cambridge: Cambridge University Press, 1998) pp. 69–77.

62. In similar vein, the theorist Robert A. Dahl saw 'democracy' as an ultimate ideal, and 'polyarchy' as its real-world variant with high levels of participation and contestation: see Robert A. Dahl, *Polyarchy: Participation and Opposition* (New Haven: Yale University Press, 1971).

63. See Patricia Springborg, *Western Republicanism and the Oriental Prince* (Oxford: Polity Press, 1992) pp. 261–9; see also Ira M. Lapidus, *A History of Islamic Societies* (Cambridge: Cambridge University Press, 2002) pp. 147–55; Patricia Crone, *God's Rule: Government and Islam. Six Centuries of Medieval Islamic Political Thought* (New York: Columbia University Press, 2004) pp. 148–96.

64. For discussion of a rigidly totalitarian Taliban text, *Al Imarat al Islamiah wa Nizamuha*, authored by Taliban 'chief justice' Abdul Hakim Haqqani and released in May 2022, see Maryam Baryalay and Abdul Mateen Imran, 'Do the Taliban have transnational ambitions?', *The Diplomat*, 29 July 2022.

65. Walter Ullmann, *Medieval Political Thought* (London: Penguin, 1975) pp. 145–6.

66. BBC *Newshour*, 13 November 2001.

67. Carter Malkasian, 'What America Didn't Understand About Its Longest War', *Politico*, 6 July 2021.

68. *A Survey of the Afghan People: Afghanistan in 2019* (Kabul: The Asia Foundation, 2019) pp. 19, 315.

69. Susannah George, Missy Ryan, Tyler Pager, Pamela Constable, John Hudson and Griff Witte, 'Surprise, panic and fateful choices: The day America lost its longest war', *The Washington Post*, 28 August 2021.

70. Recriminations persist as to the adequacy of preparation for evacuation. See Dan Lamothe and Alex Horton, 'Documents reveal U.S. Military's frustration

with White House, diplomats over Afghanistan evacuation', *The Washington Post*, 8 February 2022.

71. Cheryl Benard, 'What do the Taliban Really Want?', *The National Interest*, 24 August 2021. Dr Benard's biographical note at the end of this article did not mention that she was married to the architect of the 29 February 2020 agreement, Dr Khalilzad. See Zalmay Khalilzad, *The Envoy: From Kabul to the White House, My Journey Through a Turbulent World* (New York: St Martin's Press, 2016) p.49.

72. *Final Report of the Commission of Experts Established Pursuant to Security Council Resolution 780 (1992)* (New York: United Nations, S/1994/674, 27 May 1994) para.130 (emphasis added).

73. Glenn Kessler, 'The Afghan evacuation and the war—by the numbers', *The Washington Post*, 2 September 2021.

74. See Thurston Clarke, *Honorable Exit: How a Few Brave Americans Risked All to Save Our Vietnamese Allies at the End of the War* (New York: Doubleday, 2019).

75. Gerry Shih, Niha Masih and Dan Lamothe, 'The story of an Afghan man who fell from the sky', *The Washington Post*, 26 August 2021. One of the authors witnessed these events from a plane that was stranded for 3–4 hours because civilians had taken over the runway; the plane departed only after NATO forces had cleared the runway.

76. Yaroslav Trofimov, Nancy A. Youssef and Sune Engel Rasmussen, 'Kabul Airport Attack Kills 13 U.S. Service Members, at Least 90 Afghans', *The Wall Street Journal*, 27 August 2021; Helene Cooper, Eric Schmitt and Thomas Gibbons Neff, 'As U.S. troops searched Afghans, a bomber in the crowd moved in', *The New York Times*, 27 August 2021.

77. Carlotta Gall, 'As the Taliban tighten their grip, fears of retribution grow', *The New York Times*, 29 August 2021. See also Shuja Jamal, 'When Diplomacy is More Harmful to Human Rights than Conflict: The Effects of America's Deal with the Taliban', *Australian Journal of Human Rights*, 2022, DOI: 10.1080/1323238X.2022.2135168.

78. For background to this network, see Vahid Brown and Don Rassler, *Fountainhead of Jihad: The Haqqani Nexus, 1973–2012* (New York: Oxford University Press, 2013).

79. Elisabeth Bumiller and Jane Perlez, 'Pakistan's spies are tied to raid on U.S. embassy', *The New York Times*, 23 September 2011.

80. See https://www.fbi.gov/wanted/terrorinfo/sirajuddin-haqqani. For further discussion of Haqqani's influence, see Abdul Sayed and Colin P. Clarke, 'With Haqqanis at the Helm, the Taliban Will Grow Even More Extreme', *Foreignpolicy. com*, 4 November 2021.

81. 'Didar-e wazir-e dakhela-i Taliban ba khanehwadaha-i muhajiman-e koshta shoda-e intehari', *BBC Persian*, 19 October 2021; Thomas Gibbons-Neff, Sharif Hassan and Ruhullah Khapalwak, 'Taliban honor suicide bombers' "sacrifices" in bid to rewrite history', *The New York Times*, 23 October 2021.

82. For overviews, see *Human Rights in Afghanistan 15 August 2021–15 June 2022* (Kabul: United Nations Assistance Mission in Afghanistan, July 2022); *Situation of Human Rights in Afghanistan: Report of the Special Rapporteur on the Situation of Human Rights in Afghanistan* (Geneva: Human Rights Council, United Nations, A/HRC/51/6, 6 September 2022).

83. Alissa J. Rubin, 'Threats and fear cause Afghan women's protections to vanish overnight', *The New York Times*, 4 September 2021; *Afghanistan: Taliban Abuses Cause Widespread Fear* (New York: Human Rights Watch, 23 September 2021); *Afghanistan: Death in slow motion: Women and girls under Taliban rule* (London: Amnesty International, ASA 11/5685/2022, 27 July 2022).

84. Amanda Taub, 'Why the Taliban's repression of women may be more tactical than ideological', *The New York Times*, 4 October 2021.

85. Heather Barr, 'For Afghan Women, the Frightening Return of "Vice and Virtue"', *Foreign Policy in Focus*, 29 September 2021.

86. Erin Cunningham and Claire Parker, 'Taliban hunting for "collaborators" in major cities, threat assessment prepared for the United Nations warns', *The Washington Post*, 20 August 2021.

87. Charlie Faulkner, 'Afghanistan's "disappeared" women: an arrest by the Taliban, then a bullet-riddled body', *The Times*, 27 January 2022.

88. *Afghanistan: Taliban responsible for brutal massacre of Hazara men—new investigation* (London: Amnesty International, 19 August 2021). See also *The Situation of the Hazara in Afghanistan* (London: The Hazara Inquiry, August 2022); *Afghanistan: ISIS Group Targets Religious Minorities: Taliban Need to Protect, Assist Hazara, Other At-Risk Communities* (New York: Human Rights Watch, 6 September 2022).

89. Sune Engel Rasmussen and Ehsanullah Amiri, 'Taliban Evict Hazara Shiite Muslims From Villages, Rewarding Loyalists', *The Wall Street Journal*, 30 September 2021; *Afghanistan: Taliban Forcibly Evict Minority Shia* (New York: Human Rights Watch, 22 October 2021); Thomas Gibbons-Neff and Yaqoob Akbary, 'In Afghanistan, "who has the guns gets the land"', *The New York Times*, 3 December 2021.

90. 'Blast hits mosque in northeastern Afghanistan, killing worshippers', *Reuters*, 8 October 2021.

91. Ezzatullah Mehrdad, Helier Cheung and Susanne George, 'Suicide bombers hit Shiite mosque in Afghanistan killing dozens—the second such attack in a week', *The Washington Post*, 15 October 2021.

92. Ali Yawar Adili, *A Community Under Attack: How successive governments failed west Kabul and the Hazaras who live there* (Kabul: Afghanistan Analysts Network, 17 January 2022).

93. Christina Goldbaum and Yaqoob Akbary, 'Over a million flee as Afghanistan's economy collapses', *The New York Times*, 3 February 2022.

94. Herbert Butterfield, *The Whig Interpretation of History* (London: G. Bell & Sons, 1931).

95. Zara Steiner, *The Triumph of the Dark: European International History 1933–1939* (Oxford: Oxford University Press, 2011).

96. On deductive approaches, see Carl G. Hempel, *Aspects of Scientific Explanation and other Essays in the Philosophy of Science* (New York: The Free Press, 1965) pp.231–43. On compositive explanation, see Arthur Lee Burns, 'International Theory and Historical Explanation', *History and Theory*, vol.1, no.1, 1960, pp.55–74 at pp.65–6.

97. For a broader discussion of conceptual analysis, see Terence Ball, James Farr, and Russell L. Hanson (eds), *Political Innovation and Conceptual Change* (Cambridge: Cambridge University Press, 1989).

98. Giovanni Sartori, 'Concept Misformation in Comparative Politics', *American Political Science Review*, vol.64, no.4, December 1970, pp.1033–53 at p.1035.

99. See the remarks of Adam Przeworski in Atul Kohli, Peter Evans, Peter J. Katzenstein, Adam Przeworski, Susanne Hoeber Rudolph, James C. Scott and Theda Skocpol, 'The Role of Theory in Comparative Politics: A Symposium', *World Politics*, vol.48, no.1, October 1995, pp.1–49 at p.16.

100. Isaiah Berlin, *Four Essays on Liberty* (Oxford: Oxford University Press, 1969) p.xxix.

2.   THE PROBLEM OF POLITICAL LEGITIMACY

1. Robert Jervis, *System Effects: Complexity in Political and Social Life* (Princeton: Princeton University Press, 1997) p.6.

2. For some overviews, see Rodney Barker, *Political Legitimacy and the State* (Oxford: Oxford University Press, 1990); David Beetham, *The Legitimation of Power* (London: Macmillan, 1991); Rodney Barker, *Legitimating Identities: The Self-Presentations of Rulers and Subjects* (Cambridge: Cambridge University Press, 2001); Ian Clark, *Legitimacy in International Society* (Oxford: Oxford University Press, 2005); Bruce Gilley, *The Right to Rule: How States Win and Lose Legitimacy* (New York: Columbia University Press, 2009); Wojciech Sadurski, Michael Sevel and Kevin Walton (eds), *Legitimacy: The State and Beyond* (Oxford: Oxford University Press, 2019); Srinjoy Bose, 'Legitimacy in Statebuilding', in Scott Romaniuk and Péter Marton (eds), *The Palgrave Encyclopedia of Global Security Studies* (London: Palgrave Macmillan, 2022).

3. John Milton, *Paradise Lost* (London: The Folio Society, 2015) p.21.

4. Jean-Jacques Rousseau, *The Social Contract and Discourses* (London: J.M. Dent, 1973) p.168.

5. Edmund Burke, 'Speech on Moving Resolutions for Conciliation with the Colonies', in *Select Works of Edmund Burke* (Indianapolis: Liberty Fund, 1999) Vol.I, p.236.

6. See Brian Barry, *Sociologists, Economists and Democracy* (Chicago: University of Chicago Press, 1970) pp.70–1.

7. Jan Pakulski, 'Legitimacy and Mass Compliance: Reflections on Max Weber and Soviet-Type Societies', *British Journal of Political Science*, vol.16, no.1, 1986, pp.35–56.

8. Richard J. Evans, *The Third Reich at War: How the Nazis Led Germany from Conquest to Disaster* (London: Penguin, 2009) pp.420–3, 447–50.

9. See Ian Kershaw, *The End: Hitler's Germany, 1944–45* (London: Allen Lane, 2011) pp.390–1, 398–400.

10. Lucian W. Pye, 'The Legitimacy Crisis', in Leonard Binder, James S. Coleman, Joseph LaPalombara, Lucian W. Pye, Sidney Verba and Myron Weiner, *Crises and Sequences in Political Development* (Princeton: Princeton University Press, 1971) pp.135–58 at p.136.

11. Max Weber, *Economy and Society: An Outline of Interpretive Sociology* (Berkeley & Los Angeles: University of California Press, 1978) Vol.I, p.215.

12. See Harry Eckstein, *Regarding Politics: Essays on Political Theory, Stability and Change* (Berkeley & Los Angeles: University of California Press, 1992) p.188.

13. See Graeme Gill, 'Changing Patterns of Systemic Legitimation in the USSR', *Coexistence*, vol.23, no.3, 1986, pp.247–66.

14. T.H. Rigby, 'Introduction: Political Legitimacy, Weber, and Communist Mono-organisational Systems', in T.H. Rigby and Ferenc Fehér (eds), *Political Legitimation in Communist States* (London: Macmillan, 1982) pp.1–26.

15. Graeme Gill, *Symbols and Legitimacy in Soviet Politics* (Cambridge: Cambridge University Press, 2011).

16. Graeme Gill, 'Personality Cult, Political Culture and Party Structure', *Studies in Comparative Communism*, vol.17, no.2, Summer 1984, pp.111–21.

17. Blaise Pascal, *Pensées* (London: Penguin, 1995) p.127.

18. See Keith Stanski, '"So These Folks are Aggressive": An Orientalist Reading of "Afghan Warlords"', *Security Dialogue*, vol.40, no.1, February 2009, pp.73–94.

19. See Romain Malejacq, *Warlord Survival: The Delusion of State Building in Afghanistan* (Ithaca: Cornell University Press, 2020); Matthew P. Dearing, *Militia Order in Afghanistan: Guardians or Gangsters?* (London: Routledge, 2022).

20. Haroun Rahimi, 'Lessons from Afghanistan's history: how not to fix a failed state', *The Diplomat*, 6 October 2021.

21. See William Maley, 'Political Legitimation in Contemporary Afghanistan', *Asian Survey*, vol.27, no.6, June 1987, pp.705–25; Amin Saikal and William Maley, *Regime Change in Afghanistan: Foreign Intervention and the Politics of Legitimacy* (Boulder: Westview Press, 1991); Abdul Warath Radman, 'Mashruiat-e siasi chist?', *Hasht-e Sobh*, 24 October 2021.

22. See Robert E. Goodin, 'Institutions and their design', in Robert E. Goodin (ed.), *The Theory of Institutional Design* (Cambridge: Cambridge University Press, 1996) pp.1–53.

23. S. Frederick Starr, 'Sovereignty and Legitimacy in Afghan Nation-Building', in Francis Fukuyama (ed.), *Nation-Building: Beyond Afghanistan and Iraq* (Baltimore: The Johns Hopkins University Press, 2006) pp.107–24 at p.112.

24. See Francis Fukuyama, *State-Building: Governance and World Order in the 21ˢᵗ Century* (Ithaca: Cornell University Press, 2004).

25. Joel S. Migdal, *State in Society: Studying How States and Societies Transform and Constitute One Another* (Cambridge: Cambridge University Press, 2001) p.145. On the diverse factors that can underpin regime breakdown, see Vilde Lunnan Djuve, Carl Henrik Knutsen and Tore Wig, 'Patterns of Regime Breakdown Since the French Revolution', *Comparative Political Studies*, vol.53, no.6, May 2020, pp.923–58.

26. Russell Hardin, *One for All: The Logic of Group Conflict* (Princeton: Princeton University Press, 1995) p.57.

27. See *Shenasnamah-e mukhtasar-e edarat-e mahali-e Afghanistan* (Kabul: Islamic Republic of Afghanistan, 2018).

28. See Ehsan Qaane and Thomas Ruttig, *A Half-Solution: Provincial Councils get oversight authority back—for the time being* (Kabul: Afghanistan Analysts Network, 12 May 2015).

29. Mohammad Qadam Shah, 'The politics of budgetary capture in rentier states: who gets what, when and how in Afghanistan', *Central Asian Survey*, vol.41, no.1, March 2022, pp.138–60.

30. Frances Z. Brown, *Aiding Afghan Local Governance: What Went Wrong?* (Washington DC: Carnegie Endowment for International Peace, 8 November 2021).

31. John Stuart Mill, *Utilitarianism, Liberty and Representative Government* (London: J.M. Dent, 1910) p.346.

32. See Hamish Nixon, *Subnational State-Building in Afghanistan* (Kabul: Afghanistan Research and Evaluation Unit, April 2008).

33. John Stuart Mill, *Utilitarianism, Liberty and Representative Government* (London: J.M. Dent, 1910) pp.354–9.

34. James N. Rosenau, 'Governance, order, and change in world politics', in James N. Rosenau and Ernst-Otto Czempiel (eds), *Governance Without Government: Order and Change in World Politics* (Cambridge: Cambridge University Press, 1992) pp.1–29 at pp.4–5.

35. Ilia Murtazashvili and Jennifer Brick Murtazashvili, 'The political economy of state building', *Journal of Public Finance and Public Choice*, vol.34, no.2, October 2019, pp.189–207 at p.199. See also Jennifer Brick Murtazashvili, *Informal Order and the State in Afghanistan* (Cambridge: Cambridge University Press, 2016); Suzanne Levi-Sanchez, *Bridging State and Civil Society: Informal Organizations in Tajik/Afghan Badakhshan* (Ann Arbor: University of Michigan Press, 2021).

36. Astri Suhrke, *When More Is Less: The International Project in Afghanistan* (New York: Columbia University Press, 2011) p.169.

37. Juan Linz, 'The Perils of Presidentialism', *Journal of Democracy*, vol.1, no.1, Winter 1990, pp.51–69. See also Matthew Soberg Shugart and John M. Carey, *Presidents and Assemblies: Constitutional Design and Electoral Dynamics* (Cambridge: Cambridge University Press, 1992); Alfred Stepan and Cindy Skach, 'Constitutional Frameworks and Democratic Consolidation: Parliamentarianism versus Presidentialism', *World Politics*, vol.46, no.1, October 1993, pp.1–22; Giovanni Sartori, *Comparative Constitutional Engineering: An Inquiry into Structures, Incentives and Outcomes* (London: Macmillan, 1997); M. Steven Fish, 'Stronger Legislatures, Stronger Democracies', *Journal of Democracy*, vol.17, no.1, January 2006, pp.5–20.

38. Carlotta Gall, 'Afghan talks adjourn, deeply divided on ethnic lines', *The New York Times*, 2 January 2004.

39. See Douglass C. North, John Joseph Wallis and Barry R. Weingast, *Violence and Social Orders: A Conceptual Framework for Interpreting Recorded Human History* (Cambridge: Cambridge University Press, 2009) pp.137–40. More generally on the contributions of institutional dysfunctionality to failings in state performance and to diminutions in legitimacy, see Daron Acemoglu and James A. Robinson, *Why Nations Fail: The Origins of Power, Prosperity and Poverty* (London: Profile Books, 2012) pp.368–403; Francis Fukuyama, *Political Order and Political Decay: From the Industrial Revolution to the Globalization of Democracy* (New York: Farrar, Straus & Giroux, 2014) pp.461–6.

40. Timor Sharan and Srinjoy Bose, 'Political networks and the 2014 Afghan presidential election: power restructuring, ethnicity and state stability', *Conflict, Security and Development*, vol.16, no.6, November 2016, pp.613–33 at p.615.

41. Timor Sharan, 'The Dynamics of Informal Political Networks and Statehood in Post-2001 Afghanistan: A Case Study of the 2010–2011 Special Election

Court Crisis', *Central Asian Survey*, vol.32, no.3, September 2013, pp.336–52 at p.336.

42. Timor Sharan, 'The Dynamics of Informal Political Networks and Statehood in Post-2001 Afghanistan: A Case Study of the 2010–2011 Special Election Court Crisis', *Central Asian Survey*, vol.32, no.3, September 2013, pp.336–52 at p.337. For further details of Sharan's arguments, see Timor Sharan, 'The Dynamics of Elite Networks and Patron-Client Relations in Afghanistan', *Europe-Asia Studies*, vol.63, no.6, August 2011, pp.1109–27; Timor Sharan, *Dawlat-e shabakahi: Rabeta-i qodrat wa sarwat dar Afghanistan pas az sal-e 2001* (Kabul: Vazhah Publications, 2017); Timor Sharan, 'Webs and Spiders: Four Decades of Violence, Intervention, and Statehood in Afghanistan (1978–2016)', in M. Nazif Shahrani (ed.), *Modern Afghanistan: The Impact of 40 Years of War* (Bloomington: Indiana University Press, 2018) pp.102–20; Timor Sharan, *Inside Afghanistan: Political Networks, Informal Order, and State Disruption* (London: Routledge, 2023).

43. Timor Sharan, *Inside Afghanistan: Political Networks, Informal Order, and State Disruption* (London: Routledge, 2023) p.292.

44. William Maley, *Transition in Afghanistan: Hope, Despair and the Limits of Statebuilding* (London: Routledge, 2018) pp.37–40.

45. Sarah Chayes, *Thieves of State: Why Corruption Threatens Global Security* (New York: W.W. Norton, 2015) pp.59–60.

46. See Whit Mason (ed.), *The Rule of Law in Afghanistan: Missing in Inaction* (Cambridge: Cambridge University Press, 2011); William Maley, *Transition in Afghanistan: Hope, Despair and the Limits of Statebuilding* (London: Routledge, 2018) pp.129–45; William Maley, 'State Strength and the Rule of Law', in Srinjoy Bose, Nishank Motwani and William Maley (eds), *Afghanistan—Challenges and Prospects* (London: Routledge, 2018) pp.63–77.

47. *A Survey of the Afghan People: Afghanistan in 2019* (Kabul: The Asia Foundation, 2019) p.305.

48. *A Survey of the Afghan People: Afghanistan in 2019* (Kabul: The Asia Foundation, 2019) p.311.

49. Max Weber, *Economy and Society: An Outline of Interpretive Sociology* (Berkeley & Los Angeles: University of California Press, 1978) Vol.I, p.56.

50. See M. Nazif Shahrani, 'The future of the state and the structure of community governance in Afghanistan', in William Maley (ed.), *Fundamentalism Reborn? Afghanistan and the Taliban* (London: Hurst & Co., 1998) pp.212–42 at p.238; M. Nazif Shahrani, 'The state and community self-governance: paths to stability and human security in post-2014 Afghanistan', in Srinjoy Bose, Nishank Motwani and William Maley (eds), *Afghanistan—Challenges and Prospects* (London: Routledge, 2018) pp.43–62.

51. See William Maley, *Rescuing Afghanistan* (London: Hurst & Co., 2006) pp.57–8.

52. *A Survey of the Afghan People: Afghanistan in 2019* (Kabul: The Asia Foundation, 2019) pp.279, 280.

53. *A Survey of the Afghan People: Afghanistan in 2019* (Kabul: The Asia Foundation, 2019) p.282.

54. *A Survey of the Afghan People: Afghanistan in 2019* (Kabul: The Asia Foundation, 2019) p.298.

55. *A Survey of the Afghan People: Afghanistan in 2019* (Kabul: The Asia Foundation, 2019) pp.295, 296.

56. *A Survey of the Afghan People: Afghanistan in 2019* (Kabul: The Asia Foundation, 2019) p.295.

57. See Lucien W. Pye, *Warlord Politics: Conflict and Coalition in the Modernization of Republican China* (New York: Praeger, 1971); Hsi-Sheng Ch'i, *Warlord Politics in China 1916–1928* (Stanford: Stanford University Press, 1976).

58. See Antonio Giustozzi, *Empires of Mud: War and Warlords in Afghanistan* (London: Hurst & Co., 2008); Dipali Mukhopadhyay, *Warlords as Bureaucrats: The Afghan Experience* (Washington DC: Carnegie Endowment for International Peace, August 2009); Dipali Mukhopadhyay, *Warlords, Strongman Governors and the State in Afghanistan* (New York: Cambridge University Press, 2014); Romain Malejacq, *Warlord Survival: The Delusion of State Building in Afghanistan* (Ithaca: Cornell University Press, 2020).

59. Romain Malejacq, *Warlord Survival: The Delusion of State Building in Afghanistan* (Ithaca: Cornell University Press, 2020) p.169.

60. See, for example, Sarah Chayes, *On Corruption in America and What Is at Stake* (New York: Vintage Books, 2020) pp.3–9.

61. Hasan Kakar, 'The Fall of the Afghan Monarchy in 1973', *International Journal of Middle East Studies,* vol.9, no.2, April 1978, pp.195–214 at p.200.

62. Leslie Holmes, *Rotten States? Corruption, Post-Communism and Neoliberalism* (Durham: Duke University Press, 2006) pp.17–31. See also Michael Johnston, *Syndromes of Corruption: Wealth, Power and Democracy* (Cambridge: Cambridge University Press, 2005).

63. Georg Cremer, *Corruption and Development Aid: Confronting the Challenges* (Boulder: Lynne Rienner, 2008) p.9.

64. Georg Cremer, *Corruption and Development Aid: Confronting the Challenges* (Boulder: Lynne Rienner, 2008) pp.10, 14.

65. Pamela Constable, 'Inexplicable wealth of Afghan elite sows bitterness', *The Washington Post*, 12 January 2009.

66. Eric M. Uslaner, *The Historical Roots of Corruption: Mass Education, Economic Inequality, and State Capacity* (Cambridge: Cambridge University Press, 2017) p.2.

67. Eric M. Uslaner, *Corruption, Inequality, and the Rule of Law* (Cambridge: Cambridge University Press, 2008) p.235.

68. Eric M. Uslaner, *Corruption, Inequality, and the Rule of Law* (Cambridge: Cambridge University Press, 2008) p.236. See also Alina Mungiu-Pippidi, *The Quest for Good Governance: How Societies Develop Control of Corruption* (Cambridge: Cambridge University Press, 2015).

69. Jennifer Brick Murtazashvili, 'The Collapse of Afghanistan', *Journal of Democracy*, vol.33, no.1, January 2022, pp.40–54 at p.52.

70. Mancur Olson, *The Logic of Collective Action: Public Goods and the Theory of Groups* (Cambridge: Harvard University Press, 1965).

71. See Rajiv Chandrasekaran, 'Karzai seeks to limit role of U.S. corruption investigators', *The Washington Post*, 9 September 2010.

72. See Joshua Partlow, *A Kingdom of Their Own: The Family Karzai and the Afghan Disaster* (New York: Alfred A. Knopf, 2016) pp.247–53.

73. See Timor Sharan, *Inside Afghanistan: Political Networks, Informal Order, and State Disruption* (London: Routledge, 2023) p.275.

74. *Corruption Perception Index 2020* (Berlin: Transparency International, 2021) pp.3, 4, 14.

75. *Corruption in Afghanistan: Recent patterns and trends. Summary findings* (Vienna: United Nations Office on Drugs and Crime, 2012) p.5.

76. *Fighting Corruption in Afghanistan: Stepping Up Transparency, Integrity and Accountability* (Kabul: United Nations Assistance Mission in Afghanistan, August 2021) p.10.

77. On the potential threat to legitimacy arising from disrespect for the dignity of the individual, see Florian Weigand, *Waiting for Dignity: Legitimacy and Authority in Afghanistan* (New York: Columbia University Press, 2022) pp.272–94.

78. *A Survey of the Afghan People: Afghanistan in 2019* (Kabul: The Asia Foundation, 2019) pp.142, 143.

79. Quoted in James M. Minifie, *Who's Your Fat Friend? Style in Politics* (Philadelphia: J.B. Lippincott, 1968) p.104.

80. John Emerich Edward Dalberg-Acton, First Baron Acton, *Historical Essays and Studies* (London: Macmillan & Co., 1907) p.504.

81. See Iavor Rangelov and Marika Theros, 'Abuse of power and conflict persistence in Afghanistan', *Conflict, Security and Development*, vol.12, no.3, July 2012, pp.227–248.

82. See *Blood-Stained Hands: Past Atrocities in Kabul and Afghanistan's Legacy of Impunity* (New York: Human Rights Watch, 2005) pp.70–100.

83. Rama Mani, *Ending Impunity and Building Justice in Afghanistan* (Kabul: Afghanistan Research and Evaluation Unit, 2003) p.20.

84. *A Survey of the Afghan People: Afghanistan in 2019* (Kabul: The Asia Foundation, 2019) pp.300–1.

85. William Maley, *Transition in Afghanistan: Hope, Despair and the Limits of Statebuilding* (London: Routledge, 2018) pp.129–45.

86. Joseph Raz, *The Authority of Law: Essays on Law and Morality* (Oxford: Oxford University Press, 1979) pp.214–218.

87. *A Survey of the Afghan People: Afghanistan in 2019* (Kabul: The Asia Foundation, 2019) p.303. For discussion of ways in which the roles of traditional institutions could be enhanced without violating human rights standards, see Ali Wardak, 'Building a post-war justice system in Afghanistan', *Crime, Law and Social Change*, vol.41, no.4, May 2004, pp.319–41; *Afghanistan Human Development Report 2007. Bridging Modernity and Tradition: Rule of Law and the Search for Justice* (Kabul: United Nations Development Programme, 2007); Ali Wardak, 'State and Non-State Justice Systems in Afghanistan: The Need for Synergy', *University of Pennsylvania Journal of International Law*, vol.32, no.5, 2011, pp.1305–24. On Taliban steps to exploit the weaknesses of the state-based 'justice system', see Adam Baczko, *La Guerre par le Droit: Les Tribunaux Taliban en Afghanistan* (Paris: CNRS Éditions, 2021). See also Geoffrey Swenson, *Contending Orders: Legal Pluralism and the Rule of Law* (New York: Oxford University Press, 2022).

88. On land issues, see Jennifer Brick Murtazashvili and Ilia Murtazashvili, *Land, the State, and War: Property Institutions and Political Order in Afghanistan* (Cambridge: Cambridge University Press, 2021).

89. See Timor Sharan, *Inside Afghanistan: Political Networks, Informal Order, and State Disruption* (London: Routledge, 2023) p.265.

90. On challenges of accountability, see Carol Wang, 'Rule of Law in Afghanistan: Enabling a Constitutional Framework for Local Accountability', *Harvard International Law Journal*, vol.55, no.1, Winter 2014, pp.211–49.

91. See Geoffrey Swenson, 'Why U.S. Efforts to Promote the Rule of Law in Afghanistan Failed', *International Security*, vol.42, no.1, Summer 2017, pp.114–51.

92. *Afghanistan: Repeal Amnesty Law. Measure Brought into Force by Karzai Means Atrocities Will Go Unpunished* (New York: Human Rights Watch, 10 March 2010); Aziz Hakimi and Astri Suhrke, 'A Poisonous Chalice: The Struggle for Human Rights and Accountability in Afghanistan', *Nordic Journal of Human Rights*, vol.31, no.2, 2013, pp.201–23 at p.214. Article 94 of the 2004 Constitution set out circumstances in which a bill could become law without presidential endorsement.

93. See Adam Przeworski, *Why Bother with Elections?* (Oxford: Polity Press, 2018).

94. Jørgen Elklit and Palle Svensson, 'What Makes Elections Free and Fair?', *Journal of Democracy*, vol.8, no.3, July 1997, pp.32–46 at p.35.

95. Jørgen Elklit and Michael Maley, 'Why Ballot Secrecy Still Matters', *Journal of Democracy*, vol.30, no.3, July 2019, pp.61–75.

96. See Nic Cheeseman and Brian Klaas, *How to Rig an Election* (New Haven: Yale University Press, 2018); Richard L. Hasen, *Election Meltdown: Dirty Tricks, Distrust, and the Threat to American Democracy* (New Haven: Yale University Press, 2020).

97. William Maley, *Transition in Afghanistan: Hope, Despair and the Limits of Statebuilding* (London: Routledge, 2018) p.114.

98. See William Maley and Michael Maley, 'Appraising Electoral Fraud: Tensions and Complexities', *Conflict, Security and Development*, vol.16, no.6, 2016, pp.653–671; William Maley, *Transition in Afghanistan: Hope, Despair and the Limits of Statebuilding* (London: Routledge, 2018) pp.105–25; Timor Sharan, *Inside Afghanistan: Political Networks, Informal Order, and State Disruption* (London: Routledge, 2023) pp.188–213.

99. Robert M. Gates, *Duty: Memoirs of a Secretary at War* (New York: Alfred A. Knopf, 2014) pp.340–1.

100. For varying perspectives, see *Press Statement: EU EOM urges immediate action against large-scale fraudulent results* (Kabul: European Union Election Observation Mission to Afghanistan, 2009); Jean Mackenzie, 'Afghanistan's sham vote', *The New York Times*, 26 August 2009; Jerome Starkey and Jon Swain, 'President Hamid Karzai takes 100% of votes in opposition stronghold', *The Sunday Times*, 6 September 2009; Jon Boone, 'Afghanistan: anatomy of an election disaster', *The Guardian*, 20 October 2009.

101. Mikhail Myakgov, Peter C. Ordeshook and Dimitri Shakin, *The Forensics of Election Fraud: Russia and Ukraine* (Cambridge: Cambridge University Press, 2009).

102. See Nils B. Weidmann and Michael Callen, 'Violence and Election Fraud: Evidence from Afghanistan', *British Journal of Political Science*, vol.43, no.1, January 2013, pp.53–75 at p.74.

103. See William Maley and Michael Maley, 'Appraising Electoral Fraud: Tensions and Complexities', *Conflict, Security and Development*, vol. 16, no. 6, 2016, p. 661.

104. Dexter Filkins, 'The Great American Arm-Twist in Afghanistan', *The New York Times*, 25 October 2009.

105. Robert M. Gates, *Duty: Memoirs of a Secretary at War* (New York: Alfred A. Knopf, 2014) p. 358; George Packer, *Our Man: Richard Holbrooke and the End of the American Century* (New York: Vintage Books, 2019) pp. 475–88.

106. Kai Eide, *Power Struggle Over Afghanistan: An Inside Look at What Went Wrong—and What We Can Do to Repair the Damage* (New York: Skyhorse Publishing, 2012) p. 249.

107. '2010 Elections: IEC Announcement, International Views', Cable Reference ID 10KABUL10_a, U.S. Embassy, Kabul, 3 January 2010.

108. Thomas H. Johnson, 'The myth of Afghan electoral democracy: the irregularities of the 2014 presidential election', *Small Wars and Insurgencies*, vol. 29, nos. 5–6, November 2018, pp. 1006–39 at p. 1014.

109. Nuristani, who resigned on 26 March 2016, was later appointed by Ghani to the Upper House of Parliament, the *Meshrano Jirga*, but in 2019, he was convicted of fraud offences in the US, unrelated to the 2014 Afghan election: see United States Department of Justice, *Afghan Senator Convicted of Federal Welfare Fraud* (San Diego: The United States Attorney's Office, Southern District of California, 11 December 2019).

110. Thomas H. Johnson, 'The myth of Afghan electoral democracy: the irregularities of the 2014 presidential election', *Small Wars and Insurgencies*, vol. 29, nos. 5–6, November 2018, pp. 1006–39.

111. Thomas H. Johnson, 'The myth of Afghan electoral democracy: the irregularities of the 2014 presidential election', *Small Wars and Insurgencies*, vol. 29, nos. 5–6, November 2018, pp. 1006–39, p. 1022.

112. Emma Graham-Harrison, 'Afghan Election Crisis: "Stuffed Sheep" Recordings Suggest Large-scale Fraud', *The Guardian*, 23 June 2014.

113. Azam Ahmed, 'Claim of fraud in Afghan vote leads official to step down', *The New York Times*, 24 June 2014. President Ghani in May 2020 appointed Amarkhil as State Minister for Parliamentary Affairs, and then Governor of Nangahar; Amarkhil switched sides to the Taliban shortly before Kabul fell in August 2021.

114. Carter Malkasian, *The American War in Afghanistan: A History* (New York: Oxford University Press, 2021) pp. 360–5.

115. *A Survey of the Afghan People: Afghanistan in 2015* (Kabul: The Asia Foundation, 2015) p. 96.

116. Thomas Johnson, 'The 2019 Afghan Presidential Election: An Assessment of Problematic Processes and Results', *Afghanistan*, vol. 4, no. 1, April 2021, pp. 19–46 at pp. 29, 40.

117. Thomas Johnson, 'The 2019 Afghan Presidential Election: An Assessment of Problematic Processes and Results', *Afghanistan*, vol. 4, no. 1, April 2021, pp. 19–46 pp. 25–8.

118. For further discussion, see Arend Lijphart (ed.), *Parliamentary versus Presidential Government* (Oxford: Oxford University Press, 1992).

119. Andrew Wilder, *A House Divided? Analysing the 2005 Afghan Elections* (Kabul: Afghanistan Research and Evaluation Unit, 2005) p.14.

120. Thomas H. Johnson and and Ronald J. Barnhart, 'An Examination of Afghanistan's 2018 Wolesi Jirga Elections: Chaos, Confusion and Fraud', *Journal of Asian Security and International Affairs*, vol.7, no.1, April 2020, pp.57–100 at p.67.

121. Giovanni Sartori, *Parties and Party Systems: A Framework for Analysis* (Cambridge: Cambridge University Press, 1976) p.41.

122. David Hume, 'Of Parties in General', in Eugene F. Miller (ed.), *David Hume: Essays Moral, Political, and Literary* (Indianapolis: Liberty Fund, 1985) pp.54–63.

123. Thomas Ruttig, *Islamists, Leftists—and a Void in the Center: Afghanistan's Political Parties and where they come from (1902–2006)* (Kabul: Konrad Adenauer Stiftung, 2006) p.43.

124. See Marvin G. Weinbaum, 'Afghanistan: Nonparty Parliamentary Democracy', *Journal of Developing Areas*, vol.7, no.1, October 1972, pp.57–74; Marvin G. Weinbaum, 'The Legislator as Intermediary: Integration of the Center and Periphery in Afghanistan', in Albert F. Eldridge (ed.), *Legislatures in Plural Societies: The Search for Cohesion in National Development* (Durham: Duke University Press, 1977) pp.95–121.

125. Astri Suhrke, 'Democratizing a Dependent State: The Case of Afghanistan', *Democratization*, vol.15, no.3, June 2008, pp.630–48 at p.641.

126. Donald Rumsfeld, *Known and Unknown: A Memoir* (New York: Sentinel, 2011) p.408.

127. https://dcas.dmdc.osd.mil/dcas/pages/report_ofs_month.xhtml. By contrast, the United States in 2020 alone experienced on average more than 53 deaths per day in non-suicide gun violence: https://www.gunviolencearchive.org/past-tolls.

128. 'Afghanistan's Ghani says 45,000 security personnel killed since 2014', *BBC News* (Asia), 25 January 2019.

129. See Nicholas O. Alozie and Andrew I.E. Ewoh, 'Citizen Evaluation of Government and Confidence in Public Institutions in Emergent Islamic Democracies: Evidence from Afghanistan', *Journal of Public Management and Social Policy*, vol.23, no.2, Fall 2016, pp.103–30.

130. See Lauren Kay Johnson, 'I helped write the official lies to sell the Afghanistan war', *The Washington Post*, 14 December 2019.

131. *A Survey of the Afghan People: Afghanistan in 2015* (Kabul: The Asia Foundation, 2015) p.6.

132. *A Survey of the Afghan People: Afghanistan in 2019* (Kabul: The Asia Foundation, 2019) pp.279, 280.

133. *The Global State of Democracy Indices: Afghanistan* (Stockholm: International IDEA, 2020).

134. *The State of Democracy in Asia and the Pacific 2021* (Stockholm: International IDEA, 2021) p.16.

135. Timur Kuran, 'Sparks and prairie fires: A theory of unanticipated political revolution', *Public Choice*, vol.61, no.1, April 1989, pp.41–74 at pp.69–70

136. Julian Jackson, *The Fall of France: The Nazi Invasion of 1940* (Oxford: Oxford University Press, 2003) pp.212–13.

3. PATHOLOGIES OF AID AND DEVELOPMENT

1. Michael Carnahan, 'Next Steps in Reforming the Ministry of Finance', in Michael Carnahan, Nick Manning, Richard Bontjer and Stéphane Guimbert (eds), *Reforming Fiscal and Economic Management in Afghanistan* (Washington DC: The World Bank, 2004) pp.123–49.

2. See P.T. Bauer, *Equality, The Third World, and Economic Delusion* (London: Methuen, 1981); Doug Porter, Bryant Allen and Gaye Thompson, *Development in Practice: Paved with Good Intentions* (London: Routledge, 1991).

3. William Maley, 'The Reconstruction of Afghanistan', in Ken Booth and Tim Dunne (eds), *Worlds in Collision: Terror and the Future Global Order* (London and New York: Palgrave, 2002) pp.184–93 at p.184.

4. Quoted in William Maley, *The Afghanistan Wars* (London: Macmillan/Red Globe Press, 2021) p.238.

5. See Erna Solberg, 'From MDGs to SDGs: The Political Value of Common Global Goals', *Harvard International Review*, vol.37, no.1, Fall 2015, pp.58–61.

6. *The Next Frontier: Human Development and the Anthropocene. Briefing note for countries on the 2020 Human Development Report: Afghanistan* (New York: United Nations Development Programme, 2020) p.3.

7. See Nematullah Bizhan, 'Revenue and state building in Afghanistan', in Srinjoy Bose, Nishank Motwani and William Maley (eds), *Afghanistan—Challenges and Prospects* (London: Routledge, 2018) pp.78–89.

8. See Paul Seabright, 'Conflicts of objectives and task allocation in aid agencies', in Bertin Martens, Uwe Mummert, Peter Murrell and Paul Seabright, *The Institutional Economics of Foreign Aid* (Cambridge: Cambridge University Press, 2002) pp.34–68.

9. For some discussion of these challenges, see Ashraf Ghani, Clare Lockhart and Michael Carnahan, *Closing the Sovereignty Gap: An Approach to State-Building* (London: Working Paper no.253, Overseas Development Institute, September 2005); Peter Blunt, Farid Mamundzay, Nader Yama, and Hamidullah Afghan, 'Policy paradigms, subnational governance and the state sovereignty gap in Afghanistan', *Progress in Development Studies*, vol.15, no.3, July 2015, pp.270–85.

10. Niamatullah Ibrahimi and William Maley, *Afghanistan: Politics and Economics in a Globalising State* (London: Routledge, 2020) pp.17–21.

11. See, in particular, Barnett R. Rubin, *The Fragmentation of Afghanistan: State Formation and Collapse in the International System* (New Haven: Yale University Press, 2002).

12. On this point, see Baheer Wardak, 'Motivation in the War in Afghanistan: Building Security Forces and the Counterinsurgency Campaign', unpublished MA thesis, Department of International Relations, The Australian National University, 2011.

13. Nan Tian, *20 years of US military aid to Afghanistan* (Stockholm: SIPRI, 22 September 2021).

14. *Divided Responsibility: Lessons from U.S. Security Sectors Assistance Efforts in Afghanistan* (Arlington: SIGAR 19-39-LL, Special Inspector General for Afghanistan Reconstruction, 13 June 2019) pp.144–7.

15. See Antonio Giustozzi and Mohammed Isaqzadeh, *Policing Afghanistan: The Politics of the Lame Leviathan* (London: Hurst & Co., 2013); Matteo Tondini, *Statebuilding and Justice Reform: Post-Conflict Reconstruction in Afghanistan* (London: Routledge, 2010) pp.47–9.

16. Pashtoon Atif, 'The Impact of Culture on Policing in Afghanistan', in Aaron B. O'Connell (ed.), *Our Latest Longest War: Losing Hearts and Minds in Afghanistan* (Chicago: University of Chicago Press, 2017) pp.131–55 at pp.132–3.

17. Andrew Wilder, *Cops or Robbers?: The Struggle to Reform the Afghan National Police* (Kabul: Afghanistan Research and Evaluation Unit, July 2007).

18. Nan Tian, *20 years of US military aid to Afghanistan* (Stockholm: SIPRI, 22 September 2021).

19. Barnett R. Rubin, *Afghanistan from the Cold War Through the War on Terror* (New York: Oxford University Press, 2013) p.186. Some data collected by the Office of the National Security Council in October 2019 highlight this problem. Afghanistan could only afford National Directorate of Security and Presidential Protection Service salaries in full. The domestic budget paid a minuscule portion of the salaries for police and army. The Office's calculation of defence and security expenditure was as follows. Total security spending amounted to US$5.9 billion, while total domestic revenue was US$2.5 billion. By sector, 66% of security spending was via the Ministry of Defence, 29% via the Ministry of Interior, and 5% via other channels. Of the Defence Ministry's budget, 78% was 'off-budget' in origin, and only 22% 'on-budget'—of which 4% was Afghanistan's contribution. Of the Interior Ministry's budget, 51% was 'off-budget' in origin, and 49% 'on-budget'—of which 14% was Afghanistan's contribution.

20. For details, see Sten Rynning, *NATO in Afghanistan: The Liberal Disconnect* (Stanford: Stanford University Press, 2012) p.57.

21. David Kilcullen and Greg Mills, *The Ledger: Accounting for Failure in Afghanistan* (London: Hurst & Co., 2021) p.174.

22. For detailed discussions, see Nikola Hynek and Péter Marton (eds), *Statebuilding in Afghanistan: Multinational Contributions to Reconstruction* (London: Routledge, 2011); David P. Auerswald and Stephen M. Saideman, *NATO in Afghanistan: Fighting Together, Fighting Alone* (Princeton: Princeton University Press, 2014); William Maley and Susanne Schmeidl (eds), *Reconstructing Afghanistan: Civil-Military Experiences in Comparative Perspective* (London: Routledge, 2015).

23. See, for a careful discussion, David Savage, 'AusAID stabilisation', in John Blaxland, Marcus Fielding and Thea Gellerfy (eds), *Niche Wars: Australia in Afghanistan and Iraq, 2001–2014* (Canberra: ANU Press, 2020) pp.229–47.

24. Renard Sexton, 'Aid as a Tool Against Insurgency: Evidence from Contested and Controlled Territory in Afghanistan', *American Political Science Review*, vol.110, no.4, November 2016, pp.731–49.

25. See Stephen Hoadley, 'New Zealand civil-military relations in Afghanistan: Aims, assessments, and lessons', in William Maley and Susanne Schmeidl (eds), *Reconstructing Afghanistan: Civil-Military Experiences in Comparative Perspective* (London: Routledge, 2015) pp.43–54.

26. See Rory Stewart, 'The Last Days of Intervention: Afghanistan and the Delusions of Maximalism', *Foreign Affairs*, vol.100, no.6, November–December 2021, pp.60–73 at p.70.

27. See William Maley, *Transition in Afghanistan: Hope, Despair and the Limits of Statebuilding* (London: Routledge, 2018) p.v.

28. *Afghanistan Development Update April 2021: Setting Course to Recovery* (Washington DC: The World Bank, April 2021) p.18.

29. Roxanna Shapour, *Realpolitik and the 2021 National Budget: The toxic struggle for money and power that undermined Afghanistan's Republic* (Kabul: Afghanistan Analysts Network, 21 December 2021).

30. Nematullah Bizhan, *Aid Paradoxes in Afghanistan: Building and Undermining the State* (London: Routledge, 2018) p.91.

31. Nematullah Bizhan, *Aid Paradoxes in Afghanistan: Building and Undermining the State* (London: Routledge, 2018) p.97.

32. See Joshua Partlow, *A Kingdom of Their Own: The Family Karzai and the Afghan Disaster* (New York: Alfred A. Knopf, 2016) pp.234–55; Grant McLeod, *Responding to Corruption and the Kabul Bank Collapse* (Washington DC: Special Report no.398, United States Institute of Peace, December 2016); Abdul Qadeer Fitrat, *The Tragedy of Kabul Bank* (New York: Page, 2018); Timor Sharan, *Inside Afghanistan: Political Networks, Informal Order, and State Disruption* (London: Routledge, 2023) pp.247–52.

33. Independent Joint Anti-Corruption Monitoring and Evaluation Committee, *Report of the Public Inquiry into the Kabul Bank Crisis* (Kabul: Independent Joint Anti-Corruption Monitoring and Evaluation Committee, 2012) p.3.

34. James Fontanella-Khan and Robin Wigglesworth, 'Kabul steps in to stop run on biggest bank', *The Financial Times*, 6 September 2010.

35. Astri Suhrke, *When More is Less: The International Project in Afghanistan* (London: Hurst & Co., 2011) p.127.

36. See *Afghanistan National Development Strategy: An Interim Strategy For Security, Governance, Economic Growth and Poverty Reduction* (Kabul: Islamic Republic of Afghanistan, 2006); *The Afghanistan Compact* (Kabul: Government of Afghanistan, 2006) Annex I.

37. Nematullah Bizhan, *Aid Paradoxes in Afghanistan: Building and Undermining the State* (London: Routledge, 2018) p.141.

38. Fariba Nawa, *Afghanistan, Inc.: A CorpWatch Investigative Report* (Oakland: CorpWatch, 2006).

39. Dion Nissenbaum, Jessica Donati and Alan Cullison, 'Who Won in Afghanistan? Private Contractors', *The Wall Street Journal*, 31 December 2021.

40. *Afghanistan Reconstruction: Deteriorating Security and Limited Resources Have Impeded Progress; Improvements in U.S. Strategy Needed* (Washington DC: Report to Congressional Committees, GAO–04–403, United States General Accounting Office, June 2004) p.10.

41. Joe Stephens and David B. Ottaway, 'A rebuilding plan full of cracks', *The Washington Post*, 20 November 2005.

42. See Jennifer Murtazashvili, 'Gaming the state: consequences of contracting out state building in Afghanistan', *Central Asian Survey*, vol.34, no.1, 2015, pp.78–92.

43. Tobias Haque and Nigel Roberts, *Afghanistan's Aid Requirements: How much aid is required to maintain a stable state?* (London: Lessons for Peace, Overseas Development Institute, October 2020) pp.5, 4 fn.1.

44. Roxanna Shapour, *Realpolitik and the 2021 National Budget: The toxic struggle for money and power that undermined Afghanistan's Republic* (Kabul: Afghanistan Analysts Network, 21 December 2021).

45. *Afghanistan–State Building, Sustaining Growth, and Reducing Poverty* (Washington DC: The World Bank, 2005) pp.47–8.

46. See Neal Blewett, *The Peers, the Parties and the People: The General Election of 1910* (Basingstoke: Macmillan, 1972); George Winterton, *Parliament, the Executive and the Governor-General: A Constitutional Analysis* (Melbourne: Melbourne University Press, 1983).

47. This is detailed exhaustively in Roxanna Shapour, *Realpolitik and the 2021 National Budget: The toxic struggle for money and power that undermined Afghanistan's Republic* (Kabul: Afghanistan Analysts Network, 21 December 2021).

48. C.P.W. Gammell, *The Pearl of Khorasan: A History of Herat* (London Hurst & Co., 2016) p.346.

49. C.P.W. Gammell, *The Pearl of Khorasan: A History of Herat* (London Hurst & Co., 2016) p.344.

50. See Kate Clark and Roxanna Shapour, *The Khalid Payenda Interview (1): An insider's view of politicking, graft and the fall of the Republic* (Kabul: Afghanistan Analysts Network, 27 September 2021); also Kate Clark and Roxanna Shapour, *The Khalid Payenda Interview (2): Reforms, regrets and the final bid to save a collapsing Republic* (Kabul: Afghanistan Analysts Network, 9 October 2021).

51. See *The Evaluation of the 'National Solidarity Program' in Afghanistan* (Kabul: Center for Regional and Strategic Studies, 18 March 2017).

52. See Andrew Beath, Fotini Christia and Ruben Enikolopov, 'The National Solidarity Programme: Assessing the Effects of Community-Driven Development in Afghanistan', *International Peacekeeping*, vol.22, no.4, August 2015, pp.302–20.

53. Mohammad Qadam Shah, 'The politics of budgetary capture in rentier states: who gets what, when and how in Afghanistan', *Central Asian Survey*, vol.41, no.1, March 2022, pp.138–60 at p.139.

54. David Mansfield, *A Taxing Narrative: Miscalculating Revenues and Misunderstanding the Conflict in Afghanistan* (Kabul: Afghanistan Research and Evaluation Unit, October 2021).

55. See James Tharin Bradford, *Poppies, Politics, and Power: Afghanistan and the Global History of Drugs and Diplomacy* (Ithaca: Cornell University Press, 2019); Ibrahimi and Maley, *Afghanistan: Politics and Economics in a Globalising State*, pp.105–11.

56. See David Mansfield, *A State Built on Sand: How Opium Undermined Afghanistan* (London: Hurst & Co., 2016) pp.225, 242; also David Mansfield, *The Helmand Food Zone: The Illusion of Success* (Kabul: Afghanistan Research and Evaluation Unit, November 2019).

57. David Mansfield, *Denying Revenue or Wasting Money? Assessing the Impact of the Air Campaign Against 'Drugs Labs' in Afghanistan* (London: LSE International Drug Policy Unit, April 2019) p.8.

58. Robert Jackson, *A Study of the Capacity of the United Nations Development System* (Geneva: United Nations, 1969) pp.iv–v.

59. William Maley, 'Institutional Design, Neopatrimonialism, and the Politics of Aid in Afghanistan', *Asian Survey*, vol.58, no.6, November–December 2018, pp.995–1015.

60. *Special Inspector General for Afghanistan Reconstruction: Stabilization: Lessons from the U.S. Experience in Afghanistan* (Arlington: SIGAR 18-48-LL, Special Inspector General for Afghanistan Reconstruction, 17 May 2018) pp.64, 191.

61. Douglas A. Wissing, *Hopeless but Optimistic: Journeying through America's Endless War in Afghanistan* (Bloomington: Indiana University Press, 2016) p.159. See also Douglas A. Wissing, *Funding the Enemy: How US Taxpayers Bankroll the Taliban* (Amherst: Prometheus Books, 2012).

62. *The Next Frontier: Human Development and the Anthropocene. Briefing note for countries on the 2020 Human Development Report: Afghanistan* (New York: United Nations Development Programme, 2020) p.3.

63. Martine van Bijlert, *Between Hope and Fear: Rural Afghan women talk about peace and war* (Kabul: Special Report, Afghanistan Analysts Network, July 2021) p.7. See also Althea-Maria Rivas and Mariam Safi, 'Women and the Afghan peace and reintegration process', *International Affairs*, vol.98, no.1, January 2022, pp.85–104 at pp.96–8.

64. See Susanne Schmeidl, 'Internal displacement in Afghanistan: The tip of the iceberg', in Srinjoy Bose, Nishank Motwani and William Maley (eds), *Afghanistan—Challenges and Prospects* (London: Routledge, 2018) pp.169–87.

4.   PROBLEMS OF INSURGENCY

1.   See Raj Desai and Harry Eckstein, 'Insurgency: The Transformation of Peasant Rebellion', *World Politics*, vol.42, no.4, July 1990, pp.441–65 at p.442.

2.   Theda Skocpol, *States and Social Revolutions: A Comparative Analysis of France, Russia, and China* (Cambridge: Cambridge University Press, 1979) p.4.

3.   Jack A. Goldstone, *Revolution and Rebellion in the Early Modern World* (Berkeley & Los Angeles: University of California Press, 1992) p.460.

4.   On earlier episodes of rebellion in Afghanistan, see Leon B. Poullada, *Reform and Rebellion in Afghanistan, 1919–1929: King Amanullah's Failure to Modernize a Tribal Soceity* (Ithaca: Cornell University Press 1973); M. Nazif Shahrani and Robert L. Canfield (eds), *Revolutions and Rebellions in Afghanistan: Anthropological Perspectives* (Berkeley: Institute of International Studies, University of California, 1984).

5.   See Richard Pipes, *Russia under the Old Regime* (Harmondsworth: Penguin, 1977) p.155; David J. Silbey, *The Boxer Rebellion and the Great Game in China* (New York: Hill and Wang, 2012).

6.   See E.J. Hobsbawn, *Primitive Rebels: Studies in Archaic Forms of Social Movement in the 19th and 20th Centuries* (New York: W.W. Norton, 1959); Ted Robert Gurr, *Why Men Rebel* (Princeton: Princeton University Press, 1970); Jeremy M. Weinstein, *Inside Rebellion: The Politics of Insurgent Violence* (Cambridge: Cambridge University Press, 2007).

7. On understandings of 'civil war', see Edward Newman, *Understanding Civil Wars: Continuity and Change in Intrastate Conflict* (New York: Routledge, 2014) pp.58–62; David Armitage, *Civil Wars: A History in Ideas* (New York: Alfred A. Knopf, 2017) pp.196–239.

8. See Stathis N. Kalyvas, *The Logic of Violence in Civil War* (Cambridge: Cambridge University Press, 2006) p.389.

9. See Jon Elster, 'Norms of Revenge', *Ethics*, vol.100, no.4, July 1990, pp.862–85.

10. See Stefan Barriga and Claus Kreß (eds), *The Travaux Préparatoires of the Crime of Aggression* (Cambridge: Cambridge University Press, 2012) p.103.

11. See Abbas Farasoo, 'Rethinking Proxy War Theory in IR: A Critical Analysis of Principal-Agent Theory', *International Studies Review*, vol.23, no.4, December 2021, pp.1835–58; Chris Alexander, *Ending Pakistan's Proxy War in Afghanistan* (Ottawa: Macdonald-Laurier Institute, 2021).

12. William Maley, *What is a Refugee?* (London: Hurst & Co., 2016) pp.104–5. See also William Maley, 'Confronting Creeping Invasions: Afghanistan, the UN and the World Community', in K. Warikoo (ed.), *The Afghanistan Crisis: Issues and Perspectives* (New Delhi: Bhavana Books, 2002) pp.256–74.

13. See Abdulkader H. Sinno, 'Partisan Intervention and the Transformation of Afghanistan's Civil War', *American Historical Review*, vol.120, no.5, December 2015 pp.1811–28 at pp.1814–16; Antonio Giustozzi, *The Taliban at War 2001–2018* (London: Hurst & Co., 2019) pp.77–107.

14. Muhammad Qasim Zaman, *The Ulama in Contemporary Islam: Custodians of Change* (Princeton: Princeton University Press, 2002) p.137.

15. See Barbara D. Metcalf, *Islamic Revival in British India: Deoband, 1860–1900* (Princeton: Princeton University Press, 1982).

16. Ahmed Rashid, *Taliban: Militant Islam, Oil and Fundamentalism in Central Asia* (New Haven: Yale University Press, 2000) p.32.

17. See Robert L. Bussard, 'The "dangerous class" of Marx and Engels: The rise of the idea of the Lumpenproletariat', *History of European Ideas*, vol.8, no.6, 1987, pp.675–92.

18. Karl Marx and Friedrich Engels, 'Manifesto of the Communist Party', in Eugene Kamenka (ed.), *The Portable Karl Marx* (Harmondsworth: Penguin, 1983) pp.203–41 at p.215.

19. Karl Marx and Friedrich Engels, 'Manifesto of the Communist Party', in Eugene Kamenka (ed.), *The Portable Karl Marx* (Harmondsworth: Penguin, 1983) pp.203–41 at p.215.

20. Kristian Berg Harpviken, 'The transnationalization of the Taliban', *International Area Studies Review*, vol.15, no.3, 2012, pp.203–29 at p.211. See also *The 'Ten-Dollar Talib' and Women's Rights* (New York: Human Rights Watch, July 2010) p.4.

21. See Barrington Moore, Jr., *Moral Purity and Persecution in History* (Princeton: Princeton University Press, 2000).

22. See Lynne O'Donnell, 'As Taliban Expand Control, Concerns About Forced Marriage and Sex Slavery Rise', *Foreignpolicy.com*, 23 July 2021; Sabawoon Samim, *Who Gets to Go to School? (3): Are Taleban attitudes starting to change from within?* (Kabul: Afghanistan Analysts Network, 7 February 2022).

23. On such engagements, see Ashley Jackson, *Negotiating Survival: Civilian-Insurgent Relations in Afghanistan* (London: Hurst & Co., 2021). The phenomenon of pragmatic local engagement emerging between local residents and autocratic powerholders—of a kind that would be unlikely at higher levels—is not new. See, for example, Merle Fainsod, *Smolensk under Soviet Rule* (Boston: Unwin Hyman, 1989) pp.446–8; Julia Boyd and Angelika Patel, *A Village in the Third Reich: How Ordinary Lives Were Transformed by the Rise of Fascism* (London: Elliott and Thompson, 2022).

24. All too often, the views of Taliban political officials with lines to spin were amplified in ways that exaggerated their significance. Problems of selection bias and sampling bias are discussed in Borhan Osman and Anand Gopal, *Taliban Views on a Future State* (New York: Center on International Cooperation, New York University, July 2016) p.10.

25. On such usages, see Leonard Schapiro, *Totalitarianism* (London: Macmillan, 1972) pp.18–20.

26. T.H. Rigby, *The Changing Soviet System: Mono-Organisational Socialism From its Origins to Gorbachev's Restructuring* (Aldershot: Edward Elgar, 1990) p.108.

27. Daniel Chirot, *Modern Tyrants: The Power and Prevalence of Evil in Our Age* (Princeton: Princeton University Press, 1994) p.2–3. See also Charles Kimball, *When Religion Becomes Evil* (New York: HarperCollins, 2002).

28. 'Taliban leader calls for help in first Afghan address', *DW News*, 27 November 2021.

29. Sakhi Khalid, 'The Taliban Have Not Set Perfect Standards for Governance', *Hasht-e Sobh*, 28 November 2021.

30. Marjana Sadat, 'Taliban Prime Minister to the Afghans: "Pray to God you survive the famine"', *La Repubblica*, 29 November 2021.

31. Susannah George, 'Taliban struggles to respond to earthquake amid international isolation', *The Washington Post*, 24 June 2022.

32. Mike Martin, *An Intimate War: An Oral History of the Helmand Conflict* (London: Hurst & Co., 2014) p.244.

33. David Kilcullen, *Blood Year: Islamic State and the Failures of the War on Terror* (Melbourne: BlackInc, 2016) p.177. Subsequently, Taliban combatants also had access to sophisticated night-vision goggles, although how they were obtained remained a matter for debate: see Thomas Gibbons-Neff and Jawad Sukhanyar, 'The Taliban have gone high-tech. That poses a dilemma for the U.S.', *The New York Times*, 1 April 2018.

34. See Antonio Giustozzi (ed.), *Decoding the New Taliban: Insights from the Afghan Field* (London: Hurst & Co., 2009).

35. For background, see Vahid Brown and Don Rassler, *Fountainhead of Jihad: The Haqqani Nexus, 1973–2012* (New York: Oxford University Press, 2013).

36. See Thomas Ruttig, 'How Tribal are the Taliban?', in Shahzad Bashir and Robert D. Crews (eds), *Under the Drones: Modern Lives in the Afghanistan-Pakistan Borderlands* (Cambridge: Harvard University Press, 2012) pp.102–35.

37. See Neil Krishan Aggarwal, *The Taliban's Virtual Emirate: The Culture and Psychology of an Online Militant Community* (New York: Columbia University Press, 2016); Thomas H. Johnson, *Taliban Narratives: The Use and Power of Stories*

in the Afghanistan Conflict (London: Hurst & Co., 2017); Weeda Mehran, Umniah Al Bayati, Matthew Mottet and Anthony F. Lemieux, 'Deep Analysis of Taliban Videos: Differential Use of Multimodal, Visual and Sonic Forms across Strategic Themes', *Studies in Conflict and Terrorism*, 2021, DOI:10.1080/10576 10X.2020.1866739.

38. Carlotta Gall, 'Mullah Muhammad Omar, enigmatic leader of Afghan Taliban, is dead', *The New York Times*, 31 July 2015.

39. Michael Semple, *Rhetoric, Ideology, and Organizational Structure of the Taliban Movement* (Washington DC: Peaceworks Report no.102, United States Institute of Peace, 2014) p.17.

40. Carlotta Gall and Ruhullah Khapalwak, 'Taliban leader feared Pakistan before he was killed', *The New York Times*, 9 August 2017.

41. See Zachary Shore, *A Sense of the Enemy: The High-Stakes History of Reading Your Rival's Mind* (New York: Oxford University Press, 2014).

42. *Afghanistan: Harrowing Accounts Emerge of the Taliban's Reign of Terror in Kunduz* (London: Amnesty International, 2015).

43. See Abdul Waheed Wafa, 'Blast at Kabul hotel kills 6', *The New York Times*, 15 January 2008; Emma Graham-Harrison, 'Taliban gunmen kill nine civilians in attack at Kabul's Serena hotel', *The Guardian*, 22 March 2014; Fatima Faizi and Rod Nordland, 'At least 5 killed in Afghan hotel attack that trapped hundreds of guests', *The New York Times*, 20 January 2018; Azam Ahmed and Matthew Rosenberg, 'Deadly attack at Kabul restaurant hints at changing climate for foreigners', *The New York Times*, 18 January 2014; Sune Engel Rasmussen, 'American University attack: at least 12 dead and 44 injured in Afghanistan', *The Guardian*, 25 August 2016.

44. Mujib Mashal, Fahim Abed and Jawad Sukhanyar, 'Deadly bombing is among worst of Afghan war', *The New York Times*, 1 June 2017; *Afghanistan: Kabul bombing is horrific act of deliberate violence* (London: Amnesty International, 2017).

45. Anthony Richards, *Conceptualizing Terrorism* (Oxford: Oxford University Press, 2015) p.146. See also Stephen Nathanson, *Terrorism and the Ethics of War* (Cambridge: Cambridge University Press, 2010) pp.24–9; William Maley, 'Terrorism and insurgency in Afghanistan', in M. Raymond Izarali and Dalbir Ahlawat (eds), *Terrorism, Security and Development in South Asia: National, Regional and Global Implications* (London: Routledge, 2021) pp.140–56.

46. *Twelfth report of the Analytical Support and Sanctions Monitoring Team submitted pursuant to resolution 2557 (2020) concerning the Taliban and other associated individuals and entities constituting a threat to the peace stability and security of Afghanistan* (New York: United Nations, S/2021/486, 1 June 2021) para.40. See also Barbara Elias, 'Why rebels rely on terrorists: The persistence of the Taliban–al-Qaeda battlefield coalition in Afghanistan', *Journal of Strategic Studies*, vol.45, no.2, April 2022, pp.234–57; Bryce Loidolt, 'How the al-Qaeda–Taliban Alliance Survived', *Survival*, vol.64, no.3, June-July 2022, pp.133–52.

47. Shane Harris, Dan Lamothe, Karen DeYoung, Souad Mekhennet and Pamela Constable, 'U.S kills al-Qaeda leader Ayman al-Zawahiri in drone strike in Kabul', *The Washington Post*, 1 August 2022.

48. See Taimoor Shah and Carlotta Gall, 'Afghan rebels find aid in Pakistan, Musharraf admits', *The New York Times*, 13 August 2007.

49. Ambassador Karl W. Eikenberry, 'COIN Strategy: Civilian Concerns' (Kabul: U.S. Department of State Cable no. Kabul 03572, November 2009).

50. Theo Farrell and Michael Semple, 'Making Peace with the Taliban', *Survival*, vol. 57, no. 6, December 2015 to January 2016, pp. 79–110 at p. 92.

51. See Ahmad Shayeq Qassem, *Afghanistan's Political Stability: A Dream Unrealised* (Aldershot: Ashgate, 2009) pp. 47–50.

52. On these events, see G. W. Choudhury, *The Last Days of United Pakistan* (Bloomington: Indiana University Press, 1974).

53. See Stephen Philip Cohen, *The Idea of Pakistan* (Washington DC: Brookings Institution Press, 2004); Farzana Shaikh, *Making Sense of Pakistan* (New York: Columbia University Press, 2009); Ayesha Jalal, *The Struggle for Pakistan: A Muslim Homeland and Global Politics* (Cambridge: Harvard University Press, 2014).

54. See Mariam Abou Zahab and Olivier Roy, *Islamist Networks: The Afghan-Pakistan Connection* (London: Hurst & Co., 2004); Rizwan Hussain, *Pakistan and the Emergence of Islamic Militancy in Afghanistan* (Aldershot: Ashgate, 2005); Abdulkader Sinno, *Organizations at War in Afghanistan and Beyond* (Ithaca: Cornell University Press, 2008).

55. See Shirin Tahir-Kheli, *The United States and Pakistan: The Evolution of an Influence Relationship* (New York: Praeger, 1982).

56. See Sumit Ganguly, *The Crisis in Kashmir: Portents of War, Hopes of Peace* (Cambridge: Cambridge University Press, 1997); Sumantra Bose, *Kashmir: Roots of Conflict, Paths to Peace* (Cambridge: Harvard University Press, 2003); Christopher Snedden, *Understanding Kashmir and Kashmiris* (London: Hurst & Co., 2015).

57. David E. Cunningham, 'Blocking resolution: How external states can prolong civil wars', *Journal of Peace Research*, vol. 47, no. 2, March 2010, pp. 115–27.

58. For background, see Hein G. Kiessling, *Faith, Unity, Discipline: The ISI of Pakistan* (London: Hurst & Co., 2016); Owen L. Sirrs, *Pakistan's Inter-Services Intelligence Directorate: Covert Action and Internal Operations* (New York: Routledge, 2017). See also C. Christine Fair, *Fighting to the End: The Pakistan Army's Way of War* (New York: Oxford University Press, 2014).

59. Mohammad Yousaf and Mark Adkin, *The Bear Trap: Afghanistan's Untold Story* (London: Leo Cooper, 1992).

60. Riaz Mohammad Khan, *Afghanistan and Pakistan: Conflict, Extremism, and Resistance to Modernity* (Washington DC: Woodrow Wilson Center Press, 2011) p. 59.

61. See Steve Coll, *Directorate S: The C.I.A. and America's Secret Wars in Afghanistan and Pakistan* (New York: Penguin Press, 2018).

62. Daniel S. Markey, *No Exit from Pakistan: America's Tortured Relationship with Islamabad* (Cambridge: Cambridge University Press, 2013) p. 202.

63. Muhammad Qasim Zaman, *Islam in Pakistan: A History* (Princeton: Princeton University Press, 2018) p. 247.

64. Idean Salehyan, 'Transnational Rebels: Neighboring States as Sanctuary for Rebel Groups', *World Politics*, vol. 59, no. 2, January 2007, pp. 217–42 at p. 219.

65. Idean Salehyan, 'Transnational Rebels: Neighboring States as Sanctuary for Rebel Groups', *World Politics*, vol. 59, no. 2, January 2007, pp. 217–42 at p. 242.

66. See *Security Council Resolution 1383 (2001)* (New York: S/RES/1383 (2001), 6 December 2001) para.1.

67. Carlotta Gall, *The Wrong Enemy: America in Afghanistan, 2001–2014* (New York: Houghton Mifflin Harcourt, 2014) pp.19–21.

68. See Laura King, 'Pakistani city serves as refuge for the Taliban', *The Los Angeles Times*, 21 December 2006.

69. Ahmed Rashid, *Descent into Chaos: The United States and the Failure of Nation Building in Pakistan, Afghanistan, and Central Asia* (New York: Viking Press, 2008) pp.249–50.

70. Carlotta Gall, 'Rough treatment for 2 journalists in Pakistan', *The New York Times*, 21 January 2007.

71. Mark Mazetti and Dexter Filkins, 'Secret joint raid captures Taliban's top commander', *The New York Times*, 16 February 2010.

72. See Hamid Mir, 'Why 2022 is shaping up to be a nightmare year for Imran Khan', *The Washington Post*, 12 January 2022.

73. Craig Whitlock, 'Number of U.S. casualties from roadside bombs in Afghanistan skyrocketed from 2009 to 2010', *The Washington Post*, 25 January 2011.

74. See *Jamming the IED Assembly Line: Impeding the Flow of Ammonium Nitrate in South and Central Asia* (Washington DC: Hearing before the Subcommittee on Near Eastern and South and Central Asian Affairs of the Committee on Foreign Relations, United States Senate, Senate Hearing 111–782, 18 November 2010), especially the joint testimony of David S. Sedney and BG Michael H. Shields, where it was noted that the 'Joint Improvised Explosive Device Defeat Organization … assesses that the vast majority of significant precursors for HME [homemade explosives] in Afghanistan—ammonium nitrate fertilizers and potassium chlorate industrial chemicals—originate in, or transit through, Pakistan'.

75. See William Shawcross, *Sideshow: Kissinger, Nixon and the Destruction of Cambodia* (London: Hogarth Press, 1991).

76. See Marvin G. Weinbaum and Jonathan B. Harder, 'Pakistan's Afghan policies and their consequences', *Contemporary South Asia*, vol.16, no.1, March 2008, pp.25–38.

77. Quoted in Antonio Giustozzi, *The Taliban at War 2001–2018* (London: Hurst & Co., 2019) p.53.

78. Joshua Partlow, *A Kingdom of Their Own: The Family Karzai and the Afghan Disaster* (New York: Alfred A. Knopf, 2016) p.111.

79. *The Concise Oxford Dictionary of Quotations* (London: Oxford University Press, 1964) p.233

80. See Seth G. Jones, 'Pakistan's Dangerous Game', *Survival*, vol.49, no.1, Spring 2007, pp.15–32; Seth G. Jones, *Counterinsurgency in Afghanistan* (Santa Monica: RAND National Defense Research Institute, 2008); Seth G. Jones, *In the Graveyard of Empires: America's War in Afghanistan* (New York: W.W. Norton, 2009); Shaun Gregory, 'The ISI and the War on Terrorism', *Studies in Conflict and Terrorism*, vol.30, no.12, 2007, pp.1013–31; and Matt Waldman, *The Sun in the Sky: The Relationship Between Pakistan's ISI and Afghan Insurgents* (London: Discussion Paper no.18, Crisis States Research Centre, London School of Economics and Political Science, June 2010).

81. This insight originated with the political scientist Raymond E. Wolfinger: see Nelson W. Polsby, 'The Contributions of President Richard F. Fenno, Jr.', *PS: Political Science & Politics*, vol.17, no.4, Autumn 1984, pp.778–81 at p.779.

82. *Corfu Channel case, Judgment of April 9ᵗʰ, 1949: I.C.J. Report* 1949, p.4 at p.22. See also James Crawford, *State Responsibility: The General Part* (Cambridge: Cambridge University Press, 2013) p.158.

83. *Security Council Resolution 1333 (2000)* (New York: S/RES/1333 (2000), 19 December 2000) para.5(a). Emphasis added.

84. *Security Council Resolution 1267 (1999)* (New York: S/RES/1267 (1999), 15 October 1999) para.4(b).

85. *Afghanistan Opium Survey 2020: Cultivation and Production—Executive Summary* (Kabul: United Nations Office on Drugs and Crime and Ministry of Counter Narcotics, Islamic Republic of Afghanistan, April 2021) pp.4, 9.

86. *Country Briefs: Afghanistan* (Rome: GIEWS—Global Information and Early Warning System, Food and Agriculture Organization of the United Nations, 23 December 2021).

87. *Drug Situation in Afghanistan 2021: Latest Findings and Emerging Threats* (Vienna: UNODC Research Brief, United Nations Office on Drugs and Crime, November 2021) p.9.

88. David Mansfield, *A Taxing Narrative: Miscalculating Revenues and Misunderstanding the Conflict in Afghanistan* (Kabul: Afghanistan Research and Evaluation Unit, October 2021) p.1.

89. David Mansfield, *A Taxing Narrative: Miscalculating Revenues and Misunderstanding the Conflict in Afghanistan* (Kabul: Afghanistan Research and Evaluation Unit, October 2021) p.2.

90. See Gretchen Peters, *How Opium Profits the Taliban* (Washington DC: Peaceworks no.62, United States Institute of Peace, August 2009); Lynne O'Donnell, 'The Taliban Are Breaking Bad: Meth is even more profitable than heroin—and is turbocharging the insurgency', *Foreignpolicy.com*, 19 July 2021.

91. See Ahmed Rashid, 'Pakistan and the Taliban', in William Maley (ed.), *Fundamentalism Reborn? Afghanistan and the Taliban* (London: Hurst & Co., 1998) pp.72–89 at pp.76–8.

92. See Niamatullah Ibrahimi and William Maley, *Afghanistan: Politics and Economics in a Globalising State* (London: Routledge, 2020) p.91.

93. David Mansfield, *A Taxing Narrative: Miscalculating Revenues and Misunderstanding the Conflict in Afghanistan* (Kabul: Afghanistan Research and Evaluation Unit, October 2021), p.1.

94. David Mansfield, *Managing Local Resources and Conflict: The Undeclared Economy. Value Chain Mapping and Visualisation of The Talc, Fuel and Transit Trade in Afghanistan* (Washington DC: USAID/OSDR/Alcis/, 2021) p.2.

95. David Mansfield, *Managing Local Resources and Conflict: The Undeclared Economy. Value Chain Mapping and Visualisation of The Talc, Fuel and Transit Trade in Afghanistan* (Washington DC: USAID/OSDR/Alcis/, 2021) p.4.

96. Neta C. Crawford and Catherine Lutz, *Human Cost of Post-9/11 Wars: Direct War Deaths in Major War Zones, Afghanistan & Pakistan (October 2001–August 2021); Iraq (March 2003–August 2021); Syria (September 2014–May 2021); Yemen (October*

2002–August 2021) and Other Post-9/11 War Zones (Providence: Watson Institute for International Studies, Brown University, 1 September 2021).

97. Rachel Pannett, Jennifer Hassan, Katerina Ang, Erin Cunningham, Missy Ryan, Claire Parker and Dan Lamothe, 'Biden defends decision to withdraw from Afghanistan after Taliban's rapid return to power', *The Washington Post*, 16 August 2021.

98. David Kilcullen and Greg Mills, *The Ledger: Accounting for Failure in Afghanistan* (London: Hurst & Co., 2021) p.284

99. Mark Lander, 'Afghan plan a new army of 70,000', *The New York Times*, 3 December 2002.

100. Mark Sedra, 'Security Sector Reform in Afghanistan: The Slide Towards Expediency', *International Peacekeeping*, vol.13, no.1, March 2006, pp.94–110 at p.97. See, however, Antonio Giustozzi, *The Army of Afghanistan: A Political History of a Fragile Institution* (London: Hurst & Co., 2015) pp.136–44 for a more nuanced picture of ethnic complexities and tensions within the army.

101. Ali Ahmad Jalali, *A Military History of Afghanistan: From the Great Game to the Global War on Terror* (Lawrence: University Press of Kansas, 2017) p.513.

102. Karen DeYoung, 'Afghan corruption: how to follow the money', *The Washington Post*, 29 March 2010.

103. Brad Adams, *New Afghan Defense Minister Should Face Investigation, Sanctions* (New York: Human Rights Watch, 12 January 2019).

104. The problem of 'ghost soldiers'—non-existent personnel added to payrolls so that those payrolls can be corruptly harvested—had seriously damaged the Lon Nol regime in Cambodia from 1970 to 1975: see Elizabeth Becker, *When the War Was Over: Cambodia and the Khmer Rouge Revolution* (New York: Public Affairs, 1998) p.123. It was to prove a problem in Afghanistan too, as we discuss in more detail in Chapter Eight.

105. David Kilcullen and Greg Mills, *The Ledger: Accounting for Failure in Afghanistan* (London: Hurst & Co., 2021) p.200.

106. David Kilcullen and Greg Mills, *The Ledger: Accounting for Failure in Afghanistan* (London: Hurst & Co., 2021) pp.202–3.

107. Christopher Ankersen and Mike Martin, 'The Taliban, not the West, won Afghanistan's technological war', *MIT Technology Review*, 23 August 2021.

108. Christopher Ankersen and Mike Martin, 'The Taliban, not the West, won Afghanistan's technological war', *MIT Technology Review*, 23 August 2021.

109. Charles E. Lindblom, 'The Science of "Muddling Through"', *Public Administration Review*, vol.19, no.2, Spring 1959, pp.79–88.

110. For more detailed discussion, see Sten Rynning, *NATO in Afghanistan: The Liberal Disconnect* (Stanford: Stanford University Press, 2012) pp.57–8.

111. Theo Farrell, *Unwinnable: Britain's War in Afghanistan 2001-2014* (London: The Bodley Head, 2017) p.284.

112. Katie Glueck and Thomas Kaplan, 'Joe Biden's vote for war', *The New York Times*, 12 January 2020.

113. Robert Burns, 'Mullen: Afghanistan isn't top priority', *The Washington Post*, 11 December 2007.

114. Robert M. Gates, *Duty: Memoirs of a Secretary at War* (New York: Alfred A. Knopf, 2014) p.569.

115. See *The U.S. Army Marine Corps Counterinsurgency Field Manual* (Chicago: University of Chicago Press, 2007); David Kilcullen, *The Accidental Guerrilla: Fighting Small Wars in the Midst of a Big One* (New York: Oxford University Press, 2009); David Kilcullen, *Counterinsurgency* (New York: Oxford University Press, 2010); Fred Kaplan, *The Insurgents: David Petraeus and the Plot to Change the American Way of War* (New York: Simon & Schuster, 2013).

116. *Remarks by the President in Address to the Nation on the Way Forward in Afghanistan and Pakistan* (Washington DC: The White House, 1 December 2009).

117. Barack Obama, *A Promised Land* (New York: Viking, 2020) p.443.

118. Craig Whitlock, *The Afghanistan Papers: A Secret History of the War* (New York: Simon & Schuster, 2021) p.153.

119. Jalali, *A Military History of Afghanistan*, pp.513–14. See also Paul Lushenko and John Hardy, 'Panjwai: A Tale of Two COINs in Afghanistan', *Small Wars and Insurgencies*, vol.27, no.1, January 2016, pp.106–31.

120. *Afghanistan: The Results of the Strategic Review, Part II* (Washington DC: Hearing before the Full Committee of the Committee on Armed Services, House of Representatives, H.A.S.C. 111-112, 8 December 2009).

121. *Recent Developments in Afghanistan* (Washington DC: Committee on Armed Services, House of Representatives, H.A.S.C. 113-88, 13 March 2014).

122. William C. Martel, *Victory in War: Foundations of Modern Military Policy* (Cambridge: Cambridge University Press, 2007) p.136.

123. Mary Kaldor, *New and Old Wars: Organized Violence in a Global Era* (Cambridge: Polity Press, 2012) pp.151–84.

124. Cian O'Driscoll, *Victory: The Triumph and Tragedy of Just War* (Oxford: Oxford University Press, 2020) p.124.

125. See Dominic D. P. Johnson and Dominic Tierney, *Failing to Win: Perceptions of Victory and Defeat in International Politics* (Cambridge: Harvard University Press, 2006).

126. James Dobbins, Jason H. Campbell, Sean Mann, and Laurel E. Miller, *Consequences of a Precipitous U.S. Withdrawal from Afghanistan* (Santa Monica: RAND Corporation, January 2019) p.2.

127. See John Lukacs, *Five Days in London: May 1940* (New Haven: Yale University Press, 1999).

128. Adam Roberts and Richard Guelff (eds), *Documents on the Laws of War* (Oxford: Oxford University Press, 2000) p.448.

129. Judith Gardam, *Necessity, Proportionality and the Use of Force by States* (Cambridge: Cambridge University Press, 2004) pp.85–137.

130. See William Maley, *The Afghanistan Wars* (London: Macmillan/Red Globe Press, 2021) p.274; *Afghanistan: Protection of Civilians in Armed Conflict. Annual Report 2020* (Kabul: United Nations Assistance Mission in Afghanistan and United Nations Human Rights Office of the High Commissioner, February 2021) p.17; *Afghanistan: Protection of Civilians in Armed Conflict. Midyear Update: 1 January to 30 June 2021* (Kabul: United Nations Assistance Mission in Afghanistan and United Nations Human Rights Office of the High Commissioner, July 2021) p.3.

131. *Afghanistan: Protection of Civilians in Armed Conflict. Midyear Update: 1 January to 30 June 2021* (Kabul: United Nations Assistance Mission in Afghanistan and United Nations Human Rights Office of the High Commissioner, July 2021) p.1.

132. See Niamatullah Ibrahimi, 'When few means many: The consequences of civilian casualties for civil-military relations in Afghanistan', in William Maley and Susanne Schmeidl (eds), *Reconstructing Afghanistan: Civil-military experiences in comparative perspective* (London: Routledge, 2015) pp.165–76.

133. Luke N. Condra, Joseph H. Felter, Radha K. Iyengar and Jacob N. Shapiro, *The Effect of Civilian Casualties in Afghanistan and Iraq* (Cambridge: Working Paper 16152, National Bureau of Economic Research, July 2010) p.3.

134. Jason Lyall, Graeme Blair and Kosuke Imai, 'Explaining Support for Combatants during Wartime: A Survey Experiment in Afghanistan', *American Political Science Review*, vol.107, no.4, November 2013, pp.679–705.

135. Paul Lushenko, Srinjoy Bose and William Maley, 'Conceptualizing global order in an era of remote warfare', in Paul Lushenko, Srinjoy Bose and William Maley (eds), *Drones and Global Order: The implications of remote warfare for international society* (London: Routledge, 2022) pp.1–35 at p.1.

136. Frud Bezhan, 'Taliban PsyOps: Afghan Militants Weaponize Commercial Drones', *Gandhara. Radio Free Europe / Radio Liberty*, 29 January 2021.

137. Cecilia Jacob and Nicola Mathieson, 'Drone warfare and the human protection Transnational Legal Order', in Paul Lushenko, Srinjoy Bose and William Maley (eds), *Drones and Global Order: The implications of remote warfare for international society* (London: Routledge, 2022) pp.98–116 at pp.104–5.

138. See Alex Edney-Browne, 'The Psychosocial Effects of Drone Violence: Social Isolation, Self-Objectification, and Depoliticization', *Political Psychology*, vol.40, no.6, December 2019, pp.1341–56.

139. See Eric Schmitt, 'A botched drone strike in Kabul started with the wrong car', *The New York Times*, 21 September 2021; Alex Horton, 'Pentagon releases drone video of botched Kabul strike that killed 10 civilians', *The Washington Post*, 19 January 2022.

140. Craig Whitlock, 'Members of Stryker Combat Brigade in Afghanistan accused of killing civilians for sport', *The Washington Post*, 18 September 2010.

141. *Report of Inquiry under Division 4A of Part 4 of the Inspector-General of the Australian Defence Force Regulation 2016 into Questions of Unlawful Conduct Concerning the Special Operations Task Group in Afghanistan* (Canberra: Commonwealth of Australia, November 2020) para.19. For background, see Tom Frame, *Veiled Valour: Australian Special Forces in Afghanistan and War Crimes Allegations* (Sydney: New South Publishing, 2022).

142. Hannah O'Grady and Joel Gunter, 'SAS unit repeatedly killed Afghan detainees, BBC finds', *BBC Panorama*, 12 July 2022.

143. Pervez Musharraf, *In the Line of Fire: A Memoir* (New York: The Free Press, 2006) p.201.

144. See Craig Cohen and Derek Chollet, 'When $10 Billion Is Not Enough: Rethinking U.S. Strategy toward Pakistan', *The Washington Quarterly*, vol.30, no.2, April 2007, pp.7–19.

145. Craig Whitlock, *The Afghanistan Papers: A Secret History of the War* (New York: Simon & Schuster, 2021) p.179.

146. Hein G. Kiessling, *Faith, Unity, Discipline: The ISI of Pakistan* (London: Hurst & Co., 2016) p.224.

147. Ahmed Rashid, *Pakistan on the Brink: The Future of America, Pakistan, and Afghanistan* (New York: Viking, 2012) p.6.

148. Barack Obama, *A Promised Land* (New York: Viking, 2020) p.679.

149. *Remarks by President Trump on the Strategy in Afghanistan and South Asia* (Washington DC: Office of the Press Secretary, The White House, 21 August 2017).

150. Missy Ryan and Carol Morello, 'Trump administration suspends most security aid to Pakistan', *The Washington Post*, 4 January 2018.

151. Robert Powell, 'Why Some Persistent Problems Persist', *American Political Science Review*, vol.113, no.4, November 2019, pp.980–96.

152. See Husain Haqqani, 'To win Afghanistan, get tough on Pakistan', *The New York Times*, 6 July 2017; C. Christine Fair and Sumit Ganguly, 'An Unworthy Ally: Time For Washington to Cut Pakistan Loose', *Foreign Affairs*, vol.94, no.5, September–October 2015, pp.160–70.

153. Husain Haqqani and Lisa Curtis, *A New U.S. Approach to Pakistan: Enforcing Aid Conditions without Cutting Ties* (Washington DC: Briefing Paper, The Hudson Institute, 2017) p.11.

154. See Zalmay Khalilzad, 'Why Trump is right to get tough with Pakistan', *The New York Times*, 23 August 2017.

155. James V. Schall (ed.), *The Collected Works of G.K. Chesterton* (San Francisco: Ignatius Press, 1986) Vol.4, p.61.

156. Karoun Demirjian and Alex Horton, 'U.S. lost war in Afghanistan through miscalculations spanning multiple administrations, Milley tells lawmakers', *The Washington Post*, 29 September 2021.

5.   POLITICAL LEADERSHIP

1.   *Second Part of King Henry IV*, Act III, Scene I.

2.   Jean Blondel, *Political Leadership: Towards a General Analysis* (Beverly Hills: SAGE, 1987) p.1.

3.   See Robert C. Tucker, *Politics as Leadership* (Columbia and London: University of Missouri Press, 1981) pp.18–19.

4.   Jean Blondel, *Political Leadership: Towards a general analysis* (Beverly Hills: SAGE, 1987) p.16.

5.   Nannerl O. Keohane, *Thinking about Leadership* (Princeton: Princeton University Press, 2010) p.19. Emphasis added.

6.   S. Alexander Haslam, Stephen D. Reicher, and Michael J. Platow, *The New Psychology of Leadership: Identity, Influence and Power* (New York: Routledge, 2020) p.169.

7.   Henry Kissinger, *Leadership: Six Studies in World Strategy* (London: Allen Lane, 2022) p.xv.

8.   See John Higley and Michael G. Burton, 'The Elite Variable in Democratic Transitions and Breakdowns', *American Sociological Review*, vol.54, no.1, February

1989, pp.17–32. For a more general discussion of the significance of elites, see John Higley, *Elites, Non-Elites, and Political Realism* (Lanham: Rowman and Littlefield, 2021) pp.1–38.

9. Archie Brown, *The Myth of the Strong Leader: Political Leadership in the Modern Age* (London: The Bodley Head, 2014) p.51.

10. Dipali Mukhopadhyay, *Provincial Governors in Afghan Politics* (Washington DC: Special Report no.385, United States Institute of Peace, January 2016) p.6.

11. See Thomas Goddard Bergin and Max Harold Fisch (eds), *The New Science of Giambattista Vico* (Ithaca: Cornell University Press, 1984) p.62; Bernard Mandeville, *The Fable of the Bees, Or Private Vices, Publick Benefits* (Indianapolis: Liberty Fund, 1988).

12. See Andrew Macintyre, *The Power of Institutions: Political Architecture and Governance* (Ithaca: Cornell University Press, 2003).

13. Guillermo O'Donnell, 'Delegative Democracy', *Journal of Democracy*, vol.5, no.1, January 1994, pp.55–69 at p.59.

14. For more detailed discussion of particular examples, see Kenneth R. Crispell and Carlos F. Gomez, *Hidden Illness in the White House* (Durham: Duke University Press, 1988); Robert H. Ferrell, *The Dying President: Franklin D. Roosevelt 1944–1945* (Columbia: University of Missouri Press, 1998); David Owen, *In Sickness and in Power: Illness in Heads of Government during the Last 100 Years* (London: Methuen, 2009).

15. Eliot A. Cohen, *Supreme Command: Soldiers, Statesmen, and Leadership in Wartime* (New York: The Free Press, 2002) pp.95–132.

16. Sir Robert Menzies, *Afternoon Light* (Melbourne: Cassell Australia, 1967) p.74.

17. Juliet Kaarbo, 'New directions for leader personality research: breaking bad in foreign policy', *International Affairs*, vol.97, no.2, March 2021, pp.423–41.

18. Harold D. Lasswell, *Psychopathology and Politics* (Chicago: University of Chicago Press, 1977) p.54.

19. See, for example, A.F. Davies, *Skills, Outlooks and Passions: A Psychoanalytic Contribution to the Study of Politics* (Cambridge: Cambridge University Press, 1980).

20. See Jerrold M. Post, *Leaders and Their Followers in a Dangerous World: The Psychology of Political Behavior* (Ithaca: Cornell University Press, 2004); Jerrold M. Post, *Narcissism and Politics: Dreams of Glory* (Cambridge: Cambridge University Press, 2015).

21. James David Barber, *The Presidential Character: Predicting Performance in the White House* (Englewood Cliffs: Prenctice-Hall, 1977) p.13.

22. Hastings Ismay, *The Memoirs of General The Lord Ismay* (London: Heinemann, 1960) p.269.

23. See Fred I. Greenstein, *Personality and Politics: Problems of Evidence, Inference, and Conceptualization* (New York: W.W. Norton, 1975) pp.63–93.

24. Max Weber, *Economy and Society: An Outline of Interpretive Sociology* (Berkeley & Los Angeles: University of California Press, 1978) Vol.I, p.241.

25. William Spinrad, 'Charisma: A Blighted Concept and an Alternative Formula', *Political Science Quarterly*, vol.106, no.2, Summer 1991, pp.295–311.

26. See Charles Lindholm, *Charisma* (Oxford: Blackwell, 1990) pp.93–116; Jerrold M. Post with Stephanie R. Doucette, *Dangerous Charisma: The Political*

Psychology of Donald Trump and His Followers (New York: Pegasus Books, 2019). The potential danger posed by charisma has long been recognised, notably by Thomas Mann in his chilling 1929 story 'Mario und der Zauberer': see Thomas Mann, *Mario and the Magician and Other Stories* (Harmondsworth: Penguin, 1975).

27. See Philip Morgan, *The Fall of Mussolini: Italy, the Italians, and the Second World War* (Oxford: Oxford University Press, 2007).

28. See T.H. Rigby, 'Was Stalin a Disloyal Patron?', *Soviet Studies*, vol.38, no.3, July 1986, pp.311–24; Sheila Fitzpatrick, *On Stalin's Team: The Years of Living Dangerously in Soviet Politics* (Princeton: Princeton University Press, 2015).

29. See Archie Brown, *The Myth of the Strong Leader: Political Leadership in the Modern Age* (London: The Bodley Head, 2014).

30. Richard E. Neustadt, *Presidential Power: The Politics of Leadership* (New York: Signet Books, 1964) pp.42–63.

31. Beatrice Forbes Manz, *The Rise and Rule of Tamerlane* (Cambridge: Cambridge University Press, 1989) p.108.

32. See Peter Self, *Administrative Theories and Politics* (London: George Allen & Unwin, 1977); Charles Lindblom, *The Policy-Making Process* (Englewood Cliffs: Prentice-Hall, 1980).

33. See Caroleen Marji Sayej, *Patriotic Ayatollahs: Nationalism in Post-Saddam Iraq* (Ithaca: Cornell University Press, 2018).

34. Neil Englehart and Patrick Grant, 'Governors, Governance, and Insurgency in Karzai's Afghanistan', *Asian Survey*, vol.55, no.2, March–April 2015, pp.299–324.

35. See Ahmad Shuja Jamal, 'How One Op-ed Explains American Ignorance About Afghanistan', *UN Dispatch*, 22 May 2011.

36. Neil A. Englehart, 'A Tale of Two Afghanistans: Comparative Governance and Insurgency in the North and South', *Asian Survey*, vol.50, no.4, August 2010, pp.735–58 at p.749.

37. Dexter Filkins, 'Death of an Afghan Godfather', *The New Yorker*, 12 July 2011.

38. Fabrizio Foschini, *The Commuter of Alisheng: Death of a Country District Governor* (Kabul: Afghanistan Analysts Network, 14 August 2012).

39. See Susanne Schmeidl, *The Man who would be King: The Challenges to Strengthening Governance in Uruzgan* (The Hague: Netherlands Institute of International Relation *Clingendael*, 2010); Azam Ahmed, 'Powerful Afghan police chief is killed in targeted suicide attack', *The New York Times*, 20 March 2015.

40. Taimoor Shah and Mujib Mashal, 'Taliban assassinate Afghan police chief ahead of elections', *The New York Times*, 18 October 2018.

41. James MacGregor Burns, *Leadership* (New York: Harper and Row, 1978) p.19.

42. James MacGregor Burns, *Leadership* (New York: Harper and Row, 1978) pp.257–397.

43. Archie Brown, *The Myth of the Strong Leader: Political Leadership in the Modern Age* (London: The Bodley Head, 2014) p.101.

44. Archie Brown, *The Myth of the Strong Leader: Political Leadership in the Modern Age* (London: The Bodley Head, 2014) p.148.

45. See Archie Brown, *The Gorbachev Phenomenon* (Oxford: Oxford University Press, 1996); Archie Brown, *Seven Years that Changed the World: Perestroika in Perspective* (Oxford: Oxford University Press, 2007).

46. At a conference in Paris attended by one of the authors in November 1986 at which Karzai was a speaker, Karzai's booming voice led the interpreting team to request that he speak more softly. Karzai replied that as a teacher, he had been trained to project his voice to the back of the classroom. Karzai's remarks were subsequently published: see Hamed Karzai, 'Attitude of the Leadership of Afghan Tribes towards the Regime from 1953 to 1978', *Central Asian Survey*, vol.7, nos.2–3, 1988, pp.33–9.

47. Peter Tomsen, *The Wars of Afghanistan: Messianic Terrorism, Tribal Conflicts, and the Failures of Great Powers* (New York: Public Affairs, 2011) p.642.

48. Peter Tomsen, *The Wars of Afghanistan: Messianic Terrorism, Tribal Conflicts, and the Failures of Great Powers* (New York: Public Affairs, 2011) p.642.

49. Neil A. Englehart, 'A Tale of Two Afghanistans: Comparative Governance and Insurgency in the North and South', *Asian Survey*, vol.50, no.4, August 2010, pp.735–58 at p.756.

50. James Risen, 'Reports link Karzai's brother to Afghanistan heroin trade' *The New York Times*, 4 October 2008; Joshua Partlow, *A Kingdom of Their Own: The Family Karzai and the Afghan Disaster* (New York: Alfred A. Knopf, 2016) pp.139–50.

51. Helene Cooper and Carlotta Gall, 'Cables offer shifting portrait of Karzai', *The New York Times*, 2 December 2010.

52. Craig Whitlock, *The Afghanistan Papers: A Secret History of the War* (New York: Simon & Schuster, 2021) p.183.

53. After ceasing to be president, Karzai's position became even more strident. In a 2016 interview, he stated 'Where are the Taliban from? They are Afghan. If they are Afghan, and [as an] Afghan force they come and capture an area, and we are Afghan, then *we* are capturing that area. What right to do we have [to say otherwise]? If we are all Afghans, how can one Afghan tell another Afghan that you cannot capture this area?'; 'Hamed Karzai: Taliban niru-i khodi hastand wa haq darand manateqi az Afghanistan ra tasarof konand', *JomhurNews*, 4 Mizan 1395 (25 September 2016).

54. This is a ubiquitous phenomenon. See Ian Haney López, *Dog Whistle Politics: How Coded Racial Appeals Have Reinvented Racism and Wrecked the Middle Class* (New York: Oxford University Press, 2015).

55. Phone interview with former US *chargé d'affaires* Ross Wilson, 4 February 2022.

56. Mohib meeting with former US *chargé d'affaires* Ross Wilson, 13 June 2021, Kabul. One of the authors attended this meeting and wrote the minutes for President Ghani.

57. His most notable work appeared after he had served as finance minister: Ashraf Ghani and Clare Lockhart, *Fixing Failed States: A Framework for Rebuilding a Fractured World* (New York: Oxford University Press, 2008).

58. See George Packer, 'Afghanistan's Theorist-in-Chief', *The New Yorker*, 4 July 2016.

59. See Kate Clark and Roxanna Shapour, *The Khalid Payenda Interview (1): An insider's view of Politicking, Graft and the Fall of the Republic* (Kabul: Afghanistan Analysts Network, 27 September 2021).

60. See Ashraf Ghani and Clare Lockhart, *Fixing Failed States A Framework for Rebuilding a Fractured World* (New York: Oxford University Press, 2008) pp.77–8. Experienced election professionals had earned his ire by declining to adopt his proposal, not least because they were fully aware that a tight election timetable meant that an attempt to roll out a high-technology system in a low-technology environment such as that in Afghanistan was extraordinarily risky. On this problem, see Joel D. Barkan, 'Technology is Not Democracy', *Journal of Democracy*, vol.24, no.3, July 2013, pp.156–65; Nic Cheeseman, Gabrielle Lynch and Justin Willis, 'Digital Dilemmas: The Unintended Consequences of Electoral Technology', *Democratization*, vol.25, no.8, 2018, pp.1397–1418.

61. See Ali Yawar Adili and Jelena Bjelica, *The E-Tazkera Rift: Yet Another Political Crisis Looming?* (Kabul: Afghanistan Analysts Network, 22 February 2018).

62. Emrys Schoemaker, 'The Taliban are showing us the danger of personal data falling into the wrong hands', *The Guardian*, 7 September 2021.

63. Clark and Shapour, *The Khalid Payenda Interview (1): An insider's view of politicking, graft and the fall of the Republic* (Kabul: Afghanistan Analysts Network, 27 September 2021).

64. James MacGregor Burns, *Leadership* (New York: Harper and Row, 1978) pp.257–397 at p.18.

65. Khalid Payenda's verdict on Qayoumi was striking: 'He was not listening to anyone … He lived in a different bubble and wasn't interested in the job'. See Clark and Shapour, *The Khalid Payenda Interview (1): An insider's view of politicking, graft and the fall of the Republic* (Kabul: Afghanistan Analysts Network, 27 September 2021).

66. *Julius Cæsar*, Act I, Scene I.

67. Sayed Salahuddin, 'Taliban threatens to disrupt Afghan elections, dismisses September vote as "ploy"', *The Washington Post*, 6 August 2019.

68. See Karen DeYoung, 'Afghan Official says any U.S. deal with the Taliban would "dishonor" American troops as relations sink', *The Washington Post*, 14 March 2019; Ron Nordland and Mujib Mashal, 'Afghan national security chief is sidelined in his own war', *The New York Times*, 30 March 2019.

69. As an example, when the Taliban attacked and killed five prosecutors on their way to release Taliban convicts in 2020, it was decided that releases would be suspended. One of the authors was tasked with communicating and explaining the position to NATO, the US and other international partners. He had barely finished explaining the decision when things shifted back; the Afghan government was no longer suspending the release process.

70. For background on Alipour, see Sune Engel Rasmussen and Ehsanullah Amiri, 'Afghanistan Braces for Worst as U.S. Troop Withdrawal Accelerates', *The Wall Street Journal*, 19 November 2020. Ghani's determination to move against Alipour stood in stark contrast to his welcoming back to Kabul in May 2017 of the notorious *Hezb-e Islami* leader Gulbuddin Hekmatyar, whose party was widely suspected of complicity in the 1988 assassination of the scholar Sayyid Bahauddin Majruh, who was an acquaintance of one of the authors. On the

murder of Majruh, see Chris Sands with Fazelminallah Qazizai, *Night Letters: Gulbuddin Hekmatyar and the Afghan IslamistsWho Changed theWorld* (London: Hurst & Co., 2019) pp.227–8.

71. Rahim Faiez, 'Tensions mount between Afghan government, powerful warlord', *Associated Press*, 23 March 2021.

72. 'Lecture on Peace Building by President Ashraf Ghani at Kabul University: Part 1', 14 January 2021. https://www.youtube.com/watch?v=2jOaKGZxHtA

73. Ali M. Latifi, 'Afghans chant "Allahu Akbar" in defiant protests against Taliban', *Al Jazeera English*, 3 August 2021.

74. Phone interview with former National Security Advisor Hamdullah Mohib, 13 February 2022.

75. Dipali Mukhopadhyay, 'The Afghan Stag Hunt', *Lawfare*, 25 February 2019. The original version can be found in Rousseau's *Discourse on the Origin of Inequality* in Jean-Jacques Rousseau, *The Social Contract and Discourses* (London: J.M. Dent, 1973) pp.27–113 at p.78.

6. DIPLOMATIC DISASTER

1. Walter Lord, *A Night to Remember* (New York: Bantam Books, 1956).

2. *Joint Declaration between the Islamic Republic of Afghanistan and the United States of America for Bringing Peace to Afghanistan* (Washington DC: Department of State, 29 February 2020).

3. The authors are not aware of any evidence in the public domain that any of the allies of the United States had authorised the representative of the United States to make such a commitment on their behalf. While the concept of 'sovereignty' is a complex one, the making of such a promise, unless it had been explicitly authorised, could be seen as a violation of the ally's sovereignty. On some of these complexities, see Stephen D. Krasner, *Sovereignty: Organized Hypocrisy* (Princeton: Princeton University Press, 1999) pp.14–20; James Crawford, *Brownlie's Principles of Public International Law* (Oxford: Oxford University Press, 2012) pp.447–9.

4. See William Maley, 'Talking to the Taliban', *The World Today*, vol.63, no.11, November 2007, pp.4–6; William Maley, 'Negotiating with the Taliban', in Micheline Centlivres-Demont (ed.), *Afghanistan: Identity, Society and Politics since 1980* (London: I. B. Tauris, 2015) pp.268–71; William Maley, *Transition in Afghanistan: Hope, Despair and the Limits of Statebuilding* (London: Routledge, 2018) pp.222–9; William Maley and Ahmad Shuja Jamal, 'Diplomacy of Disaster: The Afghanistan "Peace Process" and the Taliban Occupation of Kabul', *The Hague Journal of Diplomacy*, vol.17, no.1, 2022, pp.32–63.

5. Ewen MacAskill and Simon Tisdall, 'White House shifts Afghanistan strategy towards talks with Taliban', *The Guardian*, 20 July 2010.

6. 'Holbrooke on negotiating peace in Afghanistan', *NPR*, 2 November 2010.

7. Ewen MacAskill and Simon Tisdall, 'White House shifts Afghanistan strategy towards talks with Taliban', *The Guardian*, 20 July 2010.

8. Jamie Crawford, 'Clinton: U.S. would negotiate with Taliban leader', *CNN*, 27 October 2011.

9.   Dexter Filkins and Carlotta Gall, 'Taliban leader in secret talks was an imposter', *The New York Times*, 22 November 2010.

10. See Joshua Partlow, 'Karzai aide blames British for bringing Taliban imposter to talks', *The Washington Post*, 26 November 2010.

11. Steve Coll, *Directorate S: The C.I.A. and America's Secret Wars in Afghanistan and Pakistan* (New York: Penguin Press, 2018) p.640.

12. Eyder Peralta, 'A Plaque And A Flag: U.S. Tries To Rescue Taliban Peace Talks', *NPR*, 20 June 2013.

13. Michele Kelemen, Diaa Hadid and Vanessa Romo, 'Zalmay Khalilzad Appointed As U.S. Special Adviser To Afghanistan', *NPR*, 5 September 2018.

14. Carter Malkasian, *The American War in Afghanistan: A History* (New York: Oxford University Press, 2021) p.425.

15. As we have argued elsewhere (see William Maley and Ahmad Shuja Jamal, 'Diplomacy of Disaster: The Afghanistan "Peace Process" and the Taliban Occupation of Kabul', *The Hague Journal of Diplomacy*, vol.17, no.1, 2022, pp.32–63 at pp.54–6), the closest historical parallel in this respect is provided by the Munich Agreement of September 1938. For background, see Telford Taylor, *Munich: The Price of Peace* (New York: Doubleday, 1979).

16. Phone interview with Ambassador Ross Wilson, former US *chargé d'affaires* in Kabul, 4 February 2022.

17. Philipp Münch and Thomas Ruttig, 'Between Negotiations and Ongoing Resistance: The Situation of the Afghan Insurgency', *Orient* vol.55, no.3, 2014, pp.25–41 at pp.36–7.

18. Phone interview with Ambassador Ross Wilson, 4 February 2022.

19. See Mujib Mashal, 'Confusion over Afghan-Taliban talks further complicates peace process', *The New York Times*, 27 July 2019.

20. See, for example, G.R. Berridge, *Diplomacy: Theory and Practice* (Basingstoke: Palgrave Macmillan, 2015) who argues at p.52 that 'major concessions should not be made at the beginning of negotiations, since this leaves little room for later bargaining'.

21. Tom Malinowski, 'Trump's peace deal with the Taliban is a sham. Here are two honest alternatives', *The Washington Post*, 7 March 2020.

22. Phone interview with former National Security Advisor Hamdullah Mohib, 4 February 2022. Mohib observed that Ghani said as much in a letter to President Trump when he came to power. See also *Collapse and Consequences in Afghanistan: A Conversation with Hamdullah Mohib* (Stanford: The Hoover Institution, 10 January 2022).

23. National Security Advisor Mohib conveyed this to US Assistant Secretary of State Dean Thompson during the latter's visit to Kabul in April 2021. He also offered similar assurances in a May 2021 call with his US counterpart, Jake Sullivan. One of the authors was present at these exchanges and wrote the minutes for President Ghani.

24. National Security Advisor Mohib meeting with NATO Senior Civilian Representative Stefano Pontecorvo, 29 July 2020, Kabul. One of the authors attended this meeting and wrote the minutes for President Ghani.

25. National Security Advisor Mohib meeting with US Deputy Chief of Mission Karen Decker, 31 August 2020, Kabul. One of the authors attended this meeting and wrote the minutes for President Ghani.

26. Foreign Minister Atmar and National Security Advisor Mohib, meeting with Ambassadors Zalmay Khalilzad and Ross Wilson, 5 January 2021, Kabul. One of the authors attended this meeting and wrote the minutes for President Ghani.

27. National Security Advisor Mohib call with US National Security Advisor Jake Sullivan, 22 January 2021, Kabul. One of the authors attended this phone discussion and wrote the minutes for President Ghani.

28. National Security Advisor Mohib call with CIA Director William Burns, 25 March 2021, Kabul. One of the authors attended this phone discussion and wrote the minutes for President Ghani.

29. National Security Advisor Mohib call with US Deputy National Security Advisor Jonathan Finer, 5 April 2021, Kabul. One of the authors attended this phone discussion and wrote the minutes for President Ghani.

30. Terri Moon Cronk, *Biden Announces Full U.S. Troop Withdrawal From Afghanistan by Sept. 11* (Washington DC: U.S. Department of Defense, 14 April 2021).

31. *Afghanistan: Protection of Civilians in Armed Conflict. Midyear Update: 1 January to 30 June 2021* (Kabul: United Nations Assistance Mission in Afghanistan and United Nations Human Rights Office of the High Commissioner, July 2021).

32. Phone interview with National Security Advisor Hamdullah Mohib, 4 February 2022.

33. In 2019, one of the authors saw at least one document, titled 'Independent Defence', drawn up by a retired general working for the Office of the National Security Council.

34. National Security Advisor Mohib call with US National Security Advisor Jake Sullivan, 26 May 2021, Kabul. One of the authors attended this phone discussion and wrote the minutes for President Ghani.

35. National Security Advisor Mohib call with US National Security Advisor Jake Sullivan, 26 May 2021, Kabul.

36. Phone interview with former Deputy National Security Advisor Rafi Fazil, 6 January 2022.

37. Phone interview with former National Security Advisor Hamdullah Mohib, 4 February 2022.

38. Phone interview with Ambassador Ross Wilson, 4 February 2022.

39. A Turkish diplomat told one of the authors that Turkey was not going to upset Qatar by hosting the conference without the right level of participants and reasonable confidence that it would result in a tangible outcome.

40. Foreign Minister Atmar and National Security Advisor Mohib, meeting with Ambassadors Zalmay Khalilzad and Ross Wilson, 5 January 2021. One of the authors attended this meeting and wrote the minutes for President Ghani.

41. This Twitter thread by former Taliban spokesperson Suhail Shahin about Mullah Baradar's visit to Tehran in July 2020 highlights how the Taliban used the visit to bolster their credentials by talking about the situation of Afghan refugees there: https://twitter.com/suhailshaheen1/

status/1278015145483124736?s=20&t=jKB8MLZ9yU9CODqXChtCUA, 1 July 2020.

42. 'Afghanistan Expresses Concern Over Videos Of Taliban Leaders Visiting Members in Pakistan', *Gandhara*, 25 December 2020.

43. 'Chinese officials and Taliban meet, in sign of warming ties', *Aljazeera*, 28 July 2021.

44. Meeting of Chinese Ambassador Wang Yu with National Security Advisor Hamdullah Mohib, 6 July 2020, Kabul. One of the authors attended this meeting and wrote the minutes for President Ghani.

45. Bruce Pannier, 'Uzbekistan Experiences The Pitfalls Of Peacemaking In Afghanistan', *Radio Free Europe/Radio Liberty*, 24 August 2019.

46. Suhasini Haidar, 'India should talk directly to Taliban, says U.S. Special Envoy Zalmay Khalilzad', *The Hindu*, 9 May 2020.

47. Rezaul H. Laskar, 'In a huge shift, India opens channels with Afghan Taliban factions and leaders', *The Hindustan Times*, 9 June 2021.

48. One of the authors received word in June 2020 from the Afghan Foreign Ministry in Kabul and the ambassador in New Delhi that Indian officials had not pre-briefed them before their secret rendezvous with the Taliban.

49. William Maley and Ahmad Shuja Jamal, 'Diplomacy of Disaster: The Afghanistan "Peace Process" and the Taliban Occupation of Kabul', *The Hague Journal of Diplomacy*, vol.17, no.1, 2022, pp.32–63 at p.52.

50. William Maley and Ahmad Shuja Jamal, 'Diplomacy of Disaster: The Afghanistan "Peace Process" and the Taliban Occupation of Kabul', *The Hague Journal of Diplomacy*, vol.17, no.1, 2022, pp.32–63 at p.52.

51. Hamid Shalizi, 'Election rival says Afghan President Ghani hindering peace deal', *Reuters*, 1 March 2019.

52. Kathy Gannon, 'AP Interview: Karzai says Afghan election threatens peace', *AP News*, 25 September 2019.

53. 'Top challenger of Afghan president says ready to quit elections for peace', *Reuters*, 29 August 2019.

54. Radio Azadi, 'Interview: U.S. Envoy Backs Afghan Presidential Election If No Peace Deal', *Radio Free Europe/Radio Liberty*, 1 August 2019.

55. See Thomas Johnson, 'The 2019 Afghan Presidential Election: An Assessment of Problematic Processes and Results', *Afghanistan*, vol.4, no.1, April 2021, pp.19–46.

56. Mujib Mashal, Fatima Faizi and Najim Rahim, 'Ghani takes the oath of Afghan president. his rival does, too', *The New York Times*, 9 March 2020.

57. Julian Borger, 'US to cut $1bn of Afghanistan aid over failure to agree unity government', *The Guardian*, 24 March 2020.

58. Phone interview with Ambassador Ross Wilson, 4 February 2022.

59. Helene Cooper, 'Pentagon shifts $1.5 billion to border wall From Afghan war budget and other military projects', *The New York Times*, 10 May 2019.

60. Michael Semple, Robin L. Raphel and Shams Rasikh, *An Independent Assessment of the Afghanistan Peace Process June 2018–May 2021* (Edinburgh: Political Settlements Research Programme, 2021) p.2. See also S. Yaqub Ibrahimi, 'False Negotiations

and the Fall of Afghanistan to the Taliban', *International Journal*, 2022, DOI: 10.1177/0020702022135299.

61. Laurel Miller, 'Will the U.S.-Taliban deal end the war?', *The New York Times*, 18 February 2020.

62. Kate Clark, *The Taleban's Rise to Power: As the US Prepared for Peace, the Taleban Prepared for War* (Kabul: Afghanistan Analysts Network, 21 August 2021).

63. Munir Ahmed, 'US envoy lauds Pakistan's role in Afghan peace talks process', *The Washington Post*, 14 September 2020.

64. National Security Advisor Mohib call with CIA Director William Burns, 25 March 2021, Kabul. One of the authors attended this phone call and wrote the minutes for President Ghani.

65. National Security Advisor Mohib call with US National Security Advisor Sullivan, 26 May 2021, Kabul. One of the authors attended this phone call and wrote the minutes for President Ghani.

66. Phone interview with Ambassador Ross Wilson, 4 February 2022.

67. Taliban members of their so-called 'Education Commission' visited several Afghan-funded schools in the province of Baluchistan in 2021 and urged school administrators to teach the Taliban curriculum. They inspected the schools' records and promised to make frequent inspection visits. Afghanistan protested these visits through diplomatic channels and the office of its Special Representative for Pakistan. The visits did not cease.

68. National Security Advisor Mohib meeting with Qatari envoy Mutlaq Al-Qahtani, 7 July 2021, Kabul. One of the authors was present at the meeting and wrote the minutes for President Ghani.

69. Kathy Gannon and Tameem Akhgar, 'US vows to isolate Taliban if they take power by force', *ABC News*, 11 August 2021.

70. *United Nations Security Council Resolution 2513 (2020)* (New York: United Nations, S/RES/2513 (2020), 10 March 2020).

71. US Secretary of State Anthony Blinken's letter to President Ashraf Ghani, published by TOLO News in March 2020: https://tolonews.com/pdf/02.pdf.

72. Jonathan Landay and Hamid Shalizi, 'U.S. proposes interim government could run Afghanistan until new polls', *Reuters*, 9 March 2021.

73. Kate Clark, *Afghanistan's Conflict in 2021 (2): Republic Collapse and Taleban Victory in the Long View of History* (Kabul: Afghanistan Analysts Network, 30 December 2021). See also Steve Brooking, *Why Was a Negotiated Peace Always Out of Reach in Afghanistan? Opportunities and Obstacles, 2001-21* (Washington DC: Peaceworks no.184, United States Institute of Peace, August 2022).

74. Michael Crowley, 'A veteran diplomat, a "tragic figure," battles critics in the U.S. and Afghanistan', *The New York Times*, 16 November 2021. For a recent attempt to downplay the adverse consequences of the February 2020 agreement, see Laurel Miller, 'The Unwinnable War: America's Blind Spots in Afghanistan', *Foreign Affairs*, vol.101, no.6, November-December 2022, pp.174–80.

75. Carter Malkasian, *The American War in Afghanistan: A History* (New York: Oxford University Press, 2021) pp.425, 446.

76. Quoted in Henry Kissinger, *Leadership: Six Studies in World Strategy* (London: Allen Lane, 2022) p.30.

7.   CASCADE EFFECTS AND THE UNRAVELLING OF MILITARY POWER

1.   Cicero, *De Natura Deorum. Academica* (Cambridge: Harvard University Press, 1951) p.375.
2.   Niamatullah Ibrahimi and William Maley, *Afghanistan: Politics and Economics in a Globalising State* (London: Routledge, 2020) p.164.
3.   Nishank Motwani, 'For real peace, Afghanistan needs a Plan B', *The Lowy Interpreter*, 11 September 2020.
4.   William Maley, 'On the brink of disaster: how decades of progress in Afghanistan could be wiped out in short order', *The Conversation*, 8 July 2021.
5.   *Roberts-Smith v. Fairfax Media Publications Pty Limited (No.20)* [2021] FCA 824.
6.   Niccolò Machiavelli, *The Prince* (Cambridge: Cambridge University Press, 1988) p.19.
7.   Cass R. Sunstein, *Going to Extremes: How Like Minds Unite and Divide* (New York: Oxford University Press, 2009) p.90.
8.   Cass R. Sunstein, *Going to Extremes: How Like Minds Unite and Divide* (New York: Oxford University Press, 2009) p.92.
9.   Cass R. Sunstein, *Risk and Reason: Safety, Law, and the Environment* (Cambridge: Cambridge University Press, 2002) p.86.
10.   Cass R. Sunstein, *Going to Extremes: How Like Minds Unite and Divide* (New York: Oxford University Press, 2009) p.87.
11.   Hans Christian Andersen, *Stories and Tales* (London: Routledge, 2002) pp.81–5.
12.   Timur Kuran, 'Ethnic Norms and Their Transformation Through Reputational Cascades', *Journal of Legal Studies*, vol.27, no.2, June 1998, pp.623–59.
13.   Timur Kuran and Cass R. Sunstein, 'Availability Cascades and Risk Regulation', *Stanford Law Review*, vol.51, no.4, April 1999, pp.683–768 at p.683.
14.   Wilhelm von Sternburg, *Carl von Ossietzky: Es ist eine unheimliche Stimme in Deutschland* (Berlin: Aufbau Taschenbuch Verlag, 1996) pp.270–304.
15.   Timur Kuran, *Private Truths, Public Lies: The Social Consequences of Preference Falsification* (Cambridge: Harvard University Press, 1995) p.252.
16.   James C. Scott, *Domination and the Arts of Resistance: Hidden Transcripts* (New Haven: Yale University Press, 1990) p.224.
17.   See Peter Siani-Davies, *The Romanian Revolution of December 1989* (Ithaca: Cornell University Press, 2005).
18.   Timur Kuran, *Private Truths, Public Lies: The Social Consequences of Preference Falsification* (Cambridge: Harvard University Press, 1995) pp.262–88. For some earlier examples, see Timur Kuran, 'Sparks and prairie fires: A theory of unanticipated political revolution', *Public Choice*, vol.61, no.1, April 1989, pp.41–74.
19.   Carter Malkasian, 'How the Good War Went Bad: America's Slow-Motion Failure in Afghanistan', *Foreign Affairs*, vol.99, no.2, March–April 2020, pp.77–91 at p.83.
20.   *A Survey of the Afghan People: Afghanistan in 2019* (Kabul: The Asia Foundation, 2019) pp.35, 315. See also Karl Laltenthaler, Arie W. Kruglanski and Austin J. Knuppe, 'The Paradox of the Heavy-Handed Insurgent: Public Support for the

Taliban among Afghan Pashtuns', *Studies in Conflict and Terrorism*, 2022, DOI: 10.1080/1057610X.2022.2055008.

21. Henry S. Bradsher, *Afghan Communism and Soviet Intervention* (Karachi: Oxford University Press, 1999) p.346.

22. See Barnett R. Rubin, 'The Fragmentation of Afghanistan', *Foreign Affairs,* vol.68, no.5, Winter 1989–90, pp.150–68 at p.155.

23. Chris Sands with Fazelminallah Qazizai, *Night Letters: Gulbuddin Hekmatyar and the Afghan Islamists Who Changed the World* (London: Hurst & Co., 2019) p.254.

24. Thomas Hobbes, *Leviathan* (Cambridge: Cambridge University Press, 1996) p.62.

25. Edward A. Gargan, 'Afghan president agrees to step down', *The New York Times,* 19 March 1992.

26. Henry S. Bradsher, *Afghan Communism and Soviet Intervention* (Karachi: Oxford University Press, 1999) *p.379.*

27. See William Maley, *The Afghanistan Wars* (London: Macmillan/Red Globe Press, 2021) pp.211–12.

28. Andrew Roberts, *Churchill: Walking with Destiny* (London: Allen Lane, 2018) p.262.

29. *House of Commons Hansard*, vol.361, 4 June 1940, column 796.

30. Ian Kershaw, *The End: Hitler's Germany, 1944–45* (London: Allen Lane, 2011) p.323.

31. Andrew Roberts, *Churchill: Walking with Destiny* (London: Allen Lane, 2018) p.947.

32. Lawrence Freedman, *The Transformation of Strategic Affairs* (London: Adelphi Paper no.379, Routledge, 2006) p.22.

33. George Packer, 'The Betrayal', *The Atlantic*, 31 January 2022. In a March 2016 interview with the BBC, Ghani had stated that he had 'no sympathy' with Afghans fleeing the country: see Yalda Hakim, 'President Ghani calls for Afghans to remain in country', *BBC News*, 31 March 2016. It was therefore unsurprising that he won little sympathy from Afghans when he chose to flee himself.

34. Thomas Gibbons-Neff, Taimoor Shah and Najim Rahim, '"What kind of peace talks are these?": on the front lines of a 17-year war', *The New York Times*, 17 July 2019.

35. Thomas Gibbons-Neff, David Zucchino and Lara Jakes, 'U.S. pushes U.N.-led peace conference in letter to Afghan leader', *The New York Times*, 7 March 2021.

36. Steve Coll and Adam Entous, 'The Secret History of the U.S. Diplomatic Failure in Afghanistan', *The New Yorker*, 10 December 2021.

37. See Winston S. Churchill, *The World Crisis: Vol.1 1911-1914* (London: The Folio Society, 2007) p.151.

38. See *Afghanistan Study Group Final Report* (Washington DC: United States Institute of Peace, February 2021) p.2, together with the USIP announcement of the Report's publication.

39. See Jonathan Mercer, *Reputation and International Politics* (Ithaca: Cornell University Press, 1996); Barbara F. Walter, *Reputation and Civil War: Why Separatist Conflicts Are So Violent* (Cambridge: Cambridge University Press, 2009); Gregory D. Miller, *The Shadow of the Past: Reputation and Military Alliances before the First World War* (Ithaca: Cornell University Press, 2012); Keren Yarhi-Milo, *Who*

Fights for Reputation? The Psychology of Leaders in International Conflict (Princeton: Princeton University Press, 2018).

40. Timur Kuran, *Private Truths, Public Lies: The Social Consequences of Preference Falsification* (Cambridge: Harvard University Press, 1995) p.269.

41. See Niamatullah Ibrahimi, 'Rumor and Collective Action Frames: An Assessment of How Competing Conceptions of Gender, Culture and Rule Of Law Shaped Responses to Rumor and Violence in Afghanistan', *Studies in Conflict and Terrorism*, vol.45, no.1, 2022, pp.20–42.

42. Timur Kuran, *Private Truths, Public Lies: The Social Consequences of Preference Falsification* (Cambridge: Harvard University Press, 1995) p.71.

43. See F.A. Hayek, *Studies in Philosophy, Politics and Economics* (London: Routledge & Kegal Paul, 1967) pp.22–42.

44. Tim Willasey-Wilsey, *Why Did the Afghan Army Evaporate?* (London: Royal United Services Institute, 18 August 2021).

45. Jonathan Landay, Arshad Mohammed and Idrees Ali, 'Exclusive: Planned $1 billion U.S. aid cut would hit Afghan security force funds', *Reuters*, 5 April 2020.

46. 'Face the Nation', *CBS Television*, 24 October 2021.

47. Sami Sadat, 'I commanded Afghan troops this year. we were betrayed', *The New York Times*, 25 August 2021. For more detailed elaboration of these points, see Abdul Waheed Ahmad and Gabriella Lloyd, *Lessons from Afghanistan for Western State-Building in a Multipolar World* (Washington DC: Issue Brief, South Asia Center, The Atlantic Council, May 2022); *Collapse of the Afghan National Defense and Security Forces: An Assessment of the Factors That Led to Its Demise. Interim Report* (Arlington: SIGAR 22-22-IP Evaluation Report, Special Inspector General for Afghanistan Reconstruction, 12 May 2022) pp.6–24.

48. Catherine Putz, 'SIGAR on the unsustainability of the Afghan air force', *The Diplomat*, 19 January 2022.

49. *Agreement for Bringing Peace to Afghanistan between the Islamic Emirate of Afghanistan which is not recognized by the United States as a state and is known as the Taliban and the United States of America* (Washington DC: Department of State, 29 February 2020). Emphasis added.

50. See Theodore McLaughlin, *Desertion: Trust and Mistrust in Civil Wars* (Ithaca: Cornell University Press, 2020) pp.6–12.

51. Thomas Gibbons-Neff, 'U.S. leaves its last Afghan base, effectively ending operations', *The New York Times*, 2 July 2021.

52. 'Face the Nation', *CBS Television*, 31 October 2021. For similar claims from Khalilzad, see Katrina Manson, 'Ghani's escape derailed last-ditch deal with Taliban, US envoy says', *The Financial Times*, 15 September 2021.

8. THE FINAL DAYS OF KABUL

1. Unless otherwise indicated, information in this chapter comes from the personal experiences and observations of one of the authors.

2. Barnett R. Rubin, 'In long-suffering Afghanistan, this is a peace deal worth trying', *The Washington Post*, 16 February 2020.

3. Matthew Lee and Lolita C. Baldor, 'Afghanistan violence must ease for peace deal with Taliban to advance, Pompeo says', *Military Times*, 6 March 2020.

4. 'Ghani: Niruhai amniati afghan az halat-e difah-e faal ba halat-e tahajumi taghyiir mawze dehand', *Anatolia News Agency*, 12 May 2020.

5. 'Mizan-e khoshunat wa talafat', Office of the National Security Council.

6. 'Jang wa talafat dar 1399', Office of the National Security Council.

7. See Ezzatullah Mehrdad, 'Assassinations silence Afghanistan's intellectuals', *The Diplomat*, 24 March 2021.

8. *Special Report: Killing of Human Rights Defenders, Journalists and Media Workers in Afghanistan 2018-2021* (Kabul: United Nations Assistance Mission in Afghanistan, February 2021) pp.4, 12.

9. US misreading of the Taliban could be explained in various ways, and there are substantial literatures on misperception, cognitive bias, information processing, and trust that are potentially relevant. See, for example, Robert Jervis, *Perception and Misperception in International Politics* (Princeton: Princeton University Press, 1976); Robert Jervis, *How Statesmen Think: The Psychology of International Politics* (Princeton: Princeton University Press, 2017); Nicholas J. Wheeler, *Trusting Enemies: Interpersonal Relationships in International Conflict* (Oxford: Oxford University Press, 2018); Marcus Holmes, *Face-to-Face Diplomacy: Social Neuroscience and International Relations* (Cambridge: Cambridge University Press, 2018); Dominic D.P. Johnson, *Strategic Instincts: The Adaptive Advantages of Cognitive Biases in International Politics* (Princeton: Princeton University Press, 2020).

10. Those who have been gulled may be extremely reluctant to countenance the possibility that this has happened. A classic example was provided by British Prime Minister Neville Chamberlain after the Munich Agreement of September 1938. When a colleague pointed out that Hitler had routinely broken his promises in the past, Chamberlain replied 'this time it is different; this time he has made the promises to me': John W. Wheeler-Bennett, *Munich: Prologue to Tragedy* (London: Macmillan, 1948) p.182.

11. National Security Advisor Mohib meeting with US *chargé d'affaires* Ross Wilson, 28 December 2020, Kabul. One of the authors attended this meeting and wrote the minutes for President Ghani.

12. *Joint Statement Condemning Increased Violence and Targeted Killings in Afghanistan* (New York: United States Mission to the United Nations, 22 March 2021).

13. Phone interview with Dr Najibullah Wardak, former Deputy Minister of Defense, March–August 2021, 13 January 2022.

14. See Daniel R. Brunstetter and Amélie Férey, 'Armed drones and sovereignty: the arc of strategic sovereign possibilities', in Paul Lushenko, Srinjoy Bose and William Maley (eds), *Drones and Global Order: The Implications of Remote Warfare for International Society* (London: Routledge, 2022) pp.137–55 at p.143.

15. 'Afghanistan Coordinating Actions', US planning document shared with the Afghan government, August 2021.

16. See Anthony Loyd, 'West has left us at mercy of Taliban, says ex-Afghan president', *The Times*, 1 July 2021.

17. Author's note from former National Security Advisor Mohib's recounting of the meeting to British ambassador Sir Laurie Bristow, 30 June 2021. One of

the authors attended the Mohib-Bristow meeting and wrote the minutes for President Ghani.

18. Phone interview with former Deputy Minister of Defence Dr Najibullah Wardak, 13 January 2022.

19. See https://twitter.com/KarzaiH/status/1419726932695003140, July 2021.

20. 'Elam-e mawjudiyat-e hezb-e taza "Harakat-e nejat-e Afghanistan" ba rahbari-e Omar Zakhilwal', *BBC Persian*, 5 March 2021.

21. Phone interview with Deputy Minister of Defence Dr Najibullah Wardak, 13 January 2022.

22. National Security Advisor Mohib meeting with General Sir Nicholas Carter in London, July 2021. One of the authors attended this meeting and wrote the minutes for President Ghani.

23. 'Rahbaran-e siasi-e keshwar himayat-e qate-e khudra az niruha-i amniati dar nabard ba Taliban elam kardand', *Hasht-e Sobh*, 9 Asad 1400 (31 July 2021).

24. *Markaz-e Melli-e Tawheed* figures from 5 August 2021.

25. Phone interview with former Deputy Minister of Defence Dr Najibullah Wardak, 13 January 2022.

26. Phone interview with former Deputy Minister of Defence Dr Najibullah Wardak, 13 January 2022.

27. Phone interview with former Deputy Minister of Defence Dr Najibullah Wardak, 13 January 2022.

28. Phone interview with former Deputy Minister of Defence Dr Najibullah Wardak, 13 January 2022.

29. Information from former National Security Advisor Hamdullah Mohib.

30. Phone interview with former Deputy Minister of Defence Dr Najibullah Wardak, 13 January 2022.

31. Anna Coren, Sandi Sidhu, Tim Lister and Abdul Basir Bina, 'Taliban fighters execute 22 Afghan commandos as they try to surrender', *CNN*, 14 July 2021.

32. Information from former National Security Advisor Hamdullah Mohib; former Deputy National Security Advisor Rafi Fazil; Ministry of Defence sources.

33. Information from former Deputy Minister of Defence Dr Najibullah Wardak, 21 February 2022. See also *DOD's Salary Payments to the Afghan Ministry of Defense: DOD Did Not Use APPS as Intended and Internal Control Weaknesses Raise Questions About the Accuracy of $232 Million in Salary Payments* (Arlington: SIGAR 22-34 Audit Report, Special Inspector General for Afghanistan Reconstruction, 22 July 2022); Timor Sharan, *Inside Afghanistan: Political Networks, Informal Order, and State Disruption* (London: Routledge, 2023) p.275.

34. *Gozaresh-e dastawardha-i wezarat-e defa-e meli dar tei sal-e 1398 shamsi* (Kabul: Ministry of Defence, Islamic Republic of Afghanistan, 2021).

35. Author's note from a meeting in June 2021 where Norwegian Ambassador Ole Andreas Lindeman alerted former National Security Advisor Mohib that the elite police Crisis Response Unit soldiers were worried about the safety of their families.

36. Information from former Deputy Minister of Defence Dr Najibullah Wardak, 21 February 2022.

37. Phone interview with former Deputy Minister of Defence Dr Najibullah Wardak, 13 January 2022.

38. Phone interview with former Deputy Minister of Defence Dr Najibullah Wardak, 13 January 2022.

39. National Security Advisor Mohib's call with US Deputy National Security Advisor Jonathan Finer, 5 April 2021. One of the authors attended this call and wrote the minutes for President Ghani.

40. Phone interview with former Deputy National Security Advisor Fazil, 7 January 2022.

41. Phone interview with former Deputy National Security Advisor Fazil, 7 January 2022.

42. Former National Security Advisor Mohib in interview with Lieutenant-General H.R. McMaster: *Collapse and Consequences in Afghanistan: A Conversation with Hamdullah Mohib* (Stanford: The Hoover Institution, 10 January 2022).

43. Phone interview with former Deputy Minister of Defence Dr Najibullah Wardak, 13 January 2022.

44. 'Soqut-e Zaranj, markaz-e wilayat-e Nimruz-e Afghanistan ba dast-e Taliban', *BBC Persian*, 6 August 2021.

45. See Ezzatullah Mehrdad and Susannah George, 'Taliban on the verge of capturing two of Afghanistan's largest cities after taking 11th provincial capital', *The Washington Post*, 12 August 2021.

46. A former high-ranking official of the Office the National Security Council to one of the authors, 14 August 2021.

47. A former high-ranking official of the Office the National Security Council to one of the authors, 9 January 2022.

48. Phone interview with former Deputy Minister of Defence Dr Najibullah Wardak, 13 January 2022.

49. Phone interviews with former Deputy National Security Advisor Fazil and Hussain Nasrat, former Chief of Staff to Vice President Danesh, 7 and 19 January 2022, respectively.

50. Phone interview with former Deputy National Security Advisor Fazil, 7 January 2022.

51. 'Seh ruz-e akhir-e Ashraf Ghani dar arg-e Kabul', *Hasht-e Sobh*, 18 Aqrab 1400 (9 November 2021).

52. Saleh's Facebook posting announcing the resistance can be found at https://www.facebook.com/AmrullahSaleh.Afg/posts/4158952600879614, 13 August 2021.

53. Phone interview with a former high-ranking official of the Office the National Security Council, 9 January 2022.

54. Phone interview with former National Security Advisor Mohib, 13 February 2022.

55. Phone interview with a former high-ranking official of the Office of the National Security Council, 9 January 2022.

56. Phone interview with former Deputy National Security Advisor Fazil, 7 January 2022.

57. Phone interview with former Deputy Minister of Defence Dr Najibullah Wardak, 13 January 2022.

58. Phone interview with former Deputy Minister of Defence Dr Najibullah Wardak, 13 January 2022; phone interview with former National Security Advisor Mohib, 13 February 2022.

59. Phone interview with former National Security Advisor Mohib, 13 February 2022.

60. Phone interview with former National Security Advisor Mohib, 13 February 2022.

61. Phone interview with a high-ranking official of the Office of the National Security Council, 9 January 2022.

62. Phone interview with former National Security Advisor Mohib, 13 February 2022.

63. Phone interview with former US *chargé d'affaires* Ross Wilson, 4 February 2022.

64. Phone interview with former National Security Advisor Mohib, 13 February 2022.

65. Phone interview with former National Security Advisor Mohib, 13 February 2022.

66. Phone interview with former National Security Advisor Mohib, 13 February 2022.

67. Phone interview with former National Security Advisor Mohib, 13 February 2022.

68. Phone interview with former US *chargé d'affaires* Ross Wilson, 4 February 2022.

69. Phone interview with former National Security Advisor Mohib, 13 February 2022.

70. Phone interview with former US *chargé d'affaires* Ross Wilson, 4 February 2022.

71. Noor's Facebook posting on a high-level meeting to this effect can be found at https://www.facebook.com/gen.noor/posts/398146618348664, 14 August 2021.

72. Phone interview with former Deputy National Security Advisor Fazil, 7 January 2022.

73. Şeyma Çelik, 'Taliban shahr-e Mehtarlam, markaz-e wilayat-e Laghman-e Afghanistan ra tasarrof kard', *Anadolu News Agency*, 14 August 2021.

74. For a discussion of the impact on the ground of this development, see Zain Samir, 'Is this a new Taliban?', *London Review of Books*, vol.44, no.13, 7 July 2022.

75. Phone interview with former Deputy Minister of Defence Dr Najibullah Wardak, 13 January 2022.

76. https://twitter.com/bbcyaldahakim/status/1426521422457937922?lang=en 14 August 2021.

77. Phone interview with former National Security Advisor Mohib, 13 February 2022.

78. Phone interview with former Deputy National Security Advisor Fazil, 7 January 2022.

79. Phone interview with former Deputy Minister of Defence Dr Najibullah Wardak, 13 January 2022.

80. Phone interview with former Deputy Minister of Defence Dr Najibullah Wardak, 13 January 2022.

81. Phone interview with former Deputy National Security Advisor Fazil, 7 January 2022.

82.   Phone interview with former Deputy National Security Advisor Fazil, 7 January 2022.

83.   Saleh's posting saying he left the city at 9.15 am on 15 August can be found at https://www.facebook.com/AmrullahSaleh.Afg/posts/4611434802298056, 31 December 2021.

84.   Phone interview with former Deputy National Security Advisor Fazil, 7 January 2022.

85.   Phone interview with Hussain Nasrat, former Chief of Staff to Vice President Danesh, 19 January 2022.

86.   Phone interview with Hussain Nasrat, former Chief of Staff to Vice President Danesh, 19 January 2022.

87.   Former Deputy National Security Advisor Fazil's recollection of the conversation, 7 January 2022.

88.   Former Deputy National Security Advisor Fazil's recollection of the conversation, 7 January 2022.

89.   Kathy Gannon, 'The AP interview: Karzai "invited" Taliban to stop chaos', *The Associated Press*, 16 December 2021.

90.   Salam Rahimi and Matin Bek, chosen by Ghani to be part of the empowered delegation but abandoned in Kabul when Ghani fled, were on the same commercial plane as one of the authors. Also on the plane were Second Vice President Danesh, Minister of Foreign Affairs Atmar, and head of the National Directorate of Security Zia Saraj, among others.

91.   Phone interview with former Deputy Minister of Defence Dr Najibullah Wardak, 13 January 2022.

92.   Former National Security Advisor Mohib in interview with Lieutenant-General H. R. McMaster: *Collapse and Consequences in Afghanistan: A Conversation with Hamdullah Mohib* (Stanford: The Hoover Institution, 10 January 2022).

93.   Robert Greene, *The 48 Laws of Power* (London: Profile Books, 2000) p.170.

9.   CONCLUSION

1.   On these events, see T.G. Otte, *July Crisis: The World's Descent into War, Summer 1914* (Cambridge: Cambridge University Press, 2014).

2.   See William R. Thompson, 'Powderkegs, sparks and World War I', in Gary Goertz and Jack S. Levy (eds), *Explaining War and Peace: Case Studies and Necessary Condition Counterfactuals* (London: Routledge, 2007) pp.113–45; Jack S. Levy and John A. Vasquez, 'Introduction: historians, political scientists, and the causes of the First World War', in Jack S. Levy and John A. Vasquez (eds), *The Outbreak of the First World War: Structure, Politics, and Decision-Making* (Cambridge: Cambridge University Press, 2014) pp.3–29 at pp.18–19.

3.   M. Cary and H.H. Scullard, *A History of Rome down to the Reign of Constantine* (Basingstoke: Palgrave Macmillan, 1975) p.551.

4.   See Adam Ferguson, *An Essay on the History of Civil Society* (Cambridge: Cambridge University Press, 1995) p.119. See also Robert K. Merton, 'The Unanticipated Consequences of Purposive Social Action', *American Sociological Review*, vol.1, no.6, December 1936, pp.894–904.

5. See Barry A. Turner, 'The Development of Disasters—A Sequence Model for the Analysis of the Origins of Disasters', *Sociological Review*, vol. 24, no. 4, November 1976, pp. 754–74.

6. *What We Need to Learn: Lessons from Twenty Years of Afghanistan Reconstruction* (Arlington: SIGAR 21-46-LL, Special Inspector General for Afghanistan Reconstruction, August 2021) pp. 4–5.

7. *The Federal Budget in Fiscal Year 2020* (Washington DC: Congressional Budget Office, April 2021).

8. *Estimated Costs to Each U.S. Taxpayer of Each of the Wars in Afghanistan, Iraq and Syria* (Washington DC: Department of Defence, March 2021).

9. 'Overwhelming majority backs US withdrawal from Afghanistan: poll', *The Hill*, 30 April 2021.

10. Interestingly, as late as 1967, a careful study suggested that mass opinion on Vietnam did 'not seem to possess much potential for controlling or limiting the alternatives of the administration': Sidney Verba, Richard A. Brody, Edwin B. Parker, Norman H. Nie, Nelson W. Polsby, Paul Ekman and Gordon S. Black, 'Public Opinion and the War in Vietnam', *American Political Science Review*, vol. 61, no. 2, June 1967, pp. 317–33 at p. 333. The 1968 Tet Offensive did much to shift US opinion in a dovish direction: see Guenter Lewy, *America in Vietnam* (New York: Oxford University Press, 1978) p. 434.

11. Andrew Mack, 'Why Big Nations Lose Small Wars: The Politics of Asymmetric Conflict', *World Politics*, vol. 27, no. 2, January 1975, pp. 175–200 at p. 187.

12. For a sample of such thinking, see Stephen M. Walt, 'The Biden doctrine will allow America to focus on bigger goals', *The Financial Times*, 30 August 2021.

13. Michael Birnbaum, Mary Ilyushina, Paul Sonne, and Isabelle Khurshudyan, 'Russia unleashes military assault on Ukraine that Biden calls "premeditated war"', *The New York Times*, 24 February 2022. On connections between the exit from Afghanistan and the Russian invasion of Ukraine, see William Maley, 'Why Now?—The Afghanistan-Ukraine Nexus', *Australian Outlook*, 5 April 2022. Other analysts have since made similar points. Eliot A. Cohen, 'The Return of Statecraft: Back to Basics in the Post-American World', *Foreign Affairs*, vol. 101, no. 3, May–June 2022, pp. 117–29, wrote at p. 124 that 'U.S. decisions on Afghanistan, Syria, and other trouble spots were similarly treated as local and separable, with little apparent awareness that they would have global repercussions. It was surely no accident that Russia's annexation of Crimea followed less than a year after the Obama administration failed to enforce its supposed redline on Syria's use of chemical weapons. Nor was it likely a coincidence that Russia invaded Ukraine following the United States' humiliating scuttle from Afghanistan'. H.R. McMaster and Gabriel Scheinmann, 'U.S. Restraint Has Created an Unstable and Dangerous World', *Foreignpolicy.com*, 17 June 2022, argued that 'After surrendering Afghanistan to a terrorist organization and conducting a humiliating retreat from Kabul, the administration's attempts to deter the Russian invasion with threats of punishment were simply not credible'. Lawrence Freedman, 'Why War Fails: Russia's Invasion of Ukraine and the Limits of Military Power', *Foreign Affairs*, vol. 101, no. 4, July–August 2022,

pp.10–23, noted at p.18 that 'the West appeared divided and unsettled after Donald Trump's presidency, an impression that was confirmed by the botched U.S. withdrawal from Afghanistan in August 2021'. There was also considerable alarm in Ukraine at the time of the collapse of the Republican system: see Alyona Getmanchuk, 'Chomu reaktsiia Baidena na Afhanistan vazhliva dlia Ukrainy', *Ukrainska Pravda*, 16 August 2021. For further evidence as to how the exit from Afghanistan influenced Russian elite thinking, see 'Patrushev dopustil povtorenie afganskogo stsenariia na Ukraine', *Izvestiia*, 19 August 2021.

14. See, for example, Laurel Miller, 'A peace "surge" to end war in Afghanistan', *The New York Times*, 23 July 2017; Barnett R. Rubin, 'In long-suffering Afghanistan, this is a peace deal worth trying'. *The Washington Post*, 17 February 2020.

15. See, for example, Michael Wolff, *Fire and Fury: Inside the Trump White House* (New York: Henry Holt, 2018); Jerrold M. Post with Stephanie R. Doucette, *Dangerous Charisma: The Political Psychology of Donald Trump and His Followers* (New York: Pegasus Books, 2019; Daniel W. Drezner, *The Toddler in Chief: What Donald Trump Teaches us about the Modern Presidency* (Chicago: The University of Chicago Press, 2020); Mary L. Trump, *Too Much and Never Enough: How my Family Created the World's Most Dangerous Man* (New York: Simon & Schuster, 2020); Philip Rucker and Carol Leonnig, *A Very Stable Genius: Donald J. Trump's Testing of America* (London: Bloomsbury, 2020). See also Lawrence Freedman, *Command: The Politics of Military Operations from Korea to Ukraine* (London: Allen Lane, 2022) p.474.

16. See Jackson Diehl, 'Mike Pompeo is the worst secretary of state in history', *The Washington Post*, 30 August 2020.

17. See Douglas London, 'CIA's former counterterrorism chief for the region: Afghanistan, not an intelligence failure—something much worse', *JustSecurity*, 18 August 2021.

18. See Carol Leonnig and Philip Rucker, *I Alone Can Fix It: Donald J. Trump's Catastrophic Final Year* (London: Bloomsbury, 2021).

19. Peter Baker, 'At 79, Biden Is testing the boundaries of age and the presidency', *The New York Times*, 9 July 2022.

20. See Juliet Kaarbo, 'New directions for leader personality research: breaking bad in foreign policy', *International Affairs*, vol.97, no.2, March 2021, pp.423–41; also Angus McIntyre (ed.), *Aging and Political Leadership* (Melbourne: Oxford University Press, 1988).

21. Neena Satija, 'Echoes of Biden's 1987 plagiarism scandal continue to reverberate', *The Washington Post*, 5 June 2019.

22. Robert M. Gates, *Duty: Memoirs of a Secretary at War* (New York: Alfred A. Knopf, 2014) p.288.

23. See Mark Weisbrot, 'Joe Biden championed the Iraq war. Will that come back to haunt him now?', *The Guardian*, 18 February 2020.

24. See Bob Woodward, *Obama's Wars* (New York: Simon & Schuster, 2010) pp.66–70.

25. Joshua Partlow, *A Kingdom of Their Own: The Family Karzai and the Afghan Disaster* (New York: Alfred A. Knopf, 2016) p.29.

26. Jennifer Brick Murtazashvili, 'Biden Continues to Bungle Afghanistan', *The National Interest*, 14 February 2022.

27. See Thomas E. Mann and Norman J. Ornstein, *It's Even Worse Than It Looks: How the American Constitutional System Collided with the New Politics of Extremism* (New York: Basic Books, 2012).

28. See John Sides, Michael Tesler and Lynn Vavreck, *Identity Crisis: The 2016 Presidential Campaign and the Battle for the Meaning of America* (Princeton: Princeton University Press, 2018); Steven Levitsky and Daniel Ziblatt, *How Democracies Die* (New York: Random House, 2018); Pippa Norris and Ronald Inglehart, *Cultural Backlash: Trump, Brexit and Authoritarian Populism* (Cambridge: Cambridge University Press, 2019); Russell Muirhead and Nancy L. Rosenblum, *A Lot of People are Saying: The New Conspiracism and the Assault on Democracy* (Princeton: Princeton University Press, 2019); Barbara F. Walter, *How Civil Wars Start and How to Stop Them* (New York: Random House, 2022).

29. See James D. Fearon, 'Counterfactuals and Hypothesis Testing in Political Science', *World Politics*, vol.43, no.2, January 1991, pp.169–95; Richard Ned Lebow, *Forbidden Fruit: Counterfactuals and International Relations* (Princeton: Princeton University Press, 2010) pp.29–66; Richard Ned Lebow, *Archduke Franz Ferdinand Lives! A World Without World War I* (New York: Palgrave Macmillan, 2014).

30. For some discussion, see Tamim Asey, *Taliban 2.0.—Have the Taliban Really Changed and Learnt Their Lesson?* (Washington DC: The Atlantic Council, 5 January 2021).

31. Zalmay Khalilzad, 'Afghanistan: Time to Reengage', *The Washington Post*, 7 October 1996.

32. For a sample of such optimism, see Barnett R. Rubin, *Leveraging the Taliban's Quest for International Recognition* (Washington DC: Afghan Peace Process Issues Paper, United States Institute of Peace, March 2021), arguing at p.1 that the US had 'underestimated the leverage that the Taliban's quest for sanctions relief, recognition and international assistance provides'.

33. See, for example, John Bew, Ryan Evans, Martyn Frampton, Peter Neumann and Marisa Porges, *Talking to the Taliban: Hope over History?* (London: International Centre for the Study of Radicalisation and Political Violence, 2013) pp.45–6.

34. Sayed Madadi, 'Talking to the Taliban with the Wrong Assumptions: The Conundrum of Afghan Peace', *War on the Rocks*, 5 June 2019.

35. Sayed Madadi, *The Dangers of Empowering the Taliban* (Washington DC: The Middle East Institute, 14 February 2021).

36. See Kathy Gannon, 'Six months of Taliban: Afghans safer, poorer, less hopeful', *The Washington Post*, 15 February 2022.

37. See, for example, Hassan Adib, 'Ruzha-i sia-e Kabul: zindagi? Ba chi qimat?', *Etilaatroz*, 15 Dalwa 1400 (4 February 2022).

38. Richard Caplan, *Measuring Peace: Principles, Practices, and Politics* (Oxford: Oxford University Press, 2019) p.29. See also William Maley, 'Peace, Needs and Utopia', *Political Studies*, vol.33, no.4, December 1985, pp.578–91 at p.591.

39. Thomas Hobbes, *Leviathan* (Cambridge: Cambridge University Press, 1996) pp.88–9.

40. See Charles Tilly and Sidney Tarrow, *Contentious Politics* (New York: Oxford University Press, 2015).

41. See Sayed Madadi, *Dysfunctional centralization and growing fragility under Taliban rule* (Washington DC: The Middle East Institute, 6 September 2022).

42. Madina Morwat, 'Over 300 media outlets shut down in past 6 months', *Tolonews. com*, 4 February 2022.

43. UNAMA stopped reporting on civilian casualties in July 2021 after nearly 12 years of producing quarterly, annual and special reports. Then, in July 2022, it produced a text on 'human rights in Afghanistan' with a fraction of the depth and detail of its previous reports on the atrocities committed by the Taliban before their violent takeover. See *Human Rights in Afghanistan 15 August 2021–15 June 2022* (Kabul: United Nations Assistance Mission in Afghanistan, July 2022).

44. See, for example, the detailed reportage in Dari of *Etilaatroz* under the tag 'forced migration' (*Kuch-e ajbari*).

45. See, for example, *'No Forgiveness for People Like You': Executions and Enforced Disappearances in Afghanistan under the Taliban* (New York: Human Rights Watch, 30 November 2021); 'U.N. says over 100 ex-Afghan officials have been slain since the Taliban's takeover', *National Public Radio*, 31 January 2022.

46. *Afghanistan: 13 Hazara Killed by Taliban Fighters in Daykundi Province—New Investigation* (London: Amnesty International, 5 October 2021).

47. Tacitus, *Agricola. Germania. Dialogus* (Cambridge: Harvard University Press, 1970) p.81.

AFTERWORD

1. 'Statement by President Joseph R. Biden, Jr. on the International Day of Democracy' (Washington DC: The White House, 15 September 2021).

2. Avishai Margalit, *On Betrayal* (Cambridge: Harvard University Press, 2017) pp.20–3. On essentially contested concepts, see W.B. Gallie, 'Essentially Contested Concepts', *Proceedings of the Aristotelian Society*, New Series, vol.56, 1955–6, pp.167–98.

3. Judith N. Shklar, *Ordinary Vices* (Cambridge: Harvard University Press, 1984) p.141.

4. Avishai Margalit, *On Betrayal* (Cambridge: Harvard University Press, 2017) pp.47, 116.

5. A.E. Housman, *The Name and Nature of Poetry* (Cambridge: Cambridge University Press, 1933) p.47.

6. Kristen R. Monroe, Michael C. Barton and Ute Klingemann, 'Altruism and the Theory of Rational Action: Rescuers of Jews in Nazi Europe', *Ethics*, vol.101, no.1, October 1990, pp.103–22. See also J.A. Barnes, *A Pack of Lies: Towards a Sociology of Lying* (Cambridge: Cambridge University Press, 1994).

7. Quoted in Telford Taylor, *Munich: The Price of Peace* (New York: Doubleday, 1979) p.1003.

8. See J.L. Austin, *How to Do Things with Words* (Oxford: Oxford University Press, 1975) pp.10–11; also P.S. Atiyah, *Promises, Morals, and Law* (Oxford: Oxford University Press, 1981) pp.99–103.

9. Joseph Raz, *The Morality of Freedom* (Oxford: Oxford University Press, 1986) pp.175–6.

10. Cliff Goddard, *Semantic Analysis: A Practical Introduction* (Oxford: Oxford University Press, 2011) pp.138–41.

11. Russell Hardin, *Trust* (Cambridge: Polity Press, 2006) p.27.

12. Nicholas J. Wheeler, *Trusting Enemies: Interpersonal Relationships in International Conflict* (Oxford: Oxford University Press, 2018) p.2.

13. Eric M. Uslaner, *The Moral Foundations of Trust* (Cambridge: Cambridge University Press, 2002) p.23.

14. Brian C. Rathbun, *Trust in International Cooperation: International Security Institutions, Domestic Politics and American Multilateralism* (Cambridge: Cambridge University Press, 2012) p.3. See also Philip Pettit, *Rules, Reasons, and Norms: Selected Essays* (Oxford: Oxford University Press, 2002) p.344.

15. Andrew F. Cooper, *Stretching the Model of "Coalitions of the Willing"* (Waterloo: Working Paper no.1, Centre for International Governance Innovation, October 2005).

16. Andrew Linklater, *The Problem of Harm in World Politics* (Cambridge: Cambridge University Press, 2011) pp.6–7.

17. Thucydides, *History of the Peloponnesian War* (Harmondsworth: Penguin, 1972) p.402.

18. Judith N. Shklar, *Ordinary Vices* (Cambridge: Harvard University Press, 1984) p.47.

19. *Hamlet*, Act I, Scene III.

20. *Hamlet*, Act III, Scene III.

21. Quoted in Robert C. Tucker, 'Swollen State, Spent Society: Stalin's Legacy to Brezhnev's Russia', *Foreign Affairs*, vol.60, no.2, 1981–2, pp.414–35 at p.429.

22. See Robert A. Jones, *The Soviet Concept of "Limited Sovereignty" from Lenin to Gorbachev: The Brezhnev Doctrine* (Basingstoke: Macmillan, 1990).

23. For this insight we are indebted to Dr Haroro J. Ingram, a leading specialist on ISIS propaganda: see Haroro J. Ingram, Craig Whiteside and Charlie Winter, *The ISIS Reader: Milestone Texts of the Islamic State Movement* (London: Hurst & Co., 2020).

24. Matthew Rosenberg and Graham Bowley, 'U.S. grants special ally status to Afghanistan, easing fears of abandonment', *The New York Times*, 7 July 2012.

25. 'Statement by the President on the Signing of the Bilateral Security Agreement and NATO Status of Forces Agreement in Afghanistan' (Washington DC: Office of the Press Secretary, The White House, 30 September 2014).

26. Quoted in D.J. Enright and David Rawlinson (eds), *The Oxford Book of Friendship* (Oxford: Oxford University Press, 1991) p.21.

27. Preeti Aroon, 'Clinton to Afghan women: "We will not abandon you"', *Foreignpolicy.com*, 14 May 2010.

28. Alistair MacDonald and Maria Abi-Habib, 'In Kabul, Biden Vows to Sustain U.S. Role', *The Wall Street Journal*, 12 January 2011.

29. Joe Biden, *Promises to Keep: On Life and Politics* (New York: Random House, 2007) p.317.

30. Or perhaps not. A recent report described Biden as having 'a penchant for embellishment': Peter Baker, 'Biden says he confronted Saudi prince over Khashoggi. How true is that?', *The New York Times*, 16 July 2022. Richard Holbrooke

in December 2010 recorded that 'When I mentioned the women's issue, Biden erupted. "I am not sending my boy back there to risk his life on behalf of women's rights, it just won't work, it's not what we're there for"'. Holbrooke also wrote that he, Holbrooke, concerned about abandoning the US's allies, commented to Biden 'that I thought we had a certain obligation to the people who had trusted us. He said, "[expletive deleted] we don't have to worry about that. We did it in Vietnam. Nixon and Kissinger got away with it."': George Packer, *Our Man: Richard Holbrooke and the End of the American Century* (New York: Vintage Books, 2019) pp.530, 531. See also George Packer, 'The Betrayal', *The Atlantic*, 31 January 2022.

31.   W.B. Yeats, 'He wishes for the Cloths of Heaven', *Selected Poems* (London: Phoenix, 2010) p.22

32.   See Anne-Marie Slaughter, *A New World Order* (Princeton: Princeton University Press, 2004); Anne-Marie Slaughter, *The Idea That is America: Keeping Faith With Our Values in a Dangerous World* (New York: Basic Books, 2004); Anne-Marie Slaughter, *The Chessboard and the Web: Strategies of Connection in a Networked World* (New Haven: Yale University Press, 2017).

33.   https://twitter.com/SlaughterAM/status/1439592999764254720, September 19, 2021.

34.   See Sten Rynning, *NATO in Afghanistan: The Liberal Disconnect* (Stanford: Stanford University Press, 2012); David P. Auerswald and Stephen M. Saideman, *NATO in Afghanistan: Fighting Together, Fighting Alone* (Princeton: Princeton University Press, 2014).

35.   See William Maley and Susanne Schmeidl (eds), *Reconstructing Afghanistan: Civil-Military Experiences in Comparative Perspective* (London: Routledge, 2015).

36.   Ishaan Tharoor, 'As U.S leaves Afghanistan, Europe sours on Biden', *The Washington Post*, 31 August 2021.

37.   See J.S. Maloy, *The Colonial American Origins of Modern Democratic Thought* (Cambridge: Cambridge University Press, 2008); Aziz Rana, *The Two Faces of American Freedom* (Cambridge: Harvard University Press, 2010).

38.   Gideon Rachman, 'Joe Biden's credibility has been shredded in Afghanistan', *The Financial Times*, 13 August 2021.

39.   Edmund Burke, 'Speech on Moving Resolutions for Conciliation with the Colonies', in *Select Works of Edmund Burke* (Indianapolis: Liberty Fund, 1999) Volume I, p.251.

40.   John Hudson, Alex Horton, Missy Ryan and Dan Lamothe, 'Bombing at Kabul airport kills 13 U.S. service members and dozens of Afghans', *The Washington Post*, 26 August 2021.

41.   *After Kabul: Veterans, America, and the End of the War in Afghanistan* (New York: More in Common, November 2021) p.13.

42.   Friedrich Nietzsche, *Thus Spoke Zarathustra* (London: Penguin, 2003) p.75.

43.   For an excellent overview, see John Bew, *Realpolitik: A History* (New York: Oxford University Press, 2016).

44.   Quoted in Telford Taylor, *Munich: The Price of Peace* (New York: Doubleday, 1979) p.884.

45.   See Jonathan J. Koehler and Andrew D. Gershoff, 'Betrayal Aversion: When Agents of Protection Become Agents of Harm', *Organizational Behavior and*

Human Decision Processes, vol.90, no.2, March 2003, pp.244–61. Even mere suspicion of betrayal can generate powerful reactions. This is a prominent theme in literature: in Charles Dickens's 1838 novel *Oliver Twist*, Bill Sikes murders Nancy not because she has betrayed him, but because Sikes has been manipulated into believing that she has betrayed him.

46. Friedrich Nietzsche, *Beyond Good and Evil* (Harmondsworth: Penguin, 1990) p.102.
47. Niccolò Machiavelli, *The Prince* (Cambridge: Cambridge University Press, 1988) p.31.
48. *Macbeth*, Act II, Scene I.
49. *Macbeth*, Act V, Scene I.

INDEX

Note: Page numbers followed by "*n*" refer to notes, "*f*" refer to figures and "*t*" refer to tables

273